P9-DIY-492

Poisoned Love

The True Story of ER Nurse Chaz Higgs,
His Ambitious Wife, and a Shocking Murder

Carlton Smith

St. Martin's Paperbacks

POISONED LOVE

Copyright © 2008 by Carlton Smith.

Cover photo of Chaz Higgs © *Reno Gazette-Journal*/Marilyn Newton. Cover photo of Kathy Alfano © Phil Alfano. Cover photo of background image © Hans Neleman/Getty Images.

For information address St. Martin's Press, 175 Fifth Avenue, New York, NY 10010.

ISBN: 0-312-94801-8
EAN: 978-0-312-94801-6

Printed in the United States of America

St. Martin's Paperbacks edition / September 2008

St. Martin's Paperbacks are published by St. Martin's Press, 175 Fifth Avenue, New York, NY 10010.

10 9 8 7 6 5 4 3 2 1

Table of Contents

July 8, 2006

Chapter 1

By 6:30 the first rays of the morning sun were well over the rim of the Shadow Hills, the eastern, desert-starting side of the lush mountain valley known as Truckee Meadows.

At 4,400 feet above sea level, the valley floor was still cool from the overnight chill, and as the early light crept up the eastern wall of the small house at 9673 Otter Way, it seemed like the dawn of just another beautiful summer day in the one-time "Biggest Little City in the World," Reno, Nevada.

To the west, the peaks of the Sierras towered over the city, clad with evergreens along the ridges, guarded by rocky spines higher up, already golden in the unfiltered glow from the east. The Truckee River, the jewel of the Meadows, rushed down its gorge from Lake Tahoe through the city, rolling north to its disappearance in Pyramid Lake, sunk in the desolation of northern Nevada. The town that had begun 150 years before as a rickety bridge across a fast-running stream had turned into a fine place to live for more than 350,000 people.

At 6:43, one of those people, William Charles Higgs, known to his wife, his friends and his co-workers as "Chaz," punched 911 on a telephone in the same Otter Way house, and calmly requested medical assistance.

"It's my wife," Higgs told the 911 dispatcher, George Reade. "I don't know what's happened to her. She's not breathing." He'd attempted CPR, cardiopulmonary resuscitation, Higgs said, but he couldn't get a pulse.

Higgs gave Reade detailed instructions on how to get to Otter Way—what streets to take, where to turn.

"How long do you think you're going to be?" Higgs asked. "She's not responding at all. I don't know what happened to her. I came back in the room and she was sleeping. She has a mitral valve prolapse, was feeling really stressed the last month or so." As far as Reade could tell, it didn't sound as though Higgs was actually doing any CPR—usually he could hear callers gasping between delivering bits of needed information. The telephone went silent—not disconnected, just put down unattended.

Within six minutes an emergency team from the Reno Fire Department had arrived at the house, followed seconds later by two paramedics from the Regional Emergency Medical Services Authority, also known as REMSA. The REMSA paramedics saw a man outside, waving them on. Braking to a stop, they rushed inside, where they encountered four firemen in a small master bedroom. There, lying on her back in the bed, a woman in a tank top and pajama bottoms appeared to be dead. The firemen removed her from the bed and put her on the floor, where paramedics Ben Pratt and Manny Fuentes began resuscitation attempts.

Pratt saw that the woman was not breathing, and had no pulse, just as he'd been advised by the 911 dispatcher—in fact, her heart had stopped, and her pupils were fixed and dilated. But Pratt refused to give up. He inserted a plastic intubation tube into her throat to make sure the airway was clear, while his partner Fuentes began artificial respiration with a hand bellows—"bagging," it was called. Pratt put an intravenous line into the woman's right arm and injected her with epinephrine, and started a second line in the left arm for atropine, two drugs which had the effect of stimulating the heart muscle. Then Pratt began a series of chest compressions in a desperate effort to get the woman's heart and lungs going again.

At about 6:50 A.M., Kathy Augustine, the Nevada state controller, and one of the Silver State's most colorful and controversial political figures, came back to life; or at least, her heart began to beat once more, although she remained unconscious. Her husband, William Charles Higgs, himself a critical care nurse by occupation, stood in the doorway of the bedroom and watched stoically as Pratt and Fuentes accomplished the seemingly impossible. Kathy Augustine was alive; barely, it was true, but nevertheless a living person once again.

At 7:10 A.M., a comatose Kathy Augustine was wheeled into Washoe Medical Center's South Meadows hospital emergency room, less than three miles from the Otter Way house. In fact, Chaz Higgs had specifically asked that his wife be taken to the same emergency room where, up until that week, he had been employed as a specialist in emergency medicine. While South Meadows was a well-equipped, modern medical facility built to accommodate the recent population growth of the south Reno area, it was still a satellite facility of the main Washoe Regional Medical Center, known colloquially as Washoe Main, located in downtown Reno.

The emergency room crew on shift that morning was composed in part of nurses Marlene Swanbeck and Kristy McCabe, admitting nurse Cindy Baker, and Dr. John Ganser. By 7:25 A.M. they had surmised, based on the paramedics' initial description, that they were dealing with the victim of a heart attack. They had no idea of their patient's identity. All they knew was that she was a woman who was comatose and breathing with artificial respiration.

Somewhere around 7:20 A.M., Chaz Higgs arrived at the emergency room. He brushed back the privacy curtain that screened Kathy from the rest of the area and made eye contact with Swanbeck.

"What are you doing here?" Swanbeck asked, thinking that it was odd to see Chaz in so early on a Saturday morning if all he wanted was to find out next week's work schedule.

"That's my wife, Kathy," Chaz said, nodding at the supine figure in the bed, and that was when, for the first time, most of the emergency room crew at South Meadows knew that their patient was the same woman that they had all come to despise, even if very few of them had actually met her.

At 7:35, at a loss to explain what was wrong with Kathy—she didn't seem to be responding to the usual cardiac care measures—Swanbeck inserted a catheter and drew Kathy's urine. Packaging it with blood taken at 7:25, the samples were sent to the hospital's lab, where tests were conducted; a test on the blood soon produced a positive result for barbiturate, a central nervous system depressant and occasional drug of abuse known as a "red," a "downer" or a "black beauty," at least when not prescribed by a physician. At that point, with a high-ranking state politician having been admitted to the hospital with a possible illicit drug overdose, the hospital decided to throw a publicity blanket over the proceedings by assigning a false name: "Sarah Lambert." It would later be determined that this result was a "false positive," that is, a mismeasurement by the laboratory, but at the time, no one knew that.

Just after 8 A.M., it was decided more information was needed. Chaz wasn't very helpful; apart from mentioning that Kathy had a congenital heart "murmur," the mitral valve prolapse, all he could tell them was that he'd been out in the garage early that morning, working on his car. When he'd come in to rouse Kathy, he'd found her comatose in their bed, and not breathing. He'd attempted CPR, he said, but couldn't get any response, so he'd called 911. He had no idea of how long she'd been lying in bed without breathing. That was ominous—more than four minutes without oxygen meant brain damage; and the damage increased exponentially with every minute above that. If Kathy Augustine had been without air for nine minutes or more, there was no hope—she was already in the realm of the living dead.

Cardiac specialists at Washoe Medical Center downtown suggested to their South Meadows colleagues that an angiogram would determine if there was a blockage of the arteries leading to Kathy's heart. After all, at five feet nine inches in height, and at 189 pounds, Kathy was a large woman, slightly overweight, and the prospect of an occluded blood vessel couldn't be discounted. The angiogram would give the doctors literally a moving picture of Kathy's heart and its arteries.

At 8:45 A.M., Pratt and Fuentes wheeled Kathy out to their ambulance for the trip to downtown Reno and Washoe Main. Pratt climbed into the back of the ambulance, Fuentes took the wheel, and Chaz jumped into the front passenger seat. As the ambulance made its way north to the main medical facility, Chaz picked the day's newspaper off the dashboard and began to peruse it.

Chaz and Kathy were barely out of the South Meadows emergency room when tongues there began to wag. Was that really Chaz's wife, the fabled Kathy Augustine, the only statewide elected official ever to be impeached? The same woman who had twice been a finalist for the job of United States treasurer, but whose candidacy had been ruined by that impeachment? The self-same, never-say-die Republican candidate for state treasurer in that year's election? The colorful politician who had once infamously suggested that a subordinate euthanize her pet cat so she'd have more time to work on Kathy's political campaign? The woman who had repeatedly excoriated the ER staff for ignoring her when she wanted to speak to her husband, Chaz, and who had threatened to use her political influence to have them fired from their jobs? The same person who, when frustrated, had so often demanded of them: "Don't you know who I am?"

Few were the people in the emergency room who hadn't tangled with Kathy by telephone the previous year or so. Kathy never seemed to get it: the ER people were busy seeing patients, sometimes saving lives, when she called demanding to speak to Chaz, as if Chaz had nothing better to do than exchange idle chit-chat with his wife. When she was put on hold and forgotten in the midst of a crisis, she often lost her temper. On more than one occasion, Kathy had threatened to use her political influence to punish those at the hospital who thwarted her; and in fact, on one occasion—or so it was widely believed—she had caused an admitting clerk to be fired, simply because Kathy had caught Chaz sending her flirtatious emails.

Kathy, it appeared, was intensely jealous. She was certain that Chaz was playing around on her behind her back, and the principal suspects were the ER nurses with whom Chaz spent so much time. Hence the frequent telephone calls, demands to speak to Chaz, to know exactly when he would be home, to know his schedule, or alternatively, complaints about the schedule, which prevented Chaz from being with her. To the ER crew, Kathy Augustine was a pain, and not one that could be treated with any known medicine.

And Chaz himself seemed to agree: his wife the politician, he would tell anyone who would listen, was "a bitch," and worse. He was apologetic to his fellow ER workers— they had to understand that Kathy was "crazy," even if she *was* one of the biggest wheels in the state. And sometimes, when a nurse asked Chaz if he needed any help—the ER crew tended to bond together the same way cops and combat soldiers do, shared trauma having that effect—Chaz would facetiously reply, "Yeah—you can get rid of my wife for me." People laughed—then.

But now, there was Kathy Augustine, 50 years old, one of only six officials elected by all the people of the state of Nevada, comatose and on her way to intensive care at Washoe Main, brought back from the dead, but probably still on her way to the Other Side, judging from her vital signs that morning.

And there also was her husband Chaz, the same man who'd so often complained about "the bitch," displaying a weird mixture of technical medical expertise and dispassionate theorizing in the ER. To Swanbeck, at least, he seemed unnaturally calm.

All of which made Swanbeck and others in the South Meadows ER wonder: had Chaz done something to the wife he had claimed to detest so much—if, having failed to convince someone to get rid of her for him, he'd decided to do the job himself?

Across town that same morning of July 8, a woman named Jeannine Coward awoke from a strange dream. Two years before, Jeannine had been instrumental in initiating the investigation that had led to Kathy Augustine's impeachment. While Jeannine was convinced that she had done the right thing, she was still troubled by the personal unpleasantness that had then developed with Kathy. In her dream, she saw Kathy standing across from her in the state Capitol Building in Carson City. Jeannine knew she was going to have to walk past her, and she had an idea that Kathy might lash out at her.

"I was afraid she'd start yelling at me again," Jeannine said later. "But instead she came up to me, smiled and put her arms around me." It was only later that Jeannine realized that she'd been having this dream at almost the same moment Kathy Augustine was getting ready to die.

At 8:30 A.M., on the other side of the Sierras in the central California town of Turlock, not far from the city of Modesto, 41-year-old Phil Alfano, Jr., took a telephone call from his mother, Kay Alfano, a resident of the Orange County suburb of La Palma, located midway between Los Angeles and Santa Ana.

"It's Kathy," Kay told her son. His sister, Kathy Marie Alfano Augustine, was in intensive care in a Reno hospital, the victim of an apparent heart attack.

"You've got to be kidding me," Phil said. The idea of his older sister suffering a heart attack at the comparatively young age of 50 seemed incomprehensible to him. The high-energy, striving Kathy seemed, at least to him, impervious to illness. But Phil knew his mother wasn't kidding—that was only a figure of speech to cover his shock.

Kay told Phil that she'd just received a call from Chaz, informing her that Kathy was unconscious, and on her way to the hospital's ICU. Kay had then told Chaz that she and Kathy's father, Phil Alfano, Sr., would immediately fly to Reno.

Chaz had told her it wasn't necessary—there was nothing the Alfanos could do for their daughter at that point, he said; it was all up to the doctors. Kay thought that was odd. Didn't Chaz understand that Kathy's mother and father would want to be at her side as she fought for her life?

Phil Jr. and Kathy had traits in common. Both were very smart, and could be quite intense when their attention was focused on something. Both had a strong sense of humor, as well as an appreciation for dry wit. Confronted with foolishness or posturing, each could be acerbic. But where Kathy tended to be somewhat flamboyant, emotionally volatile and certainly socially adept, Phil was more like his father: phlegmatic, mentally disciplined and conservative, both socially and politically.

Moreover, as a high school administrator in Modesto, Phil had of necessity and training developed some acute skills for observing and evaluating individual motivations and behavior—not one of Kathy's stronger suits. As the next few weeks unfolded, Phil Alfano, Jr., was to employ those observational skills with great effect. Chaz's advice to Kay Alfano to stay away from Reno seemed as strange to Phil as it had to his mother.

Chaz was being dense and insensitive, Phil now told his mother. Of course they should go to Reno. They should *all* go to Reno, no matter what Chaz thought. Phil made arrangements to pick up his parents at the airport in Sacramento that same afternoon. They would drive over the mountains to Reno that evening to be with Kathy in her struggle to live.

Ten minutes later that same morning, a woman in Phoenix, Arizona, received a similar call from Kay. This was Dallas Augustine, Kathy's estranged 26-year-old daughter, and a rather colorful personality in her own right; apart from her alternative lifestyle, Dallas was a veteran professional football player, having played on the offensive and defensive lines of professional women's teams in southern California and Arizona in 2004 and 2005.

At five eleven and 180 pounds, Dallas was a large, powerful woman, not only physically, but in her personality, which tended toward the combative and confrontational. She and Kathy had not been getting along that spring. Where the Alfanos, including Kathy and her brothers, Phil and Tony, derived their strength from the closeness of their family ties, Dallas seemed to be in a stage of rebellion against family togetherness, and especially against her mother. In fact, the more successful Kathy became in her political career, the more unpredictable Dallas became in her own life, at least as far as her conservative Uncle Phil saw such matters. To Phil, Dallas saw Kathy as controlling and reveled in smashing her mother's expectations for her, no matter how destructive it was to their relationship.

Others saw this differently: to some, Kathy had used her only child as a "whipping girl" throughout her life.

Still, after getting this call from her grandmother, and learning that her mother was in the hospital with a heart attack, Dallas immediately called Chaz at the number Kay had given her, which was Kathy's cellphone. No one answered, so Dallas left a message. Forty-five minutes later, Chaz called back to confirm that Kathy had indeed suffered a heart attack, and that she was in a coma in the hospital. Dallas at once made arrangements to fly to Reno from Phoenix. She got there in the early afternoon, accompanied by her significant other, Jessie.

That same morning, Chaz made numerous cellphone calls to Mark Taylor, an official in the Nevada State Controller's Office. As assistant controller, Taylor worked closely with Kathy, and in fact, often handled her relations with the news media. Chaz thought Taylor should be notified so he could respond to the press inquiries that were certain to come, once the word got out that Kathy Augustine had collapsed.

Chaz called Taylor at 7:32 that morning, while still at South Meadows, and left a message. He called again at 8:12, then 9:28, 10:30, at 2 P.M. and again at 7 that night. Taylor did not answer or return any of the calls, for the simple reason that he was boating on a lake in the mountains with his family, and therefore out of cellphone range, a fact that Kathy knew but hadn't previously conveyed to her husband.

Chaz made other calls as well: a minute-long message for his identical twin brother, Mike, in Virginia; another one-minute message to his father, William Higgs, in North Carolina; and altogether, two calls totaling forty-seven minutes to his mother, Shirley, also in North Carolina. The first call to Shirley was interrupted by a two-minute call from Dallas, apparently to say she'd just arrived in Reno, and that she was on her way to the Washoe Main intensive care unit. After taking this call, Chaz had called his mother back for another twenty-minute conversation. Just what mother and son said to one another was never made clear. But it was only a little more than a week after this that a prominent lawyer was retained by Chaz's family to represent him.

That evening, the South Meadows admitting nurse, Cindy Baker, arrived at the Washoe Main ICU, hoping to see Kathy and Chaz. When she arrived, Chaz and Dallas were in the ICU room. Kathy was on her back in the hospital bed, connected to a respirator, IV lines and various monitors. Her sightless eyes were blinking incessantly. Cindy Baker had only worked in the South Meadows emergency room for six months, and she considered Chaz her "mentor." On seeing him there that morning, Cindy concluded that he was in shock, based on his placidity. She'd even called a social worker to see if he needed assistance. Now she wanted to make sure he was okay. She hugged him, and Chaz hugged her back, telling her it was "all right." Cindy turned to Kathy, with whom she'd exchanged sharp words in the past.

"I'm so sorry," Cindy told Kathy, holding her hand, although Kathy couldn't hear her. Cindy asked the ICU nurse why Kathy was blinking her eyes.

"She's having brain seizures," the nurse said. Then the nurse was explaining something on Kathy's chart to Chaz and Dallas, and Cindy left, feeling sick to her stomach and wondering if what people at South Meadows were saying was true, that Chaz had done something to harm his wife. She hoped it wasn't so—she really liked Chaz.

Chapter 2

Sometime around 8 that night, the three Alfanos arrived in Reno. Kay had received one other call from Chaz that morning, but they'd apparently neglected to discuss which of the several Reno-area hospitals was caring for Kathy. Kay eventually reached Chaz, again on Kathy's cellphone, and learned that Kathy was at the Washoe Main ICU. The Alfanos got to the hospital about 9 P.M. Cindy Baker had just left. Chaz and Dallas were there with Kathy and the ICU nurse. Kathy's eyes had suddenly stopped blinking.

"We went in there," Phil Jr. recalled later, "and it was just terrible. Gosh. She was on a respirator, and her eyes were just wide open. She couldn't blink, and they had to keep putting drops in. And she couldn't move, other than an involuntary twitch in her lower body. And by the next morning, *that* was gone. And then she wasn't moving at all."

The Alfanos learned that the angiogram had not shown any arterial blockage, but the heart had been severely damaged, probably from a lack of oxygen. A CAT scan was scheduled for the following day to assess the amount of brain injury, which neurologists thought had probably been extensive, based on earlier EEG readings.

"Yeah," Phil said later, "it was pretty hard to take."

The rest of the night was a blur for Phil Alfano and his parents. One of the nurses told Kay about the positive test for barbiturates, and said that Chaz had been made aware of the results. For some reason Chaz had kept this to himself.

After that, Phil remembered checking in to the Reno Hilton, but little else. Kay decided to spend the night at the ICU. Dallas went back to the Otter Way house with Chaz, and spent the night there with Chaz and Jessie.

Maybe things will be better in the morning, Phil thought. The Alfanos were natural optimists—their loyalty to one another helped make them that way.

The next morning was Sunday, and Marlene Swanbeck was back on duty at the South Meadows emergency room. Some time around 11:15 she received a telephone call from Chaz.

"Can you do me a favor? Grab my check, and meet me in ten minutes in the parking lot."

Swanbeck thought it was a little odd that Chaz had called *her*, of all possibilities in the ER. After all, they weren't particularly close friends. Every time Chaz had said something negative about his marriage in the past, Swanbeck had inwardly cringed, put off by his crudity and seeming hatefulness toward his wife. And now there was this request from Chaz to meet in the parking lot—why didn't he just come into the ER himself to pick up his own check? Was it that Chaz didn't want to look any of them in the eye?

By now suspicion that Chaz might have done something to Kathy had been well-circulated around the ER, and had even become the subject of black humor. No one had forgotten Chaz's oft-voiced pleas for help: "Take my wife—please." Before going out to meet Chaz in the parking lot at 11:30, Swanbeck told everyone where she was going and who she was going to meet.

"If I don't come back, you'll know what happened to me," she said, making another macabre joke.

In the parking lot, Chaz greeted her with a box of donuts.

"Thanks for taking care of Kathy," he told Swanbeck, and gave her the box as a gesture of appreciation.

Although she took the donuts and made the appropriate remarks to Chaz, some part of Swanbeck was registering that Chaz's behavior seemed wrong: "The timing didn't feel right to me—needing his paycheck, the donuts, it felt too weird," she said later. To Swanbeck, it was as if Chaz was acting—as if he was following some script: this is the way the grieving spouse should act. It was as if all the nasty things he'd said about Kathy had never passed his lips.

After this encounter, Chaz drove off to see Kathy and the Alfanos at Washoe Main.

After they'd arrived at the hospital around 9 that same Sunday morning, Phil later recalled, Chaz and Dallas spent much of the morning "running errands" outside the hospital, one of them apparently Chaz's parking-lot pickup of his paycheck. They arrived back at the Washoe Main ICU around noon. Kay Alfano, of course, had been there all night, and Phil and his father had come early in the morning. Just before noon, Chaz and Dallas returned to the ICU— rather cavalierly, in the Alfanos' view. Phil, at least, was getting the idea that Chaz and maybe even Dallas didn't care much whether Kathy lived or died.

"We were here all day yesterday," Chaz told Phil. When Chaz said that, Phil noticed the ICU nurse roll her eyes in contradiction.

As Phil had already noted, Kathy's condition seemed worse, not better. The involuntary leg movement was now gone. That suggested that the brain damage had been extensive, the neurologist explained to the Alfanos. The CAT scan confirmed the worst: there was massive swelling on both sides of Kathy's brain. The prospect for recovery was remote, probably nil, according to the experts.

Chaz had already explained what had happened: he'd been out in the garage, working on his car. It was early in the morning. He'd decided to let Kathy sleep in, because she was tired. She'd been under stress lately, from her campaign to be elected state treasurer, Chaz said. In fact, she'd skipped a political function the night before, because she wasn't feeling well.

He'd come into the bedroom with some coffee to wake Kathy up about 6:30. He'd first opened the curtains to let more light in, and then noticed she wasn't breathing. He could find no pulse, which showed that her heart had stopped. He'd tried to perform CPR, but she didn't respond. He'd then called the paramedics, who'd somehow resuscitated her. He had no idea of when she'd stopped breathing, but it couldn't have been too long, or the paramedics wouldn't have been able to get her heart started again. He knew that Kathy's "heart murmur" might be dangerous. The "mitral valve prolapse," as it was called, was a congenital mismatch between the size of the heart's mitral valve cover and the valve opening. The mismatch could cause blood leakage inside the heart, and the blood leakage could cause the heart to fibrillate—to suddenly convulse, leading to a heart attack. Chaz guessed this leakage had come when Kathy was asleep, leading to the heart seizure. Chaz sounded very authoritative, Phil thought.

That evening, Kay and the two Phils, father and son, asked Dallas if she wanted to have dinner with them; they hadn't seen much of her for the past year, and wanted to reconnect. But Dallas said no. She seemed curt, disinterested, or perhaps preoccupied, the Alfanos thought. It seemed unusual behavior from someone who had practically grown up in the Alfano home, and who had lived with her grandparents twice as an adult when estranged from her mother.

So far, there had been nothing in the news about Kathy's collapse, but Phil Jr. knew that wouldn't last long. The fact that the Nevada state controller was in a coma in a hospital in Reno was news, and surely someone—a nurse, a paramedic, a doctor, a fireman, someone—would tell what he or she knew, very soon. Phil suggested to Chaz that he might want to contact the controller's office to clue them in. Chaz explained that he'd been trying to reach Mark Taylor without success for two days.

"Well," Phil said, "maybe we should go down to Carson City tomorrow to let them know what's going on." Phil was politically savvy enough to realize that rumors of Kathy's collapse were certain to make their way to the office by the following morning. Chaz agreed. Kathy's executive assistant at the state controller's office, Michelle Ene, came to the hospital that night after Chaz had called her. But Phil really wanted to get into Kathy's office before anyone else. He knew that Kathy had been battling with people in her own party. He worried someone might try to remove something from her office, or worse, plant something that would make her look bad—"shenanigans," as Phil referred to political dirty tricks.

Thus, the prospect of something negative being planted on Kathy to damage her reputation was in the front of Phil's mind the next morning when Chaz, a half-hour late, pulled into the Hilton parking lot and got into Phil's car for the trip to Carson City.

"I just wanted to let you know," Chaz told Phil, "the nurse called last night. They found traces of barbiturates in Kathy's system."

Chaz's offhand remark brought Phil up short. It wasn't that the drug test had been positive, but the way Chaz was now telling him how he'd learned about it—that "the nurse" had called him "last night." Phil knew that wasn't so: Chaz had been told this Saturday morning at South Meadows, not over the telephone by "the nurse" on Sunday night.

Why would he lie about something like that? Phil wondered. *What's the point?* But Phil kept these thoughts to himself, and as they set out for Carson City, Chaz seemed oblivious to Phil's new doubts about his veracity.

"Well, it's probably nothing," Chaz went on. "It's probably an anti-depressant." Chaz rattled off some well-known anti-depressant medications, suggesting that Kathy had been taking the medications to cope with the "stress" of the political season. But the unnecessary lie had stoked Phil's suspicion of his brother-in-law, already bubbling slowly in the back of his mind.

"That, to me, was kind of a tipping point," Phil said later, "where I now began to believe something was wrong. Because he was lying about it. And it didn't seem like something he would need to lie about." From this point forward, Phil began to observe Chaz's behavior closely, watching for inconsistencies in his story, or his demeanor as the supposedly grieving husband.

At the controller's office in Carson City, Chaz and Phil confirmed to the employees that Kathy had collapsed, and that she was in intensive care. As Phil had expected, the telephones were already ringing off the hook as rumors spread. The chief deputy controller, Bill Reinhard, came in and greeted Phil and Chaz in Kathy's personal office.

"I'm so sorry," Reinhard told them. "I just want to tell you, this is really a shock. If you had told me this six months or a year ago, maybe. But Kathy had been in such great spirits, she'd been happy." Reinhard meant that a year or so earlier, after Kathy had been impeached by the Nevada State Assembly, but allowed to remain in office by the State Senate, Kathy was angry and depressed. But since she'd decided to run for the office of state treasurer, she'd been upbeat—it was as if a burden had been lifted from her, as she saw a way to clear her name after the impeachment.

And that campaign had been going well, Reinhard said—recent polls showed she was even with the main Republican opponent, a Las Vegas businessman named Mark DeStefano, even though the party bigwigs, including the governor and U.S. senator, wanted her to resign, and one legislator, the former state treasurer, no less, wanted to simply abolish the controller's office, just after she'd first been elected in 1998. Worse, the Republican Party had refused to endorse her candidacy for state treasurer, and in fact had even passed a resolution in effect condemning her at their recent state party convention. All this was well-known to Phil, Chaz and Reinhard, and didn't need to be mentioned; it was the history of Kathy Augustine in Nevada politics over the previous seven years.

Reinhard left the office, and Phil and Chaz began to look through files there to see if there was anything personal that needed to be removed for safekeeping. Almost at once Phil found a folder with documents pertaining to DeStefano, including a variety of papers about various businesses DeStefano had been affiliated with, along with complaints from customers of some of those businesses: Kathy's "opposition research" on her main primary opponent. Phil decided to take the file, just in case. Another file contained correspondence between Kathy and the Bush White House over her prospective appointment as U.S. treasurer, a job that had gone aglimmering after the impeachment. Phil thought that should be taken, as well.

Meanwhile, Chaz had been looking through things, and discovered a rubber stamp bearing Kathy's signature as controller. "I'd better take this," Chaz said.

About then, Reinhard reentered the office.

"I need to talk to you about something," he told them. He was holding a copy of the state constitution. He pointed to a section which required the governor to appoint someone, should the controller become incapacitated, and he was starting to say something about the governor's wanting to appoint—

Phil erupted at Kathy's former top associate.

"You know what? This is bullshit," he said. "First of all, you have people over here who were trying to throw her out of office, who said you don't even *need* a controller. Do you mean to tell me the wheels of government are going to come to a screeching halt if the governor doesn't appoint somebody *right now*?

"I know what's been going on over here," Phil added, ominously, "and I'll make it real clear to you, Bill: I don't trust anybody, and that comes from the governor on down."

Was it really possible that one of Kathy's political enemies—Phil knew that she had more than her share— had had something to do with Kathy's sudden collapse? In his rational mind, Phil knew that was highly unlikely, but under the stress of the circumstances—his sister in a coma, not expected to live—he wasn't ready to rule out anything or anyone. Hadn't Kathy told him of threats made to her if she persisted in her campaign for state treasurer? Phil glared at Reinhard, aware that at least part of his anger was frustration over his sister's condition, while Chaz said nothing.

Reinhard mumbled an apology and said he'd discuss the matter again with someone in the governor's office. He left.

Just before 2 P.M. that Monday, Mark Taylor finally emerged from the mountains with his family, trailing his boat behind his car. As soon as they reached a cellular coverage area, his phone went berserk. That was when Taylor first learned that Kathy Augustine had collapsed and was in a coma.

Five minutes after that, Chaz Higgs spoke to reporters hastily assembled by the controller's staff on the steps of the controller's office, telling them that Kathy had suffered a "massive heart attack."

Chaz explained that he had found Kathy unmoving, not breathing in bed early Saturday morning.

"I went to try to wake her, and I couldn't get her to wake up," he said. He couldn't find a pulse, he added. He'd given her cardiopulmonary resuscitation, and called for the paramedics.

Phil leaned against a wall and watched as Chaz spoke.

Kathy, Chaz said, had been complaining of heartburn and

indigestion in the days before she collapsed, and particularly the night before.

That's right out of WebMD, Phil thought. *Geez, he's making this up as he goes along.*

Over the past few months, Chaz continued, Kathy had been under a lot of stress from the political campaign. "I think that is probably *the* factor," he said.

What? Didn't they just hear Reinhard say that she was feeling happy, upbeat about the campaign? What is Chaz talking about? Phil was growing more and more skeptical of his brother-in-law. *He's a bullshitter*, Phil thought. *He's always been a bullshitter, as long as I've known him. But then, Kathy never did see it—or didn't want to see it, maybe.*

That evening, Phil spoke to his mother, Kay.

"You know," he said, "something doesn't seem right here."

"I was thinking the same thing," Kay told him.

As it would turn out, that was exactly what yet another nurse was thinking, too.

Kathy

Chapter 3

By the time she lay dying in the intensive care unit of Washoe Regional Medical Center that weekend, Kathy Marie Alfano Voss Hohn Augustine Higgs had already lived lifetimes unknown to the majority of Nevadans who had repeatedly elected her to high political office. Although Kathy liked to appear as a paragon of family values, a staunch wife and mother, she had in fact been married four times. With one possible exception, none of these unions could be called particularly successful, either in longevity or by the gold standard of marital bliss, mutual happiness. Even her sixteen-year marriage to Charles F. Augustine, a handsome Delta Air Lines pilot sixteen years her senior, was marked with strife and separations; by the time Chuck died of apparent complications from a massive stroke in the summer of 2003, Kathy had already served him with divorce papers, and was well known in Nevada's capital as a woman about town.

For someone who was intellectually brilliant and politically astute, Kathy seemed to have some sort of blind spot when it came to intimate relationships with men, as even her family later admitted.

"She could be very, very impulsive when it came to relationships," Phil Alfano, Jr., observed later. "And that was a pattern throughout her life, unfortunately. It even went back to when she was in high school. We had a pretty tranquil household, but one of the few arguments I remember was my mom and my sister [over] some of the guys that she was dating . . . I remember once she was dating a guy who lived in Anaheim, she must have been about eighteen or nineteen at the time . . . and we went over there, and I saw him get verbally and physically abusive with her. She left and dumped him, and on the ride home, said, 'Don't say anything to Mom and Dad.' She had very poor judgment when it came to men, yeah. I think we're all at a loss to understand it."

Nowhere was this more perplexing to Kathy's family and friends than in her last marriage, this to Chaz Higgs, exactly one month after the death of Chuck Augustine.

J ust why Kathy would tie the knot with Higgs was a mystery to nearly everyone who knew her. Were there ever two people more different?

For one thing, Chaz was just over eight years younger than Kathy. With the front of his hair permed and bleached, with his pierced ears, with his penchant for see-through body shirts, he seemed of a different generation entirely from the middle-aged Republican matron that Kathy had become.

"When we first met him," Phil later recalled, "my wife commented to me that he looked like one of the Pet Shop Boys," a reference to a 1980s–1990s popular singing duo with similar punkish hairstyles. In fact, Chaz was young enough to have been Chuck Augustine's son. As it happened, in fact, Chaz had been one of Chuck's nurses just before he died, which was how Kathy had first met him.

A hospital corpsman with sixteen years' service in the U.S. Navy, Chaz claimed to have been in combat with Navy SEALs after the first Gulf War in 1990. A few years earlier, he'd been a medic in Saudi Arabia when Al Qaeda had bombed Khobar Towers, or so he said. He'd left the Navy in the late 1990s, four years short of a twenty-year career, and had then taken classes in North Carolina to qualify as a registered nurse.

Like Kathy, Chaz had also been married three times—he

had two ex-wives in Las Vegas and a third on the East Coast. He had declared bankruptcy twice in a dozen years. Before he met Kathy, Chaz was living in a recreational vehicle park on Boulder Highway in east Las Vegas, was driving a 1966 Volkswagen, and was reputedly flat broke. In Kathy Augustine, a comparatively wealthy woman who was about to become a somewhat wealthier widow, Chaz Higgs encountered the chance for a quantum jump of possible upward material circumstance.

Within two months of the death of Chuck Augustine, the taciturn Chaz was accompanying Kathy to political functions in Las Vegas and Reno, drawing discreet stares from the political cognoscenti. It was evident to everyone that Chaz had even less interest in politics than Chuck Augustine had. Soon the gossips began to suggest, tittering behind their fingers, that Kathy had replaced her deceased husband with a hard-bodied, ex-Navy boy-toy who said next to nothing, and who was clearly bored out of his mind with politics, even if it was Kathy's own consuming interest. Or, as one of Kathy's closest friends in Reno put it later, Kathy had found herself a "stud muffin."

Kathy Marie Alfano was born May 29, 1956, the first child of Phil Alfano and his wife Kay. Phil, a veteran of back-to-back enlistments in the Marine Corps, including a combat tour in Korea, was the manager of veterans' housing at Occidental College in northeast Los Angeles when Kathy was born. He played football on the same team with future pro quarterback, congressman and vice-presidential candidate Jack Kemp, and pro football coach Jim Mora, among others.

Phil had a scientific mind, and at one point considered going to medical school. But with Kathy's birth, he decided to go into business, and soon found work as a sales representative for a major pharmaceutical company, a job he would hold until his retirement decades later.

Kathy was soon joined by her younger brothers Phil Jr. and Tony, and the family lived in several southern California communities before eventually settling in La Palma, a small town just over the Orange County line from Los Angeles County. There the Alfano children grew up, surrounded by an extended family of uncles, aunts and cousins, and strongly influenced by the Church; the family attended Mass every Sunday.

"My parents are very religious," Phil Jr. said, and they did their best to pass their faith on to their children.

When the Alfanos moved in, La Palma had recently been developed from former dairy farms, and much of the housing was new. So, too, were the schools. In fact, the town's John F. Kennedy High School was completed not long after the president's 1963 assassination; Phil Jr. was to recall that it was the first high school in the nation to be named after the murdered president.

It was at John F. Kennedy High School, according to Phil Jr., that the then dark-haired Kathy first became involved in politics.

"There is, on the wall of the main hall there, the famous quote: 'Ask not what your country can do for you, but what you can do for your country,'" Phil Jr. recalled. "There was a real emphasis of leadership, on giving back to the community, that sort of thing, at the school. And I think it affected Kathy. She got involved in lots of things there, school leadership things."

Kathy graduated from John F. Kennedy in 1974 and enrolled at the University of California, Irvine, for the fall semester. But because she found it difficult to get the classes she wanted to take, she soon transferred to Occidental College.

"I know that pleased my dad, because he was a graduate of Occidental," Phil said.

By that year, Phil Sr. had long since abandoned his youthful preference for the Democrats and Franklin D. Roosevelt, and had become a Republican, a political persuasion that

Kathy seems to have readily adopted. "We were definitely a Republican household," Phil recalled.

That fall, Kathy was selected for a Lyndon B. Johnson fellowship in the Washington, D.C., office of then Orange County Congressman Jerry Patterson, like Johnson, a Democrat. "I think Kathy was the only Republican on Patterson's staff," Phil recalled.

After the year in Washington, Kathy returned to Occidental even more enthusiastic about politics than she had been before. In the 1976 campaign, she worked for former California Governor Ronald Reagan's unsuccessful attempt to win the Republican nomination for president over incumbent Republican Gerald Ford. Phil Jr., then about 16, recalled accompanying her to Reagan's Los Angeles headquarters, where he was thrilled to collect some badges boosting Reagan.

By the end of the decade, Kathy had not only graduated from Occidental, she'd found work with Western Airlines, then operating throughout the American Southwest, as well as on longer flights to Mexico, Alaska, Hawaii and Canada. It was while working at Western that Kathy married for the first time, to an aircraft mechanic named Gary Voss. By October of 1979, Kathy had given birth to Dallas Voss. But four months later, Kathy learned for the first time that Gary Voss was seeing another woman. By the summer of 1980, Kathy and Voss had separated. Voss moved in with the other woman.

It appears that Kathy wasn't about to take this rejection without a fight. By the summer of the following year, in fact, the other woman had filed a request for a restraining order against "Kathy M. Alfano aka Kathy M. Voss," demanding that she remain at least 100 yards away from the other woman's Long Beach, California, apartment and her place of work, and that Kathy be prohibited from making any telephone calls to the woman. Both Kathy and the other woman worked at Western Airlines, as did Gary Voss. Both women worked in offices that were within walking distance.

Defendant [Kathy] calls plaintiff [the other woman] at her home and workplace. Defendant calls the plaintiff vile names and asks her questions using profanities. In her petition for the restraining order, the other woman complained: On August 29, 1980, defendant called plaintiff at workplace and asked her nonsensical and personal questions using profane language. Defendant has been coming to plaintiff's doorbell persistently late at night. On September 4, 1980, defendant knocked on plaintiff's door, tried to open door with a key, and rang doorbell for two hours and then proceeded to back of building and commenced yelling.

The "erratic behavior and harassment," the other woman added, made her "wary of defendant and what she is capable of doing to plaintiff."

Under these circumstances—with an infant daughter and an apparently philandering husband—one can readily understand Kathy's persistence in wanting to have contact with the absent Gary. Clearly, Kathy believed that he was sheltering behind the other woman's skirts. But the accusation of vile profanities hurled at the woman was pretty much classic Kathy: when she got mad, you knew it.

Kathy soon responded to the other woman's complaint with a written response to the court:

Only my husband was in contact with the plaintiff between July 1979 and February 1980. I was unaware that they were seeing each other during this period . . . my first contact with the plaintiff is when she came uninvited to my place of residence to see my husband on February 24, 1980.

In other words, Kathy claimed that she'd had no idea that her husband and the other woman were carrying on behind her back until the other woman had the nerve to show up at the marital residence and demand to speak to Gary.

She'd only wanted to have contact with the other woman, Kathy went on, because:

> I have an eleven month old child from my marriage to Gary Voss, and my husband was, and at the time of this petition, is, cohabiting with the plaintiff. I find it necessary to speak to my husband regarding our child, as well as other material matters and have no other way of contacting him in the evening hours . . . where he is living.

She'd tried to contact Voss on the evening of September 4, 1980, but not late at night.

> In fact, on September 4, 1980, I did go to plaintiff's door with my infant daughter and knocked on the door and tried to speak to my husband and child's father. When they refused to answer the door, we left.

Because the other woman was preventing her from talking to her husband, Kathy added, the other woman was causing her "extreme emotional distress."

After a hearing in Superior Court, a judge issued the temporary restraining order, and a copy of the order was sent on to the Long Beach Police Department. Kathy had to keep away from her estranged husband and his new paramour. Not long after that, Kathy and Gary Voss were divorced, and Kathy was left to care for Dallas by herself. According to her brother Phil, Gary Voss provided little child support during the 1980s, and had no contact with his daughter as a child. Eventually Voss married the other woman, and they moved to Phoenix, Arizona.

Now a single mother, Kathy had no intention of settling for the meager existence of a spurned wife. Within a year or

so she had enrolled at California State University, Long
Beach, and begun work on a master's degree in public administration. During this time, Dallas Voss often spent days
and evenings with the Alfanos in La Palma, as Kathy continued to work at Western Airlines, and attended school at
night. Her brother Phil, for one, admired her grit and deter-
mination to get ahead in life, despite the setback from her
failed marriage.

By 1984, Kathy had obtained her master's degree, and
soon began moving up the management ranks of Western
Airlines. By the mid-1980s, in fact, she was responsible for
scheduling flight crews, including pilots—a very responsible position, one that involved careful attention to flight
hours, along with an ability to work with the pilots, many of
them known for their brash, flirtatious demeanor. When
Delta Air Lines bought Western out in 1987, that meant even
more pilots and flights for Kathy to schedule.

Kathy then married again, this time to a Marine non-
com named Kevin Hohn.

Of Kathy's four marriages, this would be the shortest:
less than six months. Phil Jr. only barely remembered
it, mostly because he'd gotten married himself that summer. Preoccupied as he was, Phil didn't pay much attention
to his sister's second marriage. He did recall that the relationship with Hohn soured quickly, over "fidelity issues,"
as he put it.

By February or so of 1988, Kathy's second divorce had
been granted. Then she stunned everyone by announcing
that she intended to marry again—this time to a Delta Airlines pilot, Chuck Augustine.

Chapter 4

Born in early 1940, Charles Francis "Chuck" Augustine was more than sixteen years older than Kathy. He'd been flying for Western since 1968, just a month after he'd left the U.S. Air Force. In his six years with the service, Chuck had flown KC-135 aerial tankers for the Strategic Air Command in Texas, North Dakota, Spain and Thailand. The latter assignment had included refueling sorties over Viet Nam, where a well-directed surface-to-air missile—of which there were many—could have easily rendered the flying fuel bomb that was a KC-135 into nothing more than a fiery mist.

Chuck was a very large man—at least six feet six inches tall, and well over 250 pounds. He'd been an All-American end at Marin Catholic High School in northern California, and had a football scholarship at the University of Notre Dame from 1958 to 1962, where he played with Daryle Lamonica, later celebrated as "the Mad Bomber" for the Oakland Raiders professional football team. In addition to gaining a bachelor's degree, Chuck also came away from his major college football career with two bad knees. In fact, his last knee injury was so severe it wiped out his senior season in 1962. If it hadn't been for the knee injuries, Chuck probably could have enjoyed a professional football career of his own.

But as a member of the Air Force ROTC at Notre Dame, Chuck had gone into military service after his graduation. During his training, he was subjected to an extended survival

skills course, where "downed" pilots had to live off the land
for some weeks. According to his son Greg, by the time the
course was over, his father had lost almost forty pounds.

"I'll never go hungry again," Chuck vowed, and according to anecdotal evidence, made sure of that.

By the time he met Kathy in 1985, Chuck was coming
off his own divorce. He'd married in Texas while still in the
Air Force in 1965, and there were three children—Andrea,
Greg and Larry. But as the 1980s unfolded, Chuck and his
first wife found that they had irreconcilable differences. A
divorce ensued, said by his sons Greg and Larry to have been
quite bitter. For one thing, Chuck, as a devout Catholic, didn't
believe in divorce. On the other hand, the marital gulf between him and his mid-sixties Texas bride had grown so vast
that it was hopeless to think of repairing it.

So Chuck finally accepted the divorce as inevitable. He
moved to a condo in the Oxnard marina, and continued to
fly for Western, with all his flights—by now including Euro-
pean destinations—scheduled by a tall, willowy, beautiful,
now blond 30-year-old woman named Kathy Alfano.

Phil Alfano, Jr., later expressed surprise at learning that
his older sister was proposing yet another marriage, only
months after splitting with Kevin Hohn.

"That was kind of shocking at first," he recalled. "My first
reaction was, This guy's like, sixteen years older than you,
and you're just coming off of a divorce? Oh boy, this isn't
going to work out."

But it did, somehow—at least at first. Phil came to see his
sister's connection to Chuck Augustine as a "good fit." He
thought Chuck's laid-back, "down-home" personality bal-
anced his sister's "Type A" behavior. Whenever Kathy got
too hyper, Chuck could bring her back to earth. The opposite
was likely also true, or else Chuck would never have gotten
involved with Kathy: Kathy's intensity somehow delighted
him.

Not long after the marriage, Kathy and Dallas moved in

with Chuck at a house he owned on Pearl Street in Las Vegas. Chuck then legally adopted Dallas, which relieved Gary Voss of any responsibility for the financial support of his daughter, and the family settled down to life in Nevada. Even better, Chuck got along well with Kathy's father, Phil Sr., and her mother Kay—a critical test for the family Alfano. Often on Los Angeles layovers, Chuck had dinner with Phil Sr. and Kay. As the 1980s turned into the 1990s, the Alfanos came to believe that their beautiful, often headstrong daughter had finally settled down.

Afterward, whenever someone asked Chuck how he'd met Kathy, he enjoyed giving his laconic, Gary Cooper–esque reply. "She was my boss."

Chuck's two teenaged sons, Greg and Larry, weren't all that sold on the marriage, however. It wasn't long before both began to notice a peculiar aspect of Kathy's personality: she relished finding fault with others. Not them, though. When "the boys" visited the newly married couple in Las Vegas, Kathy made sure the red carpet was rolled out. Meanwhile, Dallas was dismissed—often sent to her room.

By this time, the late 1980s, Greg Augustine was in his late teens, and Dallas was around 9 or 10. Both Greg and his younger brother Larry thought that Kathy was terribly harsh on her daughter.

"If you've ever seen a puppy kicked a thousand times when she just wants to put her head in your lap, well, that was Dallas," Greg recalled. "Eventually she'll just give up and not care." Kathy was demanding, even cruel to her daughter, the two Augustine brothers thought. Nor were the brothers alone: the Augustines' next-door neighbors in Las Vegas, John Tsitouras and his wife, Dotty, thought so, too. Sometimes, John said later, Kathy could be downright mean when it came to Dallas, threatening her with dire punishment for the slightest transgression. It was as if Kathy wanted to prove to Chuck that she could be an effective parent.

"For a while there, when they were first married, I think she would have been content with being a wife and a mother," Phil Alfano recalled.

But with Chuck out of town three to four days a week flying for Delta, that left Kathy with a lot of time and energy on her hands. Phil gathered that Kathy had once hoped to have more children, with Chuck, but that Chuck just wasn't interested. Of course, by 1988, when Kathy and Chuck were married, Chuck was 48 years old—not exactly the right age for staying up all night with babies with colic and teething problems. From Chuck's point of view, he'd already fathered three children, and that was enough.

"I know at one point she'd talked to Chuck about adopting," Phil Jr. recalled, "and he didn't want to do that. I just think Kathy needed something to keep her busy. She was getting involved in a lot of charity work, and volunteering at Dallas' school."

But eventually Kathy's ambitions turned back to the political arena, a development that first bemused Chuck, then later alternately exasperated and alarmed him. By the end, though, Kathy's penchant for politics simply disgusted Chuck—the glad-handing and posturing so endemic to the electioneering culture was more than he could stomach.

In October of 1990, Chuck and Kathy bought a large two-story house on Maria Elena Drive in central Las Vegas. To acquire the new house, Chuck and Kathy first sold Chuck's house on Pearl Street. The old house, it turned out, had a leaky roof.

Eight months later, on July 8, 1991, the buyers of the Pearl Street house sued Chuck and Kathy. The lawsuit was eventually settled out of court. Like a weird astrological coincidence, the date the lawsuit was filed, July 8, would later be the same date Kathy was found comatose in her bed, fifteen years later, in Reno. But that wasn't the only time that particular day of the year would arise, ominously, for Kathy

Augustine. Whether it was mere coincidence depends on one's faith in superstition. While modernists eschew astrology, such coincidences can only make one wonder whether some peculiar outside influence, perhaps with a rather warped sense of humor, isn't directing human affairs after all.

Located on a cul-de-sac only a little over a mile from the downtown nexus of Las Vegas Boulevard and Fremont Street, the $329,000 Maria Elena house and its neighborhood both had histories.

Originally built in 1979 by Las Vegas bookmaking/casino legend Mel Exber, the 6,000-square-foot, two-story modern-style house had three bedrooms, four bathrooms, a family room, a wet bar, a living room, a study, a dining room and two fireplaces—a bit of an overstatement for Las Vegas. A large oval swimming pool graced the backyard.

Close to downtown Las Vegas, the neighborhood was something of an anomaly: a semi-suburban oasis in the shadow of the world of glitzy casinos.

"This was a very exclusive neighborhood, a little hidden area," recalled the Augustines' long-time neighbor, John Tsitouras. At one time, Tsitouras said, the enclave was also the home of *Las Vegas Sun* publisher Hank Greenspun, the actress Elizabeth Taylor, and at least two of Howard Hughes' lawyers. In fact, he said, the lot next to the one where Exber built his house was initially owned by Hughes, who was said to be planning to build a house there for his seldom-seen wife, Jean Peters. When Hughes died, the Tsitourases bought the lot from the Hughes estate, and built their own house on it instead.

The Augustines soon became good friends with the Tsitouras family. John was a scientist; he worked for the federal government at the Nevada Test Site, a huge expanse of sagebrush, mountains, canyons and flats northwest of Las Vegas that had been the location of almost two decades of atomic bomb tests.

As a scientist and a government administrator, John had a strong interest in aviation. At one point, in fact, the government had assigned him to select a location for a remote airstrip for the testing of experimental, secret aircraft. It was John who selected Groom Lake from the vast desert expanse, far from prying eyes; eventually the site became known as Area 51—the proving ground for the once–supersecret F-117 Stealth Fighter, and according to UFO conspiracy buffs, the place where even today the Air Force examines extraterrestrial technology.

During his days out of the Delta cockpit, Chuck enjoyed long conversations with John about flying, about the Air Force, and similar topics, often over a glass or two of scotch whisky.

"John ragged my father about putting on so much weight, and he ragged John about his smoking," Greg Augustine later recalled. The two men, both of a different generation from Kathy, enjoyed each other's company, as their razzing of each other showed.

By 1992, Kathy had decided to run for public office. At first Chuck was supportive—Kathy had a lot of energy, and it was clear that volunteering at Bishop Gorman High School, where Dallas was about to be a student, had paled. After all, Kathy did have a master's degree in public administration, and some political experience from her Washington internship. John's wife, Dotty, was initially enthusiastic about Kathy's decision to seek election as a state representative in the Nevada Assembly. At one point Dotty volunteered to help Kathy by addressing envelopes from a list of names and addresses Kathy provided.

"The next day, Kathy came over and wanted to know why Dotty hadn't finished addressing the envelopes," John recalled, with a wry grin. "Now Dotty has, let's say, a very strong sense of propriety. If someone offers to give you something, you should be appreciative, not nasty. So she told Kathy, 'I'm not your employee,' and handed her back the box of envelopes and the list." Kathy didn't say anything, but simply took the list and the blank envelopes back. To John, it didn't seem that Kathy even realized that Dotty had been offended by her imperiousness, or even that she had been seen that way.

Kathy came in for sharp criticism for her campaign tactics in the election. Among other things, she produced a campaign flyer with her photograph as a blond white woman next to a grainy image of her opponent, Dora Harris, who was African-American. The juxtaposition was condemned by many as overtly racist. It was nevertheless effective in a state with a small minority of African-Americans.

Kathy won the election in 1992, and took her place in the Nevada Assembly. Because the legislature in Nevada only meets for six months every two years, Kathy wasn't absent that much from Las Vegas; and it was possible to fly back and forth between Reno, near the Nevada capital of Carson City, and Las Vegas, with a minimum of trouble. The separations did not seem to bother either Chuck or Kathy at first, especially with Chuck often gone on long-distance flights. Greg Augustine often attended political functions with Kathy.

Like his father, Greg is a large, massive, good-looking man, and when Kathy introduced him as her "son," people would be amazed that someone as young as Kathy could have had such a handsome child in his early twenties—she had to have been only 15 at the time Greg was born! But Kathy liked to burnish a family image, and letting it be known she was the mother of four children helped, even though Andrea Augustine hadn't spoken to her father for almost a decade, and almost never to Kathy.

As the 1990s unfolded, Chuck and Kathy came to see the Tsitourases as among their closest friends. They often spent Christmas and New Year holidays together, and soon Kathy and Chuck were also friends with many of the Tsitourases' acquaintances, among them a Las Vegas plastic surgeon, Charles Vinnick and his wife, Nancy. Over the years, Kathy and Nancy Vinnick became very close friends.

In 1994, Kathy decided to run for the Nevada State Senate, a step up, since state senators had four-year terms. Kathy's opponent was an incumbent Democrat, a lawyer, Lori Lipman Brown. And it was in that campaign that Kathy's reputation for being a ruthless politician, or as her brother later put it, "a mudslinger," took root.

As this campaign unfolded, Kathy began taking campaign advice and assistance from a powerful Republican state senator from Reno, Bill Raggio, and two of Raggio's Republican allies in the senate, both from Las Vegas. The trio put Kathy in contact with a Las Vegas public relations firm, which handled the advertising for Kathy's campaign. One ad excoriated Brown, saying "the truth hurts, but the truth is still the truth," and went on to assert that Brown "actively opposes prayer and refuses to participate in the Pledge of Allegiance during legislative sessions." Prayer and the flag were both red-meat issues in a Western state like Nevada.

But it *wasn't* the truth, Brown protested. She wasn't against prayer, and certainly not against the Pledge of Allegiance. She'd only asked the legislature's leadership to ask the religious figures selected to give the daily prayers to make the invocations non-sectarian, since she was Jewish, but they had refused. So Brown simply waited outside the chamber until the prayers were over, then went in. At that point, the Pledge of Allegiance was undertaken—but because Brown hadn't yet reached her desk when the pledge began, it looked as though she hadn't participated.

Kathy soon enlisted Raggio and the other two senators to release letters confirming the charges made in the political ads. Brown was outraged by what she thought were dirty tactics, to no avail. She lost the election, with prayer and patriotism both counting against her.

But after the election, Brown sued. She named Kathy,

Raggio, the public relations firm and the other two senators as defendants, and said they had defamed her.

Suddenly Chuck was on the hook for Kathy's legal bills. Kathy's brother Phil recalled that Kathy complained that both Brown and her father Melvin were lawyers, so it wasn't costing *them* anything to pursue the lawsuit, while Chuck had to pay Las Vegas lawyer Albert Marquis to defend Kathy. The legal meter spun rapidly, and by late 1994, the Augustines filed a homestead exemption on their Maria Elena house, just in case Brown was successful in her lawsuit and won the right to seize their property to pay for the supposed defamation. Kathy and Chuck breathed a sigh of relief when a trial court judge threw out Brown's lawsuit. But that didn't stop the legal meter—Brown appealed to the Nevada Supreme Court. Two years later, that court reinstated the lawsuit.

By the following spring, the American Civil Liberties Union had joined the controversy; it turned out that Mel Lipman was a member of the ACLU's board. The ACLU threatened to sue the state if the legislature didn't stop opening its sessions with prayers mentioning Jesus Christ. At that point, the leadership of the legislature decided to take Brown's three-year-old advice and go for non-denominational prayers, in which Jesus' name was not included. Brown was invited to give one of the first such prayers. Meanwhile, a judge scheduled an arbitration hearing to see if Brown's lawsuit couldn't be settled out of court.

"By then, Chuck was sick of the whole thing," Phil Alfano recalled. "He told her [Kathy], 'Settle this!'" It seems that while Chuck was often indulgent of Kathy, there was a point when he was capable of saying enough was enough; in fact, that was exactly the sort of demeanor Kathy wanted from her husband—the same sort of no-nonsense, no argument marching orders that her father would have given.

The lawsuit was settled. Kathy, Raggio and the other two senators admitted that they were mistaken about Brown, and offered quasi-apologies. Kathy sent a letter to Brown characterizing her ad as "an unfortunate choice of words developed during the heat of an election campaign.

"I acknowledge that you had a 100 percent voting record for veterans," Kathy added, "and had never actually done anything to my knowledge which showed anything but the utmost respect for our flag and for the veterans of our nation."

For her part, Brown signed a letter saying she had no reason to believe any of those she'd sued were anti-Semitic.

Chapter 5

By late 1997, the Lori Lipman Brown imbroglio behind her, Kathy was thinking about running for Congress. Ever since working for Congressman Patterson in the nation's capital, Kathy had felt the desire to get back to Washington. True, it would mean some long separations from Chuck, but then, Chuck was usually off flying somewhere, anyhow.

Kathy began calling in her chits from various political corners. But somewhere along the line, as she later explained it, higher-ups in the party dissuaded her from a congressional campaign. Instead, they suggested she run for state controller, a statewide post whose 76-year-old Republican incumbent was retiring. After thinking it over, Kathy agreed.

To help establish her bona fides as a statewide candidate, various Republican Party organs began to extol her virtues. In one such panegyric, an outfit calling itself the National Republican Legislators Association named her one of the ten most outstanding state legislators in the country for the year 1998. A columnist for the *Las Vegas Review-Journal* newspaper couldn't believe it.

"Kathy Augustine?" wrote John Ralston. "The lawmaker who was judged one of the five worst state senators in a *Review-Journal* poll conducted near the end of the [1997] session?" Ralston first suggested that the award was someone's idea of a joke—he pointed out that the state legislature hadn't even *met* in 1998.

The whole thing was actually a political con job, Ralston

advised his readers. After the denouement of the Lori Lipman Brown affair, he said, there was no way that Kathy could win another term in the state senate, which why she was running for state controller. Winning the supposed "prestigious award," Ralston said, was nothing more than a sham to make it seem as though Kathy was qualified for higher office.

In Nevada, there are two different elected posts with control over the state's money—the state treasurer and the state controller. Essentially, the controller is the state's principal accountant, while the treasurer is the principal investment officer. However, both the controller and the treasurer's signatures are required on any official state check. While the treasurer is supposed to find the best place to deposit the state's money, meaning the safest place with a high return, the controller is supposed to audit the various government departments, including the treasurer, to make sure all the spending and investment is both legitimate and efficient. The two officers not only have to work together, they are also watchdogs over each other.

For the eight years prior to 1998, the treasurer's job had been filled by Bob Seale. In that year, Seale decided not to run for reelection, but recommended that his principal deputy and protégé, Brian Krolicki, be elected in his stead. Seale and Krolicki were extremely close; at one point, both men had survived an air crash that had killed Seale's wife; Krolicki had hiked through the wilderness for some miles to summon help. But even before Krolicki was elected to replace his mentor in 1998, Seale had been trying to do away with the job of state controller. There was no reason, he said, for the state to have two fiscal officers, when one could do the job more efficiently. Thus, when Kathy Augustine was elected state controller in November of 1998, the stage was already set: Seale, and presumably Krolicki, had no enthusiasm for any state controller, let alone a potential political rival to Krolicki, as the ever-voluble, telegenic, media-savvy Kathy could become in a state-wide elective post.

Later, Kathy would tell her brother Phil, among others, that Seale had accosted her in the Capitol building shortly after she'd been sworn in, and backed her up against a wall.

"Don't fuck it up," Seale was alleged to have said. Kathy believed that Seale meant that he and Krolicki had devised some special arrangement for the deposit of state funds that would accrue to their personal benefit; but Seale, when questioned about this much later, said he meant no such thing— only that Kathy, not being an accountant, was unqualified to be the state's principal auditor.

Afterward, Kathy told her brother not to be concerned about Seale.

"It's just the way they play politics here," she told him, meaning both government and electioneering were rough-elbowed sports in a wide-open state like Nevada, where anyone with ambition had to be prepared to give as good as they got if they hoped to survive.

Still, Seale's words would echo years later, as Kathy Augustine lay dead in a morgue in Reno.

Kathy's election as controller meant that she would have to spend far more time in Carson City, separated from Chuck. At first they tried to make the best of this, with Kathy often coming to Las Vegas, where the controller had a satellite office. At one point, questions were raised in the state legislature about eight round-trip flights between Reno and Las Vegas for Kathy, and Kathy's critics demanded better accounting for the trips. Eventually, Chuck bought Kathy a new $40,000 Lexus SUV, in part to increase her safety and comfort for the occasions when she drove from Carson City to Las Vegas, or back. But the separation was taking its toll on the marriage.

On May 10, 1999, Kathy bought a house at 9673 Otter Way in a new, gated community in southeast Reno. The sale price was $139,873, according to the Washoe County Assessor. Title was taken by both Kathy and Chuck as joint tenants, meaning that each had an equal legal share in the property. Two weeks later, the Augustines obtained a mortgage of $144,050 on the property—a loan with a rate that was subsidized by the federal Department of Veterans Affairs. Of course, Kathy wasn't a veteran, but Chuck was. The VA imprimatur helped the Augustines get a lower interest rate. Interestingly, each page of the recorded deed of trust securing the loan bears the initials "KMA," for Kathy Marie Augustine, and "CFA," for Charles Francis Augustine, and all the letters appear to have been written by the same hand. Thus, the Augustines, or Kathy at least, obtained a loan worth 103 percent of the property purchase price at a government-subsidized loan rate. Later, both Greg and Larry Augustine were to have doubts about the validity of Chuck's full signature at the end of the loan document, which was notarized in Washoe County, with the notary attesting that both Kathy and Chuck had signed the document in her presence. Chuck rarely went to Reno, Greg and Larry observed.

Six months after obtaining the loan, on December 20, 1999, a grant deed was filed showing that "Charles F. Augustine" had granted the Reno house to Kathy Augustine, "a married woman, as her sole and separate property." The signature on this deed was similar to the earlier one on the VA-subsidized loan document, although this one was notarized in Las Vegas. Thus, Kathy obtained complete control over the Reno property. It appeared to some, at least, that Kathy was taking steps to make a life for herself without Chuck.

Dallas, meanwhile, had moved out of the Las Vegas house on Maria Elena Drive, and enrolled at San Diego State University, where she had an athletic scholarship as an elite golfer. But something went wrong for Dallas in San Diego. Her Uncle Phil later learned that she'd dropped out of school, and for the first few years after Kathy was elected state controller, mother and daughter had only sporadic contact. From her brother Phil's perspective, Kathy's impatience with Dallas was clear—where she'd had to work extra hard to obtain a master's degree as a single mother, Dallas had had it all handed to her, but simply couldn't keep it together well enough to take advantage of it.

Chuck, meanwhile, was eyeing his imminent retirement. The rules required him to leave the cockpit at age 61. That would be on February 8, 2001. But by then Chuck hadn't done much flying for the previous six months—his knees were giving him such pain that it was hard to walk, let alone exercise, and his weight had begun to balloon to over 330 pounds. John Tsitouras recalled that Chuck had put on so much weight, he'd failed a flight physical, and was grounded by Delta.

Not that Chuck cared all that much about the lack of flying. The way he saw it, he'd done his time in a thousand airports, hauling tourists and business people from gate to jetway and jetway to gate, smiling, shaking hands, playing the role of the genial air captain in the handsome blue uniform, and now it was over. All Chuck wanted at this point was to sleep late, eat when he felt like it, sit in the sun by his pool, work on his crossword puzzles, sip his Scotch, swap stories with John Tsitouras, and enjoy his well-earned retirement. Gallivanting off to join Kathy in the never-ending round of political cocktail parties and rubber-chicken awards banquets was just not on.

"He was tired of traveling," Larry Augustine recalled. "He just wanted to be . . . retired."

As Chuck settled in to his life of leisure, Kathy wasn't happy.

"I think she felt when he retired that he'd spend more time up in Carson City," Phil Alfano recalled. "And he certainly had the means, and being a former pilot, he could fly for free. So that was a big disappointment for her. And I really think her job as controller played a role in their growing apart. Because when she was in the legislature, the legislature only meets for six months every two years, and she could fly home on weekends." But being controller was a full-time job, year in, year out.

For her own part, Kathy was discovering that she had a natural talent for retail politics—that is, the personal, one-to-one contact with voters and supporters. The interchange with people seemed to charge Kathy up—make life exciting.

"I've seen her work a room," John Tsitouras recalled. "She was awesome." Her brother Phil agreed: when it came to engaging with people whose support she wanted, Kathy was unstoppable: verbally acute, occasionally ribald, a charismatic personality, a live wire whom people couldn't help but remember later.

But even as Kathy became more successful as a politician, Chuck became more distant and disinterested. Soon Kathy's naturally acerbic nature asserted itself, and her target was her husband. As 2000 turned into 2001, with Chuck no longer able to escape into the cockpit, Kathy's criticism of him got worse. It was almost as if she was daring him to lose his temper with her—anything, maybe, to show he still cared.

"Kathy's big shtick was making my father feel bad," Larry Augustine recalled. "She was constantly dissing him—the way he dressed, his habits, his attitudes." Kathy made much of the fact that she was someone important, while Chuck was, now . . . nobody. But Chuck was still the down-home, good old boy he'd always been. The difference was, now he was down-home at home every day.

Chuck loved his old recliner, his place of refuge when he wanted to watch a football game; Kathy thought the chair was ratty, disgusting, certainly not something the spouse of a high state official should be caught sitting in. As Chuck grew heavier, Kathy couldn't help chide him by telling Greg: "Greg, I hope you don't get as fat as your father."

"She was constantly berating him," Greg recalled, and John Tsitouras agreed: "They had grown apart."

Not long after George W. Bush was sworn in as the 43rd President of the United States, Kathy wound up on the short list of prospective appointees to be United States treasurer. Whether this was some sort of maneuver by Republican rivals in Nevada to sidetrack Kathy into an out-of-state sinecure isn't clear, but some of Kathy's assistants at the controller's office at the time, as well as her brother Phil, agree that she was under consideration for the appointment. Kathy flew back to Washington for the interview, and thought she had a good chance. But then, according to some of her former underlings at the controller's office—admittedly, disgruntled former employees—she was confronted with an FBI photograph of her accompanying a Russian man thought to be an intelligence recruiter into a Washington, D.C., hotel. Kathy blanched, or so the story goes, and withdrew her candidacy for the federal treasurer's job.

Then, in July of 2001, Kathy attended a two-week-long seminar for state government officials at Harvard University. The $5,000 cost of the seminar was underwritten by some of Kathy's political contributors in the construction industry. While at the seminar, according to some of Kathy's underlings at the controller's office, Kathy began a brief relationship with a man from Holland. In later months, when the man came to visit in Reno, Kathy had the controller's staff call various Reno-area hotel/casinos to induce them to "comp" a room for the man. Or so some of Kathy's former employees later asserted during the investigation into her possible impeachment. Likewise, some thought that Kathy had a similar brief relationship with an Israeli she had met while traveling on state business to that country in the year 2000.

In any event, by the middle of 2001, about five months after Chuck had formally retired, it seemed that he had given up trying to make Kathy happy. He began referring to her, wryly, as "She Who Must Be Obeyed."

Then, in December of 2001, Kathy confided in her brother Phil.

"Kathy called me at work," Phil recalled. "I remember this very vividly, because it wasn't the type of conversation we normally had."

"I'm thinking of divorcing Chuck," Kathy told her brother.

"What the hell are you thinking?" Phil told her. "Kathy, why would you want to do that? You guys have been married for thirteen years . . . and he's a good guy."

"Well, he just doesn't want to do anything," Kathy said. "He doesn't want to go out, he doesn't—"

Phil cut her off.

"You knew he doesn't like that sort of stuff, he doesn't like going to the political events and that sort of thing."

Kathy started crying.

"No, you don't understand. He doesn't want to do *anything* anymore."

Phil suddenly realized that his sister meant that Chuck wasn't interested in her as a woman. But Kathy was going on.

"He's become like a hermit," Kathy continued. "He shuffles around the house in Vegas, some days he doesn't get out of his bathrobe . . ."

"Well, I think you should work it out," Phil told her. "You need to think about these things. You know, when you were married, when you got married, you were thirty-two, he was forty-eight, and you know, this shouldn't be totally unexpected." Phil Jr. could sound a lot like Phil Sr. when the occasion called for it.

"I just don't think you're getting it: he is a *recluse*," Kathy told him. "I need companionship. I just don't know what to do, I need *companionship*, I need somebody with me."

Not long afterward, Kathy gave Chuck a proposed divorce settlement. Chuck showed it to John Tsitouras, and told him that he wasn't going to agree to it. Not just because he was against divorce on moral grounds, but simply because he felt like being obstreperous. Kathy's criticism of Chuck only intensified.

"It was getting uglier and uglier," Greg Augustine recalled. But Kathy backed off on the proposed divorce, for some reason. Greg came to believe she simply didn't want a contested divorce while running for reelection as controller that year, 2002.

"Kathy wanted to project a family image," Greg said later.

But at one point that year, Chuck called him at his home in Thousand Oaks, California.

"He said, 'I've drafted a will,' or 'I'm drafting a will,' something like that," Greg recalled. Greg didn't want to hear his father discuss his future demise, even though he knew that Chuck's health was deteriorating.

"We don't need to talk about this now," Greg told him. But Chuck was adamant. He wanted to let Greg know what he was thinking.

Just then Greg could hear Kathy yelling something in the background—he couldn't quite catch what she said, but it sounded to him like Kathy was "screaming" something at Chuck.

"I'll have to call you back," Chuck said, and hung up. Although they talked numerous times after that, both in person and on the telephone, the subject of a will never came up again; Greg didn't bring it up—he didn't want to start his father thinking about his own death again.

But retirement had been good for Chuck Augustine, at least materially. He told his son Larry that having retired, he was "making more money now than when I was working." That was obviously an exaggeration, but Chuck had prepared well for his life after Delta: in addition to a $2,434 monthly pension from the airline, he also had $481,000 in a private insurance account that paid a $4,634 annuity each month for the next decade. Together this added up to an income of more than $7,000 a month—just over $84,000 a year. While this was much less than the $180,000 a year he'd been earning flying Delta's jets, he didn't have to do anything for it—he'd already done it.

By early 2003, Kathy was spending most of her days and nights in Reno and Carson City, avoiding Chuck, according to John Tsitouras. Dallas was living with Phil Sr. and Kay in La Palma while working as a security guard at Disneyland, trying to figure out what she was going to do with her life, according to her Uncle Phil.

That same spring, Greg and Larry came to visit Chuck at the Maria Elena house. Kathy was in Carson City at the time. The two younger Augustines were badgering their father about his health, especially about his ballooning weight. They noticed he seemed depressed, morose.

"You guys will just inherit, anyway," he told them.

"By now he knew that Kathy was running around on him," Greg recalled. "He knew what was going on." They encouraged him to break with Kathy, to get his health back, to start to enjoy life again—"to get back in the game," as Greg put it. Chuck brightened up, and made a joke about Viagra.

"Get her out of your life," Greg told his father. He suggested that Chuck come live with him and his family in Thousand Oaks.

"Good idea," Chuck said, and Greg was encouraged. Both sons believed their father had turned an important corner.

Not long after this, Chuck had a telephone conversation with Larry.

"Well," he said, "we've come to terms." Chuck said he and Kathy had finally agreed on a fair division of property. They'd agreed to share one lawyer for the divorce. The terms weren't what Kathy had first sought, Chuck said, but were fair for both.

A little less than a month later, Chuck Augustine suffered the stroke that was to eventually cost him his life.

Chapter 6

Even before this, troubles of another kind—political and personnel—were looming for Kathy as January 2003 came. Although she had handily won reelection as state controller in 2002, Kathy had cut some corners in doing it. Principal among these was the use of state employees and equipment on her reelection campaign in both 2001 and 2002.

This petty, although illegal, diversion of resources had been going on for some time, it appeared, in fact as early as halfway into her first four years as controller, when she'd asked the then chief deputy controller—a professional, qualified accountant—to prepare her required campaign contribution and expenditure reports. At that time the official—who was exempt from the state's civil service regulations, meaning Kathy could fire him at will—said nothing and prepared the documents.

Perhaps if this first official had refused, later events would have turned out differently. But as it happened, he acquiesced, and prepared the blatantly political documents. Kathy apparently took this compliance as an unstated perk of office—that, as an elected official, those bureaucrats who were dependent on her for their continued employment would naturally want to see her succeed. But then, Kathy had never been a bureaucrat, only a politician, and there's a big difference.

People who work for a government, whether local, state or federal, realize early on in their employment that the boundary line between legitimate government work and politics is often indistinct. To keep government from becoming too politicized, most states and localities, as well as the federal government, have enacted civil service protections for government employees. These protections essentially prevent the politicians from using their statutory power to extract personal, often political, favors from the bureaucracy.

But most elected positions also have the authority to hire and fire employees who are exempt from the civil service rules. These usually include executive officers, top deputies, executive secretaries, executive assistants and the like. Since these people are hired by the office holder directly, most have a high degree of loyalty to the person who gave them the job. And when an elected official asks such a person to do something political, often two assumptions are made: the office holder assumes the underling will perform the task out of a sense of personal loyalty to the office holder, while the underling may, though not always, feel that refusing to perform the task might well cost them their job—that it might be seen as clear evidence of disloyalty.

Such was the dilemma that Jeannine Coward confronted during the last year she worked for Kathy Augustine.

Jeannine was, like Kathy, a former member of the Nevada Assembly. She joined the controller's staff in 1999, just after Kathy was sworn in. Married to a prominent Nevada lobbyist, Jeannine was politically savvy and well-connected, having previously worked for Governor Kenny Guinn and U.S. Senator John Ensign. Unlike some on the controller's staff, Jeannine didn't need the job to pay her rent, so she wasn't reluctant to say no when Kathy asked her to cross the line and practice politics on state-paid working hours. That she nevertheless acquiesced in doing clearly political work for Kathy was only because she simply didn't want to put up with Kathy's tantrums if she refused.

"It was worse than *The Devil Wears Prada,*" Jeannine later said, only half-joking.

"The very first time she asked me to do something, [it] was to call a lobbyist who was hosting a fund-raiser for her in . . . August of 2001. And I told her I was not comfortable making a campaign phone call on state time, and she said, 'Well, just wait and make it after five o'clock, then.' So from that point on, I wasn't going to argue with her. Because it was obvious: I was expected to do what she asked me to do, and you know, she didn't care whether I did it on my own time or not . . ."

This was definitely Type A Kathy, imperious, bossy, insensitive, a personality suffused with what she thought were the perks of her office, perfectly willing to give employees their marching orders, assuming that the exempt workers understood that what was good for Kathy was good for them. As Kathy wasn't shy about pointing out, the office's exempt employees ought to be doing everything they could to see that she was reelected, because if she was voted out of office, they'd lose their jobs, too—the new controller would see to that. Politics can be a very feudal undertaking.

Although Jeannine had written most of Kathy's public speeches, once she had declined to help with the fund-raiser, Kathy knew she'd have to find a replacement for Jeannine.

Thus in October of 2001, Kathy hired a new executive assistant, Jennifer Normington. Jennifer had been working as a hotel supervisor at a hotel/casino just outside of Reno. One of her avocations was giving "presentations," toastmaster speeches to various groups. Kathy had heard her give one such speech in September and was impressed. When Kathy told Jennifer that she'd like to have her as her executive assistant, but was sure the state couldn't afford her, Jennifer told her, "Don't be too sure about that." Kathy wrote down a salary that was $10,000 a year more than what Jennifer had been earning in the hotel business. The following day, Jennifer's fiancé faxed Jennifer's résumé to Kathy, and Kathy immediately hired her.

As executive assistant, Jennifer's official duties were

fairly straight-forward. She was supposed to open all the office mail, and segregate out all the incoming checks for proper logging before delivering them to the office accounting section. Additionally, she was responsible for organizing the office's personnel files, and keeping track of Kathy's calls and appointments.

Within a week of her hiring, however, Jennifer found herself working on campaign-related activities—updating a database of Republican women, for example, or keeping track of donations to Kathy's campaign. She also became the new speech-writer, replacing Jeannine. Within a matter of weeks Jennifer was also going to political functions as Kathy's coat-holder, or even occasionally as her stand-in.

Truly, this was work that lasted from dawn to midnight. To Jennifer, it soon seemed as though Kathy expected her to be at her beck and call, as if she were some sort of 24/7 personal servant.

"I was told to be at work at eight in the morning," Jennifer said later, "and she would call me from her house in Reno, or Las Vegas, if she was down there . . . she would start calling the office at eight to make sure I was there. If I got to work at seven fifty, set up the coffee, went to use the restroom and if I missed her call, there would be a message left on the voicemail at my desk . . . screaming, 'Jennifer, where the hell are you? You're never at your desk when I need to talk to you . . . get your ass back to your desk and call me.' And that would pretty much start my morning."

Even worse, Jennifer said, Kathy often came to the office late in the morning, and stayed until late in the evening. Naturally, she expected Jennifer to stay there with her.

Jennifer said she was soon spending most of her waking hours at the controller's office, and much of her weekend doing campaign work for Kathy.

"The problem I ran into throughout my employment with her [was]," Jennifer said, "one of the cats I have is diabetic . . . and he needs insulin shots twice a day." Jennifer had been giving the cat his insulin at 7 in the morning and again at 7 at night, but Kathy's demands were wrecking the schedule. As the clock ticked away hours after 5, Jennifer grew increasingly anxious to leave.

"I'd tell her, 'Kathy, I need to leave. I need to get home to give my cat his insulin.' Her response was, 'That cat's interfering with your life. You need to kill it.'"

One of Jeannine Coward's jobs with the controller's office, besides writing speeches for Kathy, was to lobby the legislature. Unlike most states, in Nevada, state "constitutional officers" such as the treasurer or controller are permitted to introduce legislation; Kathy's bright idea was to privatize state debt collection—turning over unpaid accounts due to the state to private bill collectors. It became Coward's task to convince the legislature to approve this, and once it was approved, to set up the procedures to hire the bill collectors. After working on the project for the better part of two years, by the fall of 2002, following Kathy's reelection, Coward expected that she would be named to head the bill-collecting operation, once it was up and running. But Kathy gave the job to someone else. With that, Jeannine quit, and within a few days of quitting, talked to Nevada Attorney General Brian Sandoval about Kathy's illegal use of state resources for her personal political aggrandizement, to wit, her reelection campaign in 2002.

"I knew," Jeannine said later, "that she was planning to run for Congress [in 2004], and I wanted to make sure she was stopped." Jeannine just couldn't accept the idea of someone as imperious as Kathy going on to higher political office. If only Kathy hadn't been so mean to the office employees, the chances were that many would have willingly volunteered to work on her campaign, Jeannine thought. But when she seemed to expect it as something the employees owed her, that curdled the enthusiasm considerably.

Jeannine had made an attempt just after the 2002 election

to interest the state's personnel director in the problem of the "hostile work environment," as she called it, only to be told there was nothing anyone could do to rein Kathy in, that she was an elected official and answerable only to the electorate.

Frustrated, Jeannine then took the problem to Sandoval and essentially dumped it in his lap. "I told him everything that had been going on, and said, 'Here it is, you figure out what to do,'" Jeannine said later. She'd known Sandoval personally from her work with Governor Guinn and Senator Ensign, and in fact she and Sandoval had served in the Nevada Assembly together. Jeannine brought Sandoval proof: copies of the hard drive on the state computer used by Jennifer Normington in the controller's office. Jennifer had given her twelve floppy disks containing all the political files—fund-raising databases, addresses and phone numbers of potential supporters, campaign finance records, press releases, speeches—the works.

Primed with this information, the acting chief investigator of the attorney general's criminal investigations division began to look into Jeannine's allegations. Dale Liebherr started with Jennifer Normington, who'd quit the controller's office at the same time Jeannine did, quickly backtracked to Jeannine, and then moved on to four other former controller employees, all of whom said pretty much the same thing: Kathy Augustine was awful to work for.

Liebherr asked Jeannine what would have happened if she'd just said no to Kathy's demands.

"Well," Jeannine said, "you just didn't want to face her wrath. I mean, there was kind of a joke about 'the Wrath of Kath' . . . She's a screamer and a yeller and a pounder on the desk. So you just tried to avoid any unpleasant situation with her."

Jeannine said Kathy expected the exempt employees in her office to attend public and political events, even after hours and on their own time. They had to use their own money for admission to some events. When she told Kathy that her husband the lobbyist didn't want her out so often at night, Kathy didn't like it—she told Jeannine she wasn't "pulling [her] weight."

"Why would the controller's office be going to a ribbon cutting?" Liebherr asked. "What was the purpose of that?"

"She wanted the presence," Jeannine said. "She wanted to keep building her name . . . she wanted to increase the visibility of . . . Kathy Augustine."

When he interviewed Jennifer Normington, Liebherr asked if she'd ever "come forward and indicate[d] to her [Kathy], 'Should I be doing all this stuff on state time?' "

"I didn't feel that I could," Jennifer said. "I felt that I had to do this. I felt that if I put my foot down and said, 'Kathy, this is illegal, I'm not supposed to be doing this,' I felt I'd lose my job."

In the end, Jennifer told Liebherr, she'd quit "because I couldn't take the emotional abuse. I developed an asthmatic condition that's stress related. It would get to the point that Kathy would walk in the door and my throat would close up . . . I figured I was going to die if I stayed there, with the amount of stress I was under in that office."

Even as Liebherr was working his way down the list of former controller employees, Kathy was making a mess for herself in another area. Just before the election in 2002, she'd made it clear that the chief deputy controller, Jim Wells, needed to find another job. Kathy had asked him to prepare her campaign finance reports for the election, but Wells had declined to do this, saying it would be illegal. As soon as the 2002 election results were in, Wells quit. The controller's office exempt staff took Wells' departure as a sign of what would happen to them if they refused Kathy's demands.

To replace Wells as the chief deputy controller, the number two position in the office, Kathy asked a variety of politically connected people for recommendations. Early in January of 2003, a "headhunter," as executive recruiters are sometimes called, suggested that she consider hiring a man named Art Ingram as Wells' replacement. On paper, Ingram seemed qualified: he was a certified public accountant, an MBA, and had experience in management. He was also a lieutenant colonel in the Army Reserve.

"He had the qualifications I was looking for," Kathy said later.

On January 25, 2003, just three days before Jeannine Coward was to go to the Nevada attorney general with her complaints, Kathy flew to Albuquerque, New Mexico, to interview Ingram. Ingram came to meet her at her hotel, and Kathy invited him to have dinner with her at an Albuquerque steakhouse.

"I was impressed with him," she said.

Kathy returned to Reno the following day, and asked some of the professional staff in the controller's office what they thought of Ingram, based on his résumé. Everyone agreed with Kathy that he seemed to be a promising candidate. But as she later admitted, no one from the office checked his references.

In any event, Kathy offered the $86,153 job to Ingram, who began work in mid-February—at almost the same time that an attorney general's computer expert was examining the copies of the controller's computer files turned over by Jeannine Coward for evidence of their use in politics. On February 21, 2003, Kathy asked Ingram to accompany her to a political event in Elko, in northeastern Nevada. Eventually, there would be two stories of what happened on the trip to Elko, Ingram's and Kathy's. Ingram maintained that Kathy had tried to interest him in having sex with her, and implied that it was a condition of his employment. At one point, Ingram claimed, Kathy had pulled up her shirt to show him her bra. Kathy said that was laughable, that no impropriety had occurred, and that Ingram was making this

up only because Kathy had fired him within three months
of his taking the job.

Kathy said she'd fired Ingram because he was interfering
with her contact with the office employees. Ingram countered that she'd fired him when he'd been called to active
duty in the Army for the opening of the war in Iraq. Kathy
said she hadn't fired him for that, but had given him a letter
of reprimand because he'd failed to keep the controller's office advised as to when he would be leaving for the Middle
East. That was when Ingram accused her of trying to seduce
him. In short, it was a personnel mess of the first magnitude.

Eventually Ingram filed a lawsuit against the state al-
leging wrongful termination. When that was dismissed—
because Ingram was an "exempt" employee—he filed
another one accusing Kathy of sex discrimination. That
lawsuit was never pursued, in part because Ingram's lawyer
discovered that Ingram's exempt status made it impossible
to advance even a claim of sexual harassment. Apparently
the law in Nevada allowed politicians to seduce or attempt
to seduce exempt employees whenever they wanted to.

The Ingram fiasco, however, seemed to show that when
it came to personnel decisions, particularly decisions involving men Kathy found attractive, trouble was always just
around the corner.

The Ingram problem was still looming in the early summer of 2003 when Chuck Augustine had his first stroke.

Chapter 7

By early July of 2003, Greg Augustine was making plans to remodel his California house to accommodate the imminent move of his father from Las Vegas. It seemed clear that the marriage between Chuck and Kathy was finally, irretrievably over. All the property issues had been settled, with Chuck agreeing to give up any claim in the Reno house in return for Kathy's agreement to forgo any interest in Chuck's pension. All that remained was to sell the Maria Elena house and divide the proceeds. Kathy was spending almost all of her time in Reno and Carson City.

Then, in early July, a water heater on the second floor of the Maria Elena house ruptured, and the resultant flood damaged the ceiling and floor of the family room below. Chuck had people in to replace the heater and repair the damage. In the family room below the leak, Chuck had a deep-pile carpet installed. Not long afterward, he was walking across the new carpet when his feet caught in the high pile, and he fell.

Within a day or so of this, Chuck noticed that something seemed to be wrong. An inveterate crossword puzzle solver, suddenly he couldn't think of the words he wanted. Nor could he add numbers—he couldn't remember basic arithmetic. As a pilot, numbers had always been easy for him.

Chuck went over the Tsitouras house next door.

"I can't read the paper," Chuck told John. "I see the

words, but I can't read them. I'd go to the hospital, but I don't know where it is."

Both John and Chuck realized that Chuck had had a stroke. Chuck thought it was probably a minor problem— after all, he could still walk and talk. John wasn't so sure, though. He drove Chuck to Sunrise Hospital, a little over a mile away.

"I think I've had a minor stroke," Chuck told the admitting nurse. After he described his symptoms, the charge nurse muttered to John that she didn't think it was really a minor stroke, but something more serious. Chuck was admitted to the hospital and placed on a blood thinner. Preparations were made to give him an MRI the following day.

That afternoon, Chuck called Larry to let him know what had happened. Larry had just moved to Florida—he was in a hotel room in St. Augustine, of all places, waiting for his house to close escrow.

"I've had a little stroke," Chuck told his son. "I'll be in the hospital a few days." That was typical of Chuck, who habitually minimized health problems, a residue of the stoicism from his football-playing days. "I guess I'm just getting older," he told Larry.

Larry wasn't particularly alarmed—his father sounded cogent and vital. Greg thought so too, when Chuck called him. It isn't clear, but it appears that Chuck also called Kathy in Carson City to let her know.

The next day, July 15, Chuck went in for the MRI, and while being prepared for the test, suffered another stroke, this one a major thrombosis. The hospital rushed him back into its intensive care unit and called Kathy. This time Chuck had lost all power of speech, and also control of his musculature. His eyes appeared unseeing. In fact, he was thrashing around so wildly that the attendants had to sedate him—at six feet six inches and over 300 pounds, an unrestrained Chuck could do a lot of damage. John and Dotty came to see him, but Chuck had no idea who they were, or that they were even there.

"He was out of his mind," Tsitouras said.

Kathy heard this news while in her office in Carson City.

"Oh my God," she told her new executive assistant. "I've got to leave right away." Kathy hurried to the Reno airport and caught the first plane to Las Vegas. Along the way she called Greg Augustine, who was driving to Las Vegas. By the time he arrived from Los Angeles, Kathy had already been to the hospital. She called Greg on his cell phone as he drove into town, and told him that Chuck was out of it—that he couldn't communicate except by squeezing someone's hand. The hospital physicians had taken him off the blood thinner for the MRI, Kathy told Greg, and that's when the major stroke had occurred.

"Why did they take him off the blood thinner?" Greg asked. But Kathy didn't know.

"We all knew he was at risk," Greg said later. Chuck's weight and inability to exercise were crucial factors in his condition.

Now Greg began weekly long-distance commutes between Los Angeles and Las Vegas in July and August, spending a few days at home before getting back on the road to Las Vegas and the hospital. After three weeks in intensive care, Chuck was moved to another room. While he didn't seem to be getting any better, at least he wasn't getting any worse, the nurses told Greg. The best hope now was rehabilitation, and with that, Chuck might possibly regain his ability to talk. At least he's losing weight, Greg thought—and Chuck was. Unable to eat anything solid, the pounds began dripping away.

Matters were very awkward between Kathy and Greg. Greg knew that Kathy and Chuck had been working on a divorce, even if he didn't know the details of the proposed settlement. He could tell that Kathy was determined to avoid taking responsibility for Chuck. Greg was more than a little angry at her for wanting to abandon his father in his time of need.

"She had a panicked look," Greg recalled. "She wanted to know, 'Who's going to take care of him? *I* can't take care of him.' "

"I'll take care of him," Greg said. Kathy looked enormously relieved, Greg recalled.

A few days later, Kathy and Greg were driving to lunch together.

"Greg, don't worry," Kathy said. "I'm not going to take the money and run."

As the days turned into weeks, with Greg continuing his long-distance commuting and Kathy spending time in Las Vegas for the first time in several years, Greg began to notice that Chuck's possessions were disappearing. First to go was the ratty old recliner chair.

Greg asked Kathy, "You're going to buy him a new one?"

"Of course," Kathy said, but Greg sensed that she had no such intention. Then there were other things of Chuck's that began to turn up missing: a "Shopsmith," a sophisticated power tool Chuck had loved, which he used to make furniture—that went to Phil Alfano. Other Alfano cousins arrived in Las Vegas, and many carried things away from the house, according to Greg. Meanwhile Kathy began complaining that she was responsible for a $10,000 bill from the hospital for Chuck's treatment.

What is wrong with this woman? Greg asked himself. The complaint about the hospital bill and the disappearance of his father's things convinced him that Kathy never expected to see her husband healthy again, or even that she expected him to die. To Greg, already suspicious of Kathy, the fact that she was giving away all of Chuck's possessions seemed incredibly incriminating.

But all that was just the background: because within a

week or two of Chuck's major, incapacitating stroke, Greg realized that Kathy was interested in another man.

"Enter Chaz Higgs," Greg said later.

Greg wasn't able to say for sure exactly when he first became cognizant of Higgs. It was something that slowly seeped into his awareness. At first all he could see was his father, lying sedated in the hospital bed, connected to all the wires and patches and IVs and catheters. When the sedative wore off, Chuck began thrashing again, tearing at the leads and tubes, trying to get rid of them, wild in the way an animal might be when held against its will, until more drugs were administered. For Greg, it was gruesome.

Slowly the picture frame widened, and there was Kathy, also in the room, talking about who was going to pay the bills, giving away his father's possessions, relieved that Greg was going to assume responsibility for a husband she no longer wanted.

Then the aperture grew wider still, and on the periphery, a male nurse, someone who kept coming into the room, exchanging words with Kathy, then later coming by, repeatedly showing himself outside the door, trying to be seen by Kathy—to Greg, it was like two high school kids flirting.

Next, seeing Kathy and the nurse he had learned was named Chaz Higgs in the hospital cafeteria, heads close together, deep in conversation. Were they touching each other's feet under the table? Greg wasn't sure, but he thought so.

As the weeks wore on, and Chuck continued in his sensory limbo, Greg came to have the deepest of suspicions about Chaz Higgs, and Kathy as well.

Then came the day—August 19, 2003—that Kathy called Greg while he was in southern California.

"Your dad has died of massive organ failure," Kathy told him.

Just like that—alive one minute, dead the next. Greg

couldn't believe it—not after all that had happened, not when nurses had just told him that his father seemed to be getting better. He told Kathy they should ask for an autopsy, but Kathy was adamant—there would be no post-mortem.

"Massive organ failure"? *What does that mean?* Greg asked himself. *How would Kathy know something like that, just twenty minutes after Dad died?* Greg thought he knew the answer: *That sounds like something that guy Chaz Higgs would have said. Kathy is just parroting that gigolo nurse.*

Greg, his wife Michelle and their two children drove to Las Vegas the next day. The plan was to hold a family wake that night at the Maria Elena house; Greg and his wife planned to stay at the house after the wake, then attend the funeral the following Friday. Larry also arrived in Las Vegas. One of the first things the brothers did was go to the funeral home to make sure of the arrangements. The funeral home showed them the death notice it planned to send out. Greg and Larry looked it over, and it seemed all right to them. The notice had all the details about their father correct—his birth, his life, his death. Neither noticed that under "survivors" were listed three sons: Greg, Larry and Dallas.

The Augustine brothers left and went to the Maria Elena house. They had keys to the house. Greg was pretty sure that Chuck had made a will before he'd had the stroke—hadn't he said he was making one, or had made one? Hadn't he said his sons would inherit? So Greg and Larry and Michelle began looking for the will, opening drawers and closets and the like, in search of it.

"We looked high and low for it," Greg recalled. After all, Chuck had been living in the Maria Elena house by himself, for all practical purposes, for the previous six months, except for his stay in the hospital. It seemed logical that if Chuck had prepared a will, it would be somewhere in the house.

Some time after they started looking, Greg, Larry and Michelle heard the front door open and close. It was the older Alfanos, followed shortly thereafter by Kathy and Dallas. They had been to the funeral home, too, and they noticed the error listing Dallas as one of Chuck's "sons." Kay Alfano was furious with Greg and Larry for the "insult," as she saw it. Now Kay felt she had caught the Augustines red-handed, tossing the house for a non-existent will.

"Where's my dad's will?" Greg asked Kathy. Kathy said there was no will. Greg said Chuck had told him he'd written one, or was writing one. Again Kathy denied it.

"He intended to leave his money to Dallas and me," Kathy said, "because you're going to get an inheritance from your mother."

By that evening, a group of about twenty or thirty people, relatives of both the Alfanos and the Augustines, had arrived at the house for the wake, among them Phil Alfano, Jr. He knew that there had been some friction between the Augustine brothers and Kathy, both over the death notice and, he thought, the size of the casket. Since Chuck was such a large man, an oversize casket was needed; Greg thought Kathy was unwilling to pay for it. By the time people began arriving at the house for the wake, there was a lot of tension in the air between the two sides of the family.

"Kathy was in her giving-away mode," Greg recalled. "She allowed my dad's cousin and his sister to take whatever they wanted." Greg thought she should have at least asked Chuck's sons first. Greg and Larry wanted their father's Notre Dame class ring. No one knew where it was.

"I was appalled," Greg recalled. "I couldn't stand to look at her."

By then, Greg was behind the bar in the family room, grim, but pouring drinks. He looked up and he saw—*What!* Chaz Higgs . . . no, *two* of him . . . sitting at the bar. How could that be? That's when Greg realized that Chaz Higgs had an identical twin brother.

What the hell is he *doing here?* Greg wondered. It seemed very strange for one of his father's nurses to turn up at his wake, let alone his twin brother. But there the two identical Higgses were, both drinking Chuck Augustine's liquor. Greg felt like throwing up.

Chaz turned to Michelle Augustine with what she thought was a leer.

"What do you say we fire up the Jacuzzi?" he said. Michelle and Greg both thought Chaz was coming on to her. Michelle was disgusted, Greg furious.

Right about then, Kay, who had been suppressing her own anger at the Augustine brothers, decided that Greg had given Dallas "a dirty look," as Greg recalled it. That set Kay off, and she accused Greg and Larry of deliberately insulting Dallas by listing her as a "son" in the death notice.

"How dare you?" Kay demanded.

Greg protested it hadn't been intentional, but then Kathy jumped in. The circumstances of Chuck's death, combined with all the other elements—the botched death notice, the supposed will, the Higgs brothers, the give-away mode—all combined to ratchet up the feelings on both sides.

"I remember yelling at Kathy," Greg confessed later. "Kathy said something about Dallas, and I said something about her looking like a man . . ."

That did it.

"Get your stuff and get out!" Kathy ordered Greg.

Greg and Michelle, and Larry and his wife and their children left the Maria Elena house and went next door to the Tsitourases'. Greg told John what had happened—the part about the hot tub flabbergasted John—and Greg began calling around for hotel rooms for the night.

Two days later, the Alfanos and the Augustines attended Chuck's funeral. All were in a sullen mood. Dallas did not attend.

Afterward, Greg was more and more convinced that something foul had happened to his father, and that Kathy and Chaz Higgs were behind it. It had something to do with the missing will, and the divorce, he felt sure.

"There was monkey business there," between Kathy and Chaz, Greg said. In his mind, Greg toted up the circumstances: a pending divorce . . . a missing will . . . no autopsy . . . hanky panky between his step-mother and his father's nurse . . . then sudden "massive organ failure," which Chuck's death certificate officially described as "cardiopulmonary arrest," and "septic shock," with the underlying cause of "cerebral vascular accident, stroke."

The situation stunk, Greg thought. He began talking to lawyers in the Las Vegas area, trying to find one who could do something . . . what, he wasn't sure. Convince someone there should be an autopsy? He had no standing to insist on one. Investigate a will that no one ever saw? Good luck.

Altogether Greg Augustine consulted five different lawyers in the Las Vegas area, and none of them wanted to take the case, whatever the case was. Greg thought they were all afraid of Kathy Augustine, the state controller, and Nevada political power.

"At every turn she was there obstructing," Greg said.

At one point, increasingly suspicious of Chaz, Greg had a credit report run on his father. The report came back with a notation: "Charles Francis Augustine, aka Chaz Higgs." There it was in black and white, as far as Greg was concerned. Chaz Higgs the nurse had tried to take over Greg's father's identity, doubtless to fraudulently use his credit. That told Greg everything he needed to know about Chaz Higgs— that he was a liar and a crook, and the way he'd put his hooks into Kathy showed he was a first-class sleaze.

Still later, Greg learned that Kathy had sold Chuck's 1996 Lincoln Town Car. The buyer was Chaz's brother Mike. To Greg it seemed like the Higgs twins were using Kathy to loot his father's estate. But he couldn't find anyone willing to pick up the cudgel on the Augustine family's behalf.

After three or four months of trying, Greg finally decided that he'd spent enough time and emotion on the matter.

"I just sort of said, *'Do-over* . . . Let them have their miserable lives.' And I remember thinking: *It's karma. Whatever goes around, comes around.*"

Chaz

Chapter 8

Years later, a prosecuting attorney would call Chaz Higgs a sociopath—someone who has no conscience, a person given to habitual lying, who cares for no person other than himself. It seemed an apt description at the time, but it wasn't true—or at least, a battery of psychological tests seemed to show it wasn't true.

But Chaz Higgs was certainly an unusual individual. Perhaps his most outstanding characteristic was his chameleon-like capacity to seem as though he actually was whatever someone wanted him to be. In short, Chaz aimed to please, and was usually very successful at making people think they *were* pleased—at least for a while. But then reality caught up with the dream, and Chaz had to find a way to move on.

"I could tell right away he was a player," a fellow nurse was later to say about him. By that, Kim Ramey didn't mean that Chaz was a Lothario, hitting on women reflexively, Don Juan–style, but rather that he like to play roles—mostly to convince people to like him, or at least be impressed by him.

Even with his name, Chaz found a way to pose. Originally born William Charles Higgs, he had lived most of his life with that name. It was only over the last few years, when he sought to cut himself loose from his past failures, that William Charles was transformed to the jazzier "Chaz."

William Charles Higgs was born June 2, 1964, reportedly the older of identical twins born to career U.S. Marine William Higgs and his 24-year-old wife Shirley. When Chaz was 13, Bill and Shirley divorced. The boys grew up in Jacksonville, North Carolina, and by all accounts their childhood was pretty ordinary: school, sports, social activities, all within the norm for their time and place. Nor is there evidence that either of the twins ever had a problem with the law, often an indicator of trouble ahead.

Chaz was considered a very bright kid, probably in the top 3 percent according to intelligence scales. In high school he was an accomplished student. Some thought he had sold himself too short—that with some diligence, he could have applied himself and gone on to high accomplishment. But there was something off about Chaz, something hidden, possibly even from himself: he had a weakness for taking shortcuts, reasoning that he was smarter than most people, and that he could probably get away with it.

By the time he was full grown, Chaz was just under six feet and well-muscled, chiseled, in fact. At his best, he weighed around 200 pounds. He was very proud of his body, and proud that women found him attractive—even irresistible, Chaz was sure.

And there was one more thing: Chaz Higgs loved his mother. A lot. And his mother loved him. In her eyes, Chaz could do no wrong.

After graduating from high school in Jacksonville in 1982, Chaz joined the Navy four days before Christmas in 1983. While training as a hospital corpsman at Camp Lejeune, just outside of Jacksonville, Chaz met another corpsman in training, Dawn Renee Brown. They were married in Dillon, South Carolina, in September of 1984. Interestingly, Dawn called Chaz "Chuck."

In light of subsequent events, two reporters for the *Las Vegas Sun*, Ed Koch and Mary Manning, made a valiant effort to fill in Chaz's background. They tracked down Chaz's first wife. Neither reporter was particularly surprised to learn that the marriage broke up because of Chaz's infidelity.

"He was a little womanizer," Dawn told the reporters. At one point she caught Chaz in bed with a nursing student. Dawn decided to forgive and forget, but it was a pattern that would be repeated the following year when they were transferred to a naval base in Jacksonville, Florida.

There Chaz met the woman who would become his next wife, Kirstin Dawn Gonzalez, who was married to another man at the time. Kirstin was also the mother of an infant son. It appears that Chaz began a relationship with Kirstin Dawn Gonzalez while he was still married to Dawn Renee Brown. That was one too many Dawns, if not mornings.

"He was seeing her while he was married to me," Dawn Renee Brown told the *Sun* reporters. "He liked to be with other women. He could not be faithful."

A divorce was granted to Dawn Renee and Chaz on February 19, 1988. A little more than eighteen months later, Chaz filed the first of his two bankruptcies. Four months after that, Kirstin Dawn's divorce was granted. She and Chaz married on the first of January, 1990. Chaz adopted Kirstin's son.

The marriage was not a success, it appears. That fall, Chaz and Kirstin left Florida and came to Las Vegas. Chaz left Kirstin and the boy there, and reported for duty aboard a ship based in San Diego. On June 4, 1992, Kirstin's divorce from Chaz was granted in Las Vegas. Chaz agreed to pay $400 a month in child support. Six years later, in 1998, Kirstin's new husband, a police officer in Las Vegas, agreed to release him from the obligation.

In July 1993, Chaz was transferred to duty in Manama, Bahrain, the Persian Gulf home base of the Navy's Fifth Fleet. In all, Chaz would be in Bahrain for almost four years. By his own account, he was present at the June 25, 1996, Khobar Towers terrorist bombing in Saudi Arabia that killed 19 U.S. servicemen. Afterward, he helped care for some of the 373 others wounded in the attack.

During his tour in Bahrain, Chaz met another woman, Lorelei Sagmit Gueco. Lorelei was in her early twenties, a native of the Philippines, and the mother of an infant daughter. When Chaz finished his tour in Bahrain, he, Lorelei and the baby returned to the United States. By the fall of 1998, Chaz had filed for bankruptcy again, this time in Virginia. From the court papers, it appears that he and Lorelei were living separately. Lorelei's address was in Jacksonville, North Carolina, while Chaz was living in the enlisted men's quarters at the Marine base in Quantico, Virginia.

The bankruptcy papers showed that Chaz was about $30,000 in debt—including over $3,200 to the American Institute of Holistic Theology in Birmingham, Alabama.

According to its website, the American Institute of Holistic Theology offers "a wide range of learning options including the philosophies of metaphysics and holistic spirituality . . . AIHT is an academic institution of higher education. It is privately owned and is not a church ministry."

The curriculum at AIHT appears to link ecumenical spirituality to New Age health practices. There is, perhaps unavoidably, a certain buzzword quality to its self-description: "AIHT coursework is based on universal laws and intended to offer students a touchstone for the deep exploration of personal growth, evolution and human potential." The institute is accredited by the state of Alabama and the American Association of Drugless Practitioners, a trade organization of holistic health care providers that some in the mainstream medical establishment consider a haven for quacks.

The bankruptcy documents don't indicate whether it was Chaz or Lorelei who was in debt to the American Institute of Holistic Theology, but given his interest in matters medical, it was probably Chaz. In later years, he would claim to be suffering from hypothyroidism, a debilitating illness that can lead to depression, apathy, loss of libido, infertility and impotence, among other symptoms, even including psychosis if left untreated. Hypothyroidism is a favorite target of holistic health care providers, some of whom offer exotic cures for the malady, including seaweed diets, ingestion of coconut oil, and similar unconventional treatments. It is possible that the debt owed to AIHT was for treatment of his hypothyroidism. Six years later, while married to Kathy Augustine, Chaz's insistence on having expensive, holistic treatment of his hypothyroidism was a continuous source of contention between them, with Kathy doubting its effectiveness, and resenting the fact that the treatment was not covered by either partner's health insurance plan.

On March 1, 1999, Chaz officially left the U.S. Navy, although it appears he'd actually served his last day a month or two before that—the bankruptcy file showed that as of February 4, he had moved to Eureka, California. Two months later, there was an address in Louisville, Kentucky. Then, sometime that summer, Chaz drove Lorelei and her little girl to Las Vegas, where they began a new life without him. Chaz returned to the East Coast, and enrolled in a nursing curriculum at Craven Community College in New Bern, North Carolina, about 40 miles northeast of Jacksonville. He obtained an associate's degree in nursing from Craven in 2002.

With his degree in hand, Chaz set out for Las Vegas in an old school bus he had converted into a motor home. According to his brother Mike, Chaz chose Las Vegas so he could be closer to Lorelei's daughter, whom he had apparently adopted. Arriving late that summer, Chaz took the nursing license test in Nevada and passed. He lived in the converted bus in a recreational vehicle park on Boulder Highway in east Las Vegas. Late that fall, Chaz was employed as a nurse at Sunrise Hospital.

In the aftermath of later events, as speculation flew over how and when Chaz and Kathy first met, Clark County District Attorney David Roger told *Las Vegas Sun* reporter Abigail Goldman that he had seen Chaz at a Republican political event in Las Vegas in the fall of 2002, escorting

Kathy Augustine. Given that Chaz had only just arrived in
Las Vegas in the fall of 2002, Roger's identification of Chaz
seems unlikely—why would Chaz, by all accounts apoliti-
cal, not to mention almost stone broke, turn up as Kathy's
escort at a political event? How would they even have known
each other? But for those who later suspected that Kathy
and Chaz had conspired together to murder Chuck Augustine, Roger's report was meaningful—it gave Chaz
and Kathy eight months to have worked up to the deed.

The far more likely explanation the supposed sighting was
that Roger simply made a mistake, confusing the year 2003
with the previous year. Because Kathy attended so many political events, and because Chaz often accompanied her in the
fall of 2003, it would have been easy to get confused.

In any event, Chaz was working at Sunrise Hospital in
July of 2003 when John Tsitouras brought Chuck Augustine
in after he suffered his first stroke. Chuck spent the first
three weeks of his hospitalization in the intensive care unit,
with all but one day of that time in an incoherent state after
the second stroke on July 15. Then, on August 8, Chuck was
transferred out of the ICU to another part of the hospital, for
rehabilitation. He still was unable to talk. Chaz was assigned
to this area of the hospital, and thus became one of Chuck's
nurses. That was when he first met Kathy, according to
Kathy herself, and also John Tsitouras, who later said that
Kathy had introduced him to Chaz at the hospital.

John was not impressed by Chaz. An old-fashioned kind
of guy, John thought Chaz was untrustworthy almost from
the moment he met him.

"Anyone with diamond studs in the ears can't be all
good," John said later. "What she saw in him was beyond
anything that anyone could guess at."

Strangely, despite these accounts from John Tsitouras,
Greg Augustine and Kathy herself, Chaz was later to insist
that he didn't meet Kathy until after Chuck died, and even
that was as a result of Kathy's initial omission of him while

presenting gifts to the hospital staff for their care of Chuck after his death. It was when she realized that she'd skipped him that Kathy first invited him to have a cup of coffee, Chaz said; just why he would say this when even Kathy admitted that they'd met before Chuck died was unclear.

Chuck died on August 19. Afterward, there was the scene at the wake in the Maria Elena house, for which both Chaz and his brother Mike were present, and where Chaz made the crude remark about the Jacuzzi. The following month Kathy went to Hawaii. Chaz went with her. They married there on September 19. With Chuck's death, Kathy had become a millionaire, at least on paper.

Kathy and Chaz

Chapter 9

Phil Alfano first realized that his sister had married again a month or so after the fact, in the fall of 2003. For some reason, Kathy had kept the Hawaiian ceremony secret. Then in October, Phil saw Chaz at a political function, having no idea who he was—he had no recollection of Chaz or his brother Mike being at Chuck's wake in August.

"It was an event where she was getting an award, and I just assumed he was just a date," Phil said. The next morning, though, the extended Alfano family met for a brunch, and Chaz again was present. That was when Kathy announced that she and Chaz had been married in Hawaii the month before.

"He's just been an angel, and he swept me off my feet," Kathy said, and went on to extol Chaz's virtues excessively, according to Phil.

"And all this kind of garbage," Phil said, of his sister's praise of his new brother-in-law. "My wife and I were just looking at each other. I mean, we were dumbfounded. It was—you know, you listen to her and it sounded like a seventeen-year-old girl. And I'm like, *Kathy! What were you thinking?*"

But Phil said nothing to his sister—what good would it have done at that point?

"I wished her well . . . You know, 'I hope things work out.' And I remember after the brunch, my mom saying to him, 'Treat her right,' and that kind of stuff. It seemed like an odd combination, but he was a very polite guy, very respectful, very quiet."

Phil and his wife Mary were particularly taken aback by Chaz's appearance, which seemed so incongruous compared to Kathy's usually conservative attire.

"My wife and I joked that he looked like one of the 'Pet Shop Boys,' with his hair, you know. We're from that same generation, like 1986—he has his hair curled in the front, and bleached, and we kind of made a joke about that. And obviously, we were all concerned because it happened so quickly."

According to Chaz's later account, the first three months were unalloyed, wedded enchantment for the odd couple. There was a trip to Washington, D.C., where Kathy met with Treasury Secretary John Snow, and White House Chief of Staff Andrew Card, and learned that she was again in the running to be the U.S. treasurer. Kathy was ecstatic, according to Chaz. But not long after they returned to Reno, the serpent in the garden showed up, in the guise of three representatives from the Nevada Attorney General's Office.

On January 28, 2004, Dale Liebherr, Deputy Attorney General Shane Chesney, and Liebherr's boss, Chief Investigator Linda Honey, sat down to question Kathy about her alleged illegal use of state personnel and resources for her 2002 reelection campaign, as well as the unhappy saga of the short-lived employment of former Chief Deputy Controller Art Ingram.

Later, Chaz would pinpoint this encounter as the beginning of the end of connubial bliss with his fourth wife. From this day on, Chaz contended, Kathy became increasingly depressed and nasty. Chaz blamed the politicians for this—in his view, the other pols were so eager to see Kathy run out of public office that they would stop at nothing, and in so doing, had ruined her life. And in feeling miserable, Chaz added, Kathy had ruined his life as well.

Eventually, Chaz would claim that Kathy's political enemies were responsible for hounding her to her death, all as part of some secret plot to get her out of the way so that crooks could get control of the state's money.

At the beginning, it didn't seem as though anything all that serious was in the offing with this interview in late January of 2004. Probably the most ominous moment was when Kathy waived her right to keep silent and/or to consult with a lawyer. Kathy probably thought this was just a routine formality. She was wrong.

Linda Honey wanted to get Kathy's side of the story. She often appeared to take Kathy's side in the controversies, judging from her lack of aggressive follow-up questioning. Perhaps that lulled Kathy into giving incautious answers; she was certainly voluble in this interview, far more so than any lawyer would have advised.

Kathy was surprised that her interlocutors wanted to know about the Ingram fiasco—she'd been led to believe that the only topic of the interview would be the 2002 election allegations.

"We didn't realize that was one of the things you were going to talk to me about," she said. With the word "we," Kathy showed that she thought Chesney *was* her lawyer, even though, unbeknownst to her, Chesney had known all along about the complaints against Kathy—Jeannine Coward had told him as long as a year earlier about the use of the staff for political purposes, but Chesney apparently hadn't told Kathy about her former subordinate's complaints.

Chesney therefore represented the state of Nevada, Attorney General Sandoval, the controller's office, and possibly the controller herself, all in the same interview. These multiple clients put Chesney in a conflicted position, to say the least—had Kathy retained her own lawyer, doubtless he or she would have pointed this out, and perhaps she would have responded differently to the questions. Chesney was obligated to disclose these conflicts to Kathy before the interview. His advice to Kathy to waive her Miranda rights was riddled with legal problems which would erupt later in the year, as the Nevada State Senate considered Kathy's impeachment.

The unexpected addition of Ingram as an interview subject did not unnerve Kathy, though. She took responsibility for hiring and firing him. Although he seemed at first "very cordial, very nice . . . it turned ugly from the very beginning," Kathy said.

She told the story of Ingram's hiring, and how things had gone bad: "We started seeing some real problems. Just his whole relationship to the staff. He was forbidding me to . . . have any interaction with the rest of the staff, he insisted that I go through him. And I'm one of those hands-on people . . . when I'm over [with the staff] they see my smiling or angry or sad or whatever face I'm wearing on that particular day, and I do have personal interaction with all my staff."

Liebherr wanted to know what she meant.

"He did not want me to go over there, and if I wandered over there to see somebody, the next thing I knew he was standing behind me," demanding to know what she was doing.

"I was quite astounded by the whole thing, and told him in no uncertain terms that I was the elected state official, that I ran the office, and if I needed to see somebody I in fact was going to go over there and talk to whoever I needed to talk to."

After that, the relationship with Ingram deteriorated, Kathy said. A month or so later, Ingram received orders calling him to active duty in the Army. At that point Kathy didn't think she could legally fire him, because of federal laws protecting the jobs of reservists called to active duty. Eventually Kathy issued Ingram a letter of reprimand, which accused him of being verbally abusive as well as condescending. Later, Kathy discovered that she could legally fire Ingram, if there was reason to believe he wasn't capable of doing the job.

Honey asked Kathy about the sexual harassment complaint. Ingram had charged her with requiring him to accompany her to various political events as her "escort." When he'd put it that way in a complaint he later filed with the Equal Employment Opportunity Commission, Kathy said, he made it "seem like he was providing me with an 'escort service' rather than escorting or accompanying me to a function . . ."

As for the trip to Elko, "There was never any impropriety during the evening, nor when we returned to the hotel [in Elko] that night." The following day when they got back to Reno, Kathy attended another event, this one for her long-time ally, State Senator Raggio. There Ingram had asked her to introduce him to "an available, quote 'available woman' that evening . . . it is ludicrous for Mr. Ingram to even suggest I would lift my shirt and show him my bra or make sexual advances toward him. In fact Mr. Ingram's behavior became so erratic and unpredictable inside the office and out, invitations to any social functions were not extended to him in the weeks prior to his subsequent departure . . ."

"Was there ever any physical contact between you two?" Honey asked.

Nothing that was improper, Kathy said.

"Did you hug him?" Chesney asked.

Kathy admitted that she had hugged Ingram "maybe on occasion."

"Are you a hugger?" Chesney asked.

Kathy laughed.

"Yes, yes. I hug the women in my office too, or I'll put my arm around somebody and tell them it's okay they're having a bad day . . . I was a Catholic school teacher, and you know, I used to do that to kids sometimes, but it was never anything that was improper or had sexual overtones."

"Did you ever kiss him?"

"He . . . uh . . . said that . . . uh . . . that I gave him a kiss on the cheek that night when we got back to [the hotel in] Elko . . . I don't remember that, but it could've, it was something that was harmless, just a thanks, nothing that could have been construed as sexual harassment. I was married, by the way, I was married at the time, and I was subsequently widowed in July of last year."

Kathy began to cry.

"It's okay," Honey said, clearly feeling uncomfortable.

Kathy composed herself, and went on to say that Ingram hadn't known that her husband had just died when he filed the sexual harassment lawsuit.

Eventually, Kathy said, Ingram had become so "volatile" that she'd reported him to the Nevada Capitol Police, and had his keys to the controller's office taken away.

Having exhausted the topic, Honey moved on to the allegations by Jeannine, Jennifer and the other former employees that Kathy had forced them to work on her reelection campaign in 2002, and that she had repeatedly shouted at and vilified them.

Kathy said Jeannine and Jennifer were both disgruntled former employees who were bent on retaliation. In fact, she said, she'd given Jennifer a letter of reprimand just before she'd quit.

"Did you ever see her work on your campaign?" Honey asked.

"Yes."

"[During state] work hours?"

"Yes."

"Did you ever talk to her?" Honey meant, had Kathy warned Jennifer not to do campaign work on state time?

Kathy didn't directly answer the question, saying instead that Jennifer was "very creative," and implying that she preferred to work on the campaign rather than do the work required by her state job. In fact, Kathy said, Jennifer had let so many of her official duties slip that Kathy had to give some of Jennifer's work to other people in the office, which created other problems. But if Jennifer or anyone else worked on her reelection campaign, Kathy said, it was only because they wanted to, not because anyone had forced them to do it.

In other words, if Jennifer and Jeannine or anyone else had cheated the state, that was their fault, not hers.

As for Jeannine, Kathy said, she was "bitter, very bitter" at not being placed in charge of the new debt collection section of the controller's office after having convinced the legislature to approve it.

"She had really taken ownership of that," Kathy said. "She felt it was her baby, she had actually done a lot of work in the legislature . . ."

When Jeannine didn't get the new job, Kathy said, and then resigned from the office, she was two years short of time needed to vest for retirement. "I think she was also angry because she had left and then lost her retirement, too."

"She makes a lot of reference to you having—"

"Yeah, a 'hostile work environment,'" Kathy finished.

"And you're brow-beating people . . ."

"She was very, very bitter," Kathy said again.

Chesney asked the two investigators what was going to happen next. Honey said they would compile a report and present it to the chief of the attorney general's criminal division.

"Oh," Kathy said, her voice barely audible. This appears to be the first time that Kathy realized she could be in jeopardy of criminal prosecution for breaking the law.

"Once again, I have to reiterate, nobody was coerced, nobody was forced . . . it was strictly voluntary," Kathy said.

The very next day, Chesney sent a letter to Kathy advising her that he had a conflict of interest in the case. Kathy soon hired her own lawyer, John Arrascada of Reno, and as the spring unfolded, Arrascada began negotiations with the Nevada Attorney General's Office. It soon became clear to

Arrascada that Sandoval meant to prosecute Kathy for potential felonies, and if possible, put her in jail.

Whether it was this looming threat of possible criminal prosecution or issues closer to home, by April much of the bloom appeared to be off the marriage of Kathy and Chaz. In the first blush of the romance, Kathy had paid some $41,000 in cash for a slightly used BMW for Chaz—quite a step up for someone whose existing wheels were a beat-up, 27-year-old Volkswagen. After all, Kathy could afford it: with Chuck's Delta pension, his annuity, and her $80,000 annual salary as controller, Kathy was taking in almost $14,000 a month before taxes, far more than she needed to meet her expenses, even with two mortgages. Chaz found a full-time nursing job at the South Meadows hospital in Reno, and pooled his money together with Kathy, giving the two-person household an income of almost $18,000 every month.

Later, this would prompt some curiosity on the part of Phil Alfano, Jr., among others: where did all the money go?

"Well, that's the question," Phil said, after Kathy died. It wasn't clear what Kathy and/or Chaz did with their money, although there were some peculiar rumors about Chaz's spending habits. One of Kathy's aides later told Phil that Chaz had tried to sell her husband cocaine, and her daughter marijuana; she said Kathy knew nothing about this. Others thought Chaz was addicted to steroids. But even if this was true—Greg Augustine doubted it because Chaz simply didn't seem bloated enough—it couldn't account for all the money that seemed to vanish. No evidence was ever produced to substantiate any of these rumors, however.

By April of 2004, though, Kathy had taken steps to protect most of her assets. She met with a Reno lawyer, Mike Melarkey, who specialized in wills and trusts. On April 30, 2004, Kathy formed the Kathy M. Augustine Trust, and signed over all her property, with the exception of the BMW and her own Lexus, to the trust. Kathy's will specified that Chaz was to receive the two vehicles but nothing more, according to Phil. If Kathy died, income from Chuck's half-million-dollar annuity was to go to Dallas, along with any other assets, including a substantial money market account, as well as the two houses, which together were worth about $800,000 at then-current market prices. Phil Alfano, Jr., was to be the trust's executor. In total, the pot was worth about $1.1 million, once the mortgages were paid off. It's interesting, and possibly significant, that evidence was later produced that Chaz's unhappiness with Kathy began about the same time that Kathy had formed this trust.

Later, Chaz was to say he always knew about this trust, which essentially cut him out of the money and the real estate, from the day Kathy signed it. Phil Alfano disputed that. Eventually, Phil obtained the lawyer Melarkey's notes. These said nothing about Chaz having been present when the trust was created. While it's certainly possible that Kathy later told Chaz about it—perhaps even confronted him with its provisions—Phil was convinced that Kathy never did, based on remarks she made to him at the end of 2004. At that point, Phil said, Kathy told him that Chaz wasn't to receive anything from the trust. Phil inferred from this that Chaz knew nothing about Kathy's plans, that the marriage between Kathy and Chaz was on the rocks, and that the union wasn't likely to last.

What Chaz actually knew about the trust, and what he did not, is crucial to understanding what was to happen over the next two years: Chaz's insistence that he knew about the trust from the start would undercut his motive to murder Kathy—if he knew he wasn't going to get any of the money, why would he commit murder?

On the other hand, if he had *not* known about the trust, he might well have decided to kill Kathy to cash in, as the inheriting spouse. Whether Chaz really knew about the trust would be a secret held by Chaz alone.

By June or so of 2004, Kathy had begun to relax about the prospect of being charged with crimes by the attorney general's office. Her lawyer, Arrascada, had told her that the attorney general's office seemed willing to bargain. That month, Chaz and Kathy took a cruise to Alaska. A shipboard photograph of the couple shows them smiling, apparently relaxed. If Kathy was feeling stressed by the prospect of being arrested, it certainly didn't seem evident.

Then, on July 1, 2004, news of the attorney general's investigation leaked out to the press, and Kathy had to admit she was the target.

Kathy refused to provide any details of what was being investigated, except to contend that it had nothing to do with her campaign finances, her travel history, or any criminal acts on her part. Well, one out of three wasn't bad.

"I just want to get this over with," Kathy told a reporter for the *Las Vegas Review-Journal*. "I want to get this behind me."

But it wasn't going away. That same day, a columnist for the *Review-Journal*, Steve Sebelius, chortled in print at Kathy's discomfiture. In a piece headlined "Is this 'Bye-bye, Kathy'?" Sebelius reported that Kathy and her lawyers were negotiating with the attorney general over her resignation. If the attorney general was investigating, he added, that probably meant that felonies were involved. Sebelius reminded readers of the Lori Lipman Brown smear, by then almost ten years in the past.

On July 8—of all dates—Attorney General Sandoval formally acted. In an official request for an opinion from the Nevada Commission on Ethics, Sandoval's chief criminal deputy, Gerald Gardner, asked the commission to determine whether Kathy had violated state ethics laws prohibiting elected officials from using "governmental time, property, equipment or other facility to benefit his personal or financial interest." In a separate news conference, Sandoval said that Kathy had already agreed to admit violations of the ethics laws.

The Nevada Commission on Ethics, a creation of the state legislature, was empowered to levy a fine of $5,000 for the first violation of the laws, if the violation was proved by a "preponderance of the evidence," a very low standard. A second violation could bring a fine of up to $10,000, and a third violation might cost as much as $25,000. At the same time, nothing in the law prevented a complaint based on the same facts from going forward separately in criminal court. Finally, if a "willful violation" of the ethics laws was found by the commission, the matter had to be referred to the State Legislature for consideration of impeachment. Together, it was a potential triple punishment for the same act, one of the strongest ethics laws in the nation, and intended to prevent government corruption in a state where vice had been legalized for three generations.

With Sandoval's announcement, it appeared that Kathy Augustine's colorful, often turbulent career as a Nevada politician was over. As a future candidate, her prospects looked as appetizing as burnt toast.

Chapter 10

"I can't believe this is happening to me," Kathy told her brother Phil after the attorney general's office filed the "request for opinion" with the ethics board. It all seemed so petty to Kathy—sour grapes from Jeannine and Jennifer, plus a few others who hadn't been able to measure up to Kathy's standards. Kathy told her brother that she thought she was being set up by political rivals, "that there were some folks who wanted to see her take a fall," Phil said. "And they were using this as a vehicle."

In the aftermath of the complaint, a host of rumors swirled around the state. In one, Kathy was said to have offered to resign for "personal reasons" if Sandoval would agree not to file the ethics charges. The rumors said Sandoval rejected the proposed deal. Her lawyer, John Arrascada, said the rumors were incorrect.

The state's principal newspaper, the *Las Vegas Review-Journal*, produced an editorial calling for Kathy to avoid impeachment by resigning—forthwith:

> *Ms. Augustine was always politically ambitious, and apparently her aspirations got the best of her. Even a neophyte should understand the obvious conflict in a sitting politician forcing public-sector underlings to do campaign work on the clock . . . she should save the taxpayers the time and treasure of an impeachment hearing and step down. Immediately.*

The following day, another *Review-Journal* columnist, Jane Ann Morrison, weighed in:

> *Comeuppance is such a delightful Victorian word. It doesn't get enough use because it doesn't happen often enough. State Controller Kathy Augustine is finally going to get hers.*

Morrison thought that Kathy deserved to take her lumps because of what she had done to Lori Lipman Brown in 1994, and Dora Harris in 1992. Morrison never met Greg Augustine, but she would have understood what he meant about karma.

On August 13, 2004, John Arrascada wrote back to the ethics commission that "State Controller Augustine admits, with explanation [sic], that she reasonably should have known that the time expended by Jennifer Normington on Controller Augustine's campaign was more than that allowed by law." Campaign work by Jeannine Coward and several others was only minimal, he said, and not even the attorney general thought these acts were violations. But in any case, no one had been *forced* to do the work, Arrascada said.

Kathy waived her right to a formal hearing before the Commission on Ethics, and agreed to a stipulation admitting three violations of the ethics code: causing Jennifer Normington to work on her reelection campaign; using the state's computer, telephone and fax for the campaign; and knowingly using this equipment for the same purpose. The last two violations seemed to be the same thing, but weren't: *using* and *knowingly using* were two different things, legally.

Kathy's stipulation sealed her fate with the Commission on Ethics. But the admission may have been extorted.

"My understanding is," Phil said, "she was threatened

with, 'Well, either you plead guilty [at the Commission on Ethics] . . . or we're going to a grand jury, [and] you'll be removed from office during the hearing.' So she signed this document. And then was fined . . . Her thinking was, 'I'll pay the fine, I'll get a slap on the wrist, and that'll be the end of it.' "

Phil said his sister had told him that her lawyer, Arrascada, recommended the admission to get rid of the problem. The $15,000 fine imposed by the Commission on Ethics wasn't even the biggest sanction it could have levied—it could have demanded $40,000.

"She thought it would be over at the ethics commission level," Phil said.

But once the commission found her guilty of violations of the ethics laws, Governor Guinn, Senator John Ensign and Congressman Jim Gibbons, Republicans all, and up to then allies of Kathy, called on her to resign.

Kathy was distraught at having been abandoned by the leaders of her own party. She was increasingly convinced that someone was out to get her from her own side, for some reason. After all, she said, others had done the same thing she'd been accused of and they hadn't been pilloried the way she'd been. To Kathy, it had to be part of some plot to get rid of her—maybe someone didn't want her poking too closely into where the state had been investing its money . . .

"The governor's asked me to resign," Kathy told her brother Phil. "I don't think I should. What do you think I should do?"

"Fight it," Phil told her. "What do you have to lose?"

"I can't believe this is happening," she told Phil, again. "This is such a minor thing. There are some real serious issues over here that people don't know about."

On October 10, Kathy sent a lengthy letter to the editor of the *Las Vegas Review-Journal*, saying she would not resign.

Up to that point, Kathy said in her letter, the public had only been given fragments of information about the charges against her. The whole story, once put into context, revealed an entirely different picture, she contended:

> *During my 2002 reelection campaign, many of my staff volunteered to assist. I should have known that some of them were expending state time on the campaign. However, I had no intention or actual knowledge that any ethics rule or law was being breached.*

Without mentioning Jennifer Normington by name, Kathy referred to the letter of reprimand she had given her.

> *I was then faced with what managers and supervisors have to deal with at one time or another: a disgruntled employee with an axe to grind . . .*
>
> *In hindsight, I should have known my employees' time spent on my campaign crossed the line. That, I admit. I was not fully aware of the allegations against me until attorney general investigators questioned me over a year after my accusers lodged their complaint with that office.*

If she'd known that what she'd done was wrong, Kathy asked, why would she have reprimanded her chief accuser? Kathy concluded:

> *The truth always leaves some sort of footprint. Persons involved in a nefarious plot do not make their scheme public, or intentionally create witnesses against themselves . . . the acts to which I have admitted have nothing to do with my accomplishments in office. I will not stand silently and have my integrity dragged through the mud. I'm ready to fight.*

One month later, the governor called a special session of the legislature to consider Kathy's impeachment. The fight was on.

The 21st Special Session of the Nevada Legislature convened on November 10, 2004. The Nevada Assembly was to hear the evidence presented against Kathy, then vote on whether she should be impeached, much as a grand jury might consider an indictment. If impeachment was voted, the matter would be passed to the Nevada State Senate, which would conduct a trial, then vote on whether to remove Kathy from office. Two-thirds of the 21-member Senate, 14 votes, were required for conviction.

Because impeachment is a political act, the normal rules of evidence found in a court of law did not apply. Thus, Deputy Attorney General Gardner acted as both a prosecutor and a witness. More significantly, Kathy's lawyers, Arrascada and Dominic Gentile of Las Vegas, had no power to cross-examine anyone. In fact, as Gentile would later point out, the Assembly's proceeding was even more stacked against Kathy than a normally secret grand jury proceeding, in that witnesses were allowed to be present while other witnesses testified, and hearsay was accepted. To Kathy's lawyers, these were serious legal flaws. To Kathy herself, the whole proceeding smacked of a Soviet-style show trial, in which the outcome was foreordained.

"Kathy Augustine had no authorization whatsoever to make state employees work on her private campaign on state time," Gardner told the members of the Assembly. "She had no authorization to use state facilities and equipment and computers to run her campaign . . . Kathy Augustine's acts fall squarely into the category of malfeasance—the commission of acts that are unlawful in themselves, which are completely unauthorized, illegal and wrongful. Her acts violated the Nevada Code of Ethical Standards; they violated the Nevada Administrative Code; they violated the Nevada Revised Statutes.

"How can such acts be anything other than malfeasance? Kathy Augustine, from approximately October 2001 to November 2002, literally ran her campaign headquarters out of the Nevada State Capitol."

Like a prosecutor in a criminal case, Gardner summarized the evidence expected from the witnesses who would next testify—Jennifer and Jeannine, and five other former employees of the controller's office. In addition, Gardner had prepared thick binders of exhibits, mostly copies of documents taken from the state computers used in Kathy's office, including emails between Kathy and the staff.

"These forty-two exhibits provide documentary proof of the vast amounts of campaign work that was being done on state time by state employees," Gardner said. "Nearly twelve hundred pages of reports, letters, logs, lists, forms, labels, invitations, endorsements, candidate platforms and press rebuttals, all created, edited, drafted, worked on, on state time."

Gardner pointed out that one of the exhibits was a copy of Kathy's stipulation to the Commission on Ethics.

"Kathy Augustine's stipulations are, in themselves, sufficient to support impeachment," Gardner said. "Engaging in this willful misconduct, Kathy Augustine lost sight of her duty to the public trust. The people of Nevada deserve to have that public trust restored by seeing the Nevada Assembly issue articles of impeachment to send Kathy Augustine to the Senate for trial."

One of the first witnesses to testify was Jennifer Normington.

She was no "disgruntled employee," Jennifer told the Assembly, despite what Kathy had written in the *Las Vegas Review-Journal*. She hadn't even been the one who reported Kathy to the attorney general. She was just a state employee who did illegal political work for her boss because she feared for her job.

Jennifer told her diabetic cat story. By this point, the tale of the cat's twice-daily insulin injections and Kathy's heartless reaction to its plight had become a staple of Nevada humor. A newspaper cartoonist had even drawn a hilarious image of a maniacal, screaming Kathy trying to choke the life out of Jennifer's scrawny pet: "Die, you sick little furball!" the cartoon Kathy shrieked.

"I loved working for the state of Nevada and serving the public in my own small way," Jennifer said. "However, what I had thought was a career breakthrough turned out to be just the opposite. My health suffered greatly as a result of the stress I faced between Ms. Augustine's oppressive management style and the ethical conflict I faced on a daily basis.

"But the issue before this body is not me. It is whether or not elected officials should be allowed to misuse public resources, as Ms. Augustine has, and still remain in office. Over the course of the 2002 year, I was forced to devote at least seventy-five percent of my state time to working on the State Controller's reelection campaign. If that is not an impeachable offense, I do not know what is, Mr. Speaker."

The Assembly Speaker, Richard Perkins, a Democrat, advised Jennifer that it was for the Assembly to decide what an impeachable offense was, but thanked her for her testimony.

Jennifer was followed to the witness table by Jeannine Coward. She wanted to contradict Kathy's assertion in the *Las Vegas Review-Journal* that the staff had "volunteered" to work on the campaign.

"Never did I consider myself a volunteer," Jeannine said, "and I do not believe any others did. We were directed by her to do the tasks, and generally [did so] when she told us . . . Controller Augustine had a history and a reputation for losing her temper, throwing things, losing control by screaming and yelling when she was angry about something, which included anything from not being at your desk when she happened to phone you, to not liking the size of a label on an envelope, not liking the size of the font on a letter, and other equally immaterial things."

Jeannine had become so disturbed by Kathy's behavior with the staff that by June of 2001, she privately asked her whether she thought she'd created a "hostile work environment." Kathy said no, but added that she wasn't trying to win a popularity contest. Jeannine suggested that if she was going to lose her temper at someone, she should at least do it in private rather than humiliating them in public. That seemed to work for a while, but soon Kathy was back to bashing people in front of others—it seemed she relished having an audience for these demonstrations of control.

It certainly wasn't true that Kathy had been unaware that it was wrong to have the staff work on politics, Jeannine said. Kathy knew, because she'd approved an employee code-of-conduct Jeannine herself had written in 1999 that specifically forbade work on political matters on state time. One of the worst things about working for Kathy, she continued, was the hypocrisy evident when Kathy paid lip service to the rule, but flouted it in actual practice.

"Did you ever see Controller Augustine lose her temper?" Perkins asked.

"Many times. One day I was talking to someone [in another state department], and she had been trying to get me on the phone. And she came in and hit my 'hold' button while I was talking to him . . . She would yell and scream. She ordered one of our chief deputies to get their 'ass' back over to the Legislature one time, in the middle of the office, screaming at him. It was a regular occurrence. So, no one wanted to confront her on anything. Everybody tried to get along, tried to do their job, but no matter how hard they tried, it was impossible to please her, because she would always find something that was wrong . . . In a hostile work environment you are not particularly inclined to volunteer your time to work for someone who treats you like you are a slave."

"So, your point is that those employees that she is claiming were volunteering on her campaign would not have volunteered on a campaign for somebody who conducted himself or herself in the fashion that she did?" Perkins clarified.

"Exactly. I think if you probably asked them if they voted for her, they probably would tell you they did not. So, they hardly would be working on her campaign."

On the other side of the Sierras, Phil Alfano, Jr., was able to get the broadband audio and video of the impeachment proceedings on his computer. As he watched, he saw Jennifer and Jeannine leafing through the forty-two paper exhibits, which were contained in binders. Some of the exhibits were computer spreadsheets of campaign donors, or lists of supporters. Phil realized that while the binders looked impressive, because of the nature of the computer program, many of the sheets were blank.

"I mean, it was comical," Phil recalled. "I watched that here, I actually saw that part of it, and I'm going, 'You've got to be kidding me—they're wasting the taxpayers' dollars on this?' "

His sister had told him, Phil said later, that while Jeannine and Jennifer and some of the others had worked on the campaign on state time, they were greatly exaggerating the amount of time they had actually put in. Phil was convinced that the principal cause of the trouble was a personality clash between Jeannine and Kathy.

"I know that Jeannine Coward served in the assembly, with Kathy, and I think her career kind of faltered, and Kathy's took off, so there was some jealousy there." Phil said later. "I know there was an assignment of some sort that was in the controller's office that was given to somebody else, and Jeannine Coward was very, very bitter about that, as well."

But Phil admitted that Kathy's personnel management

skills left a lot to be desired, "and so that just adds fuel to the fire.

"It's very obvious they both had an axe to grind," Phil said, "and my take on it is, and Kathy's was, that somewhere along the line, others saw this as a way to make a mountain out of a molehill."

By the end of the first day, almost all of Gardner's witnesses had testified, and then Gardner moved for admission of investigator Dale Liebherr's report as an exhibit.

Kathy's lawyer Gentile had already objected to Gardner's testimony as inappropriate—to him, it was like allowing the prosecutor to take the stand and give his own opinion in a criminal trial, an obvious violation of the rules of evidence. Now with the acceptance of investigator Liebherr's report, another, similar violation was taking place.

"Mr. Speaker, with all due respect . . . from my point of view, [the fact] that you just had Mr. Gardner testify and present Exhibit forty-one [Liebherr's written report] has totally polluted this matter," Gentile said. "Exhibit forty-one should not be a part of this record. Other than that, I have nothing more to say at this time."

Perkins asked if Kathy's lawyers wanted to offer suggestions as to how the next day's proceedings should be structured.

"Maybe I did not articulate it well enough," Gentile said. "Given the pollution, I am not going to contribute anything to this record. We are *done*."

Gentile was disgusted with the way the impeachment was being handled. To him it had all the fairness of a kangaroo court.

The following day, Kathy's lawyers renewed their attack on the legitimacy of the proceedings, claiming that they had been initially told that the attorney general's office would play no role in presenting the matter to the Legislature, only to see that promise evaporate in the rush to charge Kathy with political crimes.

"It is clear that the attorney general has a conflict of interest," Arrascada said. When Deputy Attorney General Shane Chesney sat in on Liebherr's interview of Kathy in January of 2004, he had a conflict—he couldn't properly represent Kathy at the same time he was an employee of the attorney general's office. When Chesney had then allowed her to make a statement and waive her Miranda rights, he was essentially acting as a double agent—after all, his boss was investigating his client, and the two interests were directly adverse.

Not only that, Arrascada said, but the evidence which had been presented was the tainted fruit of a criminal investigation. Had Kathy been charged with statutory crimes like theft or bribery, she would have been entitled to many rights, not the least of which was the right to confront her accusers. In the absence of criminal charges, the claims against her should have remained confidential, he said.

"By Nevada law, the dissemination of this material is improper, and it should not have been provided to you."

The process was also fundamentally unfair, Arrascada said.

"In a preliminary hearing, we would be allowed to cross-examine witnesses to test their credibility, their reliability, and their recollection of facts. No one [who] testified here yesterday was placed under the crucible of cross-examination to address their biases, their reliability, and their credibility." He'd looked at impeachment proceedings in other states, Arrascada said, and he'd been unable to find any other state that used the procedure the Assembly had used against Kathy the day before.

"The Speaker said yesterday that we were making history," Arrascada concluded, "but [that] we are going to make history in 'the Nevada way.' As a fourth-generation Nevadan, I know that 'the Nevada way' includes fairness, a respect for fundamental rights, process, and that people are allowed to speak their mind and fight their fight, but fight it fair. I think we all must question whether yesterday was done in a 'Nevada way.'"

After a short break, a lawyer for the Legislature assured the members that despite Arrascada's criticisms, the proceedings were legal.

With that, the forty-two members of the Assembly voted on three articles of impeachment, each of them alleged to be a willful misdemeanor or malfeasance, and each of them encompassing the same language adopted by the Commission on Ethics in late September.

The Assembly approved all three articles by a unanimous vote, 42–0, setting the stage for the impeachment trial that followed.

Chapter 11

The impeachment trial of Kathy Augustine began in the Nevada State Senate on November 29, 2004. Two weeks into the process, some of the objections voiced in the Assembly by Kathy's lawyers had sunk in—for the Senate trial, the attorney general's office was benched, and a special prosecutor, Dan Greco, the chief deputy district attorney in Washoe County, where Reno was the county seat, was appointed. It appears that Kathy's long-time ally, Senator Raggio—himself a former Washoe County district attorney—played a role in the switch.

"By doing this, we are not agreeing that a conflict exists," he said. "In fact, we have been advised by our own legislative counsel and by the attorney general's office that the law clearly indicates there is no conflict of interest. But to avoid the issue, a special prosecutor has been designated . . ."

As in the Assembly, the rules of evidence used in a criminal case did not apply. That meant objections as to vagueness, hearsay, lack of proper foundation, or similar legal safeguards were out. As Special Prosecutor Greco kept insisting, the Senate had the right to decide what it would and would not consider evidence. Whenever the defense asserted privileges normally accepted under the evidence code, Greco objected, saying they had no relevance in the political proceeding of impeachment. At the same time, Greco availed himself of evidentiary privileges that normally benefited the prosecution, and when Kathy's lawyers objected to this as unfair, Greco was quick to argue that the Senate could do whatever it wanted to do—that it wasn't bound by any rules other than those it chose to make for itself.

Kathy's lawyers had previously filed a written objection to the "sufficiency," or legality, of the articles of impeachment adopted by the Assembly. The articles "suffered from duplicity," they wrote, meaning that Kathy could be accused of either a misdemeanor or malfeasance, but not both.

It was a technical argument, but one worth pursuing: since the Senate had to decide each article by a two-thirds majority, which was she guilty of—malfeasance, or misdemeanor? Some senators might say one violation was a misdemeanor, others might say the same violation was actually malfeasance. Depending on how each senator defined the violation, each article might therefore have less than the required two-thirds vote to convict.

Malfeasance and misdemeanor were entirely different legal concepts, the defense contended. So the Senate first had to decide between the two before it could even consider the issue of guilt or innocence. Or, the defense suggested, the Senate could just dismiss the case entirely, and they could all go home.

In any case, whether misdemeanor or malfeasance, to qualify as an impeachable offense, Kathy's lawyers argued, the special prosecutor still had to prove that the violations were directly related to her performance in office. Personal peccadilloes, even occasional diversions of state resources for personal purposes, did not qualify. Personality clashes were definitely out.

"What will become absolutely clear . . . is that Kathy Augustine's actions *do not* constitute either misdemeanor or malfeasance while in office," the defense contended. "Instead, Kathy Augustine's actions should be viewed as exactly what they are: poor judgment decisions by a superior who was not well-liked by her subordinates.

"In fact, not being well-liked by her subordinates is perhaps too kind—the facts reveal a group of *former* employees who were biased, disgruntled, prone to exaggeration and/or outright lies and who clearly held a grudge against their boss. The 'witnesses' against Kathy Augustine made numerous derogatory references to Kathy's personality, appearance, and personal life when presenting their testimony both to investigators with the AG's office and to the Assembly itself.

"Her actions constituted minor transgressions that fall far short of a legitimate basis to impeach her and remove her from the office to which the electorate appointed her."

If the Senate convicted Kathy and removed her, any elected official in the state would be fair game for any employee, or former employee, who wanted to get even with them for personal or political purposes, the defense argued. That was a swamp the Senate dared not enter—to approve the articles of impeachment, the senators would have to weigh Kathy's conduct against "all elected officials who are running campaigns for reelection while they are in office." Was what Kathy had done really so different from what any other elected official might?

"What Kathy Augustine did amounts to misguided judgment—plain and simple. The *only* reason her misguided actions have gotten her to the stage of the first impeachment trial in the state of Nevada is because three former, extremely biased employees . . . who were prone to hyperbole and gross exaggeration, got together and somehow convinced the powers that be within the [attorney general's] office that their mean, bitchy boss should be made an example of, for doing something that goes on at every level of government during an election year, and particularly where the candidate is already holding office."

The unholy trio's complaints had never been subjected to any critical evaluation or cross-examination, Kathy's lawyers pointed out. Most of the complaints centered on Kathy's personality, nothing more.

"Their statements to investigators from the AG's office and their orchestrated testimony before the Assembly, neither of which was subject to *any* cross-examination, is filled with absolutely irrelevant and highly inflammatory statements about how demanding of a boss Kathy was; how verbally and emotionally abusive she was towards her employees; that she had a bad temper; that Kathy flung papers at her employees when she was mad; that Kathy was computer illiterate; that Kathy hated her employees; that the controller's office was too stressful; that Kathy was greedy for campaign donations; that Kathy was a cheap boss; that Kathy remarried too quickly after her husband died; that Kathy remarried a man who was her previous deceased husband's hospital nurse; that Kathy was not very smart; that Kathy's demanding personality caused her employees to suffer from health conditions; that Kathy's employees referred to her temper as 'the Wrath of Kath'; that Kathy unfairly reassigned her employees to duties that they didn't want to do; and that Kathy just wasn't a nice person. *None* of this testimony is even remotely related to the allegations of malfeasance and misdemeanor in office."

These complaints were just griping. It was for the voters to decide to throw Kathy out of office for these complaints, not the State Legislature, said the defense.

"It was a well-known fact that Kathy was not well-liked—by her employees and by fellow government officials. Kathy speaks her mind about all issues pertaining to the duties of the controller's office, and she often took sides of an issue that were unpopular to say the least. She can be a stern, short-tempered and highly demanding boss and elected official. Nevertheless, she has always maintained the integrity of the office to which she was elected, and her primary goal as state controller has been to ensure that the responsibilities of that office are carried out completely.

"Removal from office is simply not necessary or just

based upon the law and evidence in this case, for no matter how dissatisfied her accusers are with the way they have been treated, Kathy Augustine has done nothing to harm the citizens who elected her or those that she serves that would rise to the level of such a drastic sanction."

After some discussion and another opinion from the Legislature's legal advisor, the senators voted 20–1 to reject this defense argument that the articles of impeachment were legally flawed.

Now the senators would hear from the witnesses, and for the first time, the witnesses would be subject to cross-examination.

After a day of testimony from the ethics commission staff, former Deputy Controller Jim Wells, and several of those former controller employees interviewed by Liebherr, Special Prosecutor Greco finally reached the heart of his case: Jeannine Coward and Jennifer Normington.

Jeannine testified much as she had in front of the Assembly, describing occasions when Kathy had lost her temper, and how members of the staff were afraid to thwart her, especially when it came to demands for campaign work. Eventually it was defense lawyer Arrascada's turn. He peppered Jeannine with demands for specific dates and times that Kathy had been abusive, and Jeannine said she couldn't name specific dates and times, that the behavior was so frequent that no one date or time stood out. Eventually Arrascada succeeded in forcing Jeannine to admit that as far as abuse of Jennifer Normington went, she had only heard about most of it from Jennifer herself, and that her own office was somewhat removed from Jennifer's in physical distance.

"You do not like her, do you?" Arrascada asked Jeannine, meaning Kathy.

"There is an old saying, 'Love the sinner, but hate the

sin,' " Jeannine said. "I did not like the way she treated our staff or me. It had nothing to do with my personal feelings about her. As I have said, she can be very charming in a social occasion. She was witty and a lot of fun to be with. Someone you would want to be your best friend."

"When you met with Dale Liebherr, what really concerned you was that Controller Augustine could be elected to a higher office. In your opinion, she did not deserve [this]?"

"I thought her behavior in our office indicated a complete lack of respect for the law," Jeannine said.

One of the senators wanted to know how Kathy's behavior had affected the efficiency of the controller's office.

"The atmosphere in the office was such that people came to work not knowing what was going to happen that day," Jeannine said. "Many of the employees told me they dreaded coming to work or they could not sleep the night before. The atmosphere was such, you never knew what the environment was going to be. It kept everyone on edge. It was like a domestic-abuse situation where the abused person feels as if they are walking on glass all the time. Even when they try to do what is right, it ends up being wrong. You always felt on edge. You could not relax. The controller's office had some wonderful employees. They were dedicated. They were not people who tried to slough off work or waste time. Everyone was in such a state of turmoil and frustration. There were days it was very difficult."

Jennifer Normington was next.

After describing her work for Kathy's reelection campaign while on state time, Jennifer said that she was present when Kathy made telephone calls from her office to contributors, asking for campaign money. Kathy closely scrutinized other officials' campaign finance reports, and if a donor happened to give more money to someone else,

Kathy would call them to wheedle more cash for her own campaign.

Kathy told her, Jennifer said, that she needed to make certain she won the election because "it would buy her four more years . . . she said she needed to buy herself four more years so she could set up her run for Congress. She said her place was in Washington, D.C., because she was too good for this hick little state."

Hick little state! If the senators were unconvinced of Kathy's secret arrogance by now, this was sure to drive the point home. Now it wasn't just the controller's staff who felt the bite of Kathy's contempt, it was all of Nevada, too.

Kathy's lawyer Gentile tried to call Jennifer's credibility into question, but didn't have much to work with. The forty-two exhibits were liberally smeared with Jennifer's electronic fingerprints. About the best Gentile could do was establish that Kathy had told her to make sure not to do the campaign work on state time, and that she hadn't resigned from the controller's office until after Kathy had given her the letter of reprimand. Gentile wanted to make Jennifer's complaints about Kathy look like sour grapes. He didn't go anywhere near the "hick little state" remark.

The senators seemed interested in why Jennifer had resigned, with some suggesting that Kathy's letter of reprimand was deserved because of Jennifer's own mistakes and omissions in her state duties—Jennifer had failed to open important mail, for example, or had failed to lodge copies of files with the state's personnel office. But Jennifer said it was difficult to stay on top of everything because Kathy forbade her to be away from her telephone for any substantial length of time.

Time was what was also on some senators' minds.

"Every day this goes by," said one senator near the end of the third day, after Jennifer had finished testifying, "I was told it costs about eight thousand dollars. When you add up the legal fees, it is worse than the gas prices. How long do we intend to travel this road? Has the prosecutor finished his presentation?"

That would be up to the special prosecutor, the fretting senator was told. But even that wouldn't end it—Kathy still had the right to put on a defense.

Chapter 12

The following day Majority Leader Raggio introduced a legal opinion from the Legislature's lawyer contending that it was perfectly legal for a state employee to use state time to maintain campaign finance records, if those records were required by state law. That had the effect of knocking most of the wind out of Jennifer Normington's testimony, since the bulk of Jennifer's work on the campaign had been spent filling out the required campaign finance forms.

Special Prosecutor Greco now called Deputy Attorney General Gerald Gardner as a witness. Gardner explained how the investigation of Kathy had come about in the first place—that Jeannine Coward had come forward with computer disks of political files given to her by Jennifer Normington in early 2003, and that Dale Liebherr had begun interviewing former staff members. By January of 2004, Gardner said, he was in contact with Kathy's lawyer, John Arrascada.

Gentile wanted to know what Gardner had told Arrascada.

"I told Mr. Arrascada if Controller Augustine admitted to all of the facts contained in that complaint, admitted that they were willful violations, and the ethics commission accepted that admission and stipulation, that we would not file criminal charges."

"When you were having your discussions with Mr. Arrascada, you would agree that, from the perspective of

Controller Augustine, there was a threat? Not that you articulated a threat, but the mere fact that she was being investigated by the criminal division of the attorney general's office, would put forth a threat that she might be charged with a crime?" Gentile asked.

"From the beginning . . . Mr. Arrascada was desperate to avoid criminal charges being filed against his client," Gardner said. "He provided me with a variety of offers in lieu of filing criminal charges." One of those was the offer to resign if no criminal charges were filed, but Gardner said his office rejected that—they wanted the public to know what had happened.

A senator wanted to know whether Gardner agreed with the Legislature's lawyer, that it was legal for state employees to complete campaign paperwork required by the election law.

He did not, Gardner said. "I must respectfully disagree with that statement."

Another senator thought that the decision by the attorney general not to accept Kathy's resignation when it was offered was both foolish and expensive.

"If you think about it, since that decision in March, you have cost the state of Nevada hundreds of thousands of dollars, and hours of personnel time that could have been spent on more productive, substantive policy issues," the senator said. "You have lost an opportunity for the voters to choose a new controller. It could have gone on the ballot, because it would have been prior to the close of filing. I am a strong supporter in ethics, never having been a double dipper myself. I think it is very important that we go after people who violate those laws. In this case and under these circumstances, in retrospect, do you think this has been the right way to pursue this?"

If Kathy's offer to resign had been accepted, the whole subject would simply have disappeared, Gardner said, no one the wiser. "We simply could not accept that," he said.

The attorney general's office had to keep faith with the employees who had come forward to complain.

Another senator wanted to know why the attorney general had decided to investigate Kathy's actions as possible felonies.

"The idea of prosecuting Controller Augustine and having her become a convicted felon and possibly face incarceration, certainly weighed in our analysis in determining that this was the best procedure to protect the public," Gardner said.

It was evident that Gardner's answers were beginning to disturb some senators, even the Democrats.

"Did you possibly realize that by pursuing this kind of complaint, you opened the door to selective prosecution?" asked a Democratic senator, Bob Coffin of Las Vegas. "It is widely known that political activity occurs in other elected offices in the state."

"I do not know if it is 'widely known,'" Gardner said. "In cases that are referred to me, we will review them for prosecution." Gardner said he did not believe that Jeannine Coward had met personally with Attorney General Sandoval in initiating the complaint. He was in error, however—according to Jeannine, the investigation had begun in Sandoval's own office, nowhere else. That made some in the Senate wonder whether Sandoval was doing a favor for Jeannine, or possibly some other political interest bent on using the attorney general's prestige and authority to force Kathy out.

Some noted that Sandoval had just been nominated for a federal judgeship, and Jeannine's complaint put him in an awkward position. If he ignored the complaint, Jeannine might go public, and then his confirmation as a judge might be put at risk amid accusations that he'd shown favoritism to a member of his own political party.

At the same time, Jeannine and Sandoval were long-time friends—they had served in the Nevada Assembly at the same time. As Jeannine put it later, they knew each other well enough so that Jeannine could call and get an appointment with the attorney general; that was unusual access, or "door opening" power, as Gentile described it.

"We have a record of assigning positions to the constitutional officers, including yours, that are used for a variety of purposes," Coffin persisted. "We know that they cannot spend all their time on the law and processing legal paperwork. They have to project the authority and image of the office. We have always felt there should be some flexibility. Your boss is in politics, as is the governor and so is the state controller. I cannot believe that this did not cause someone in your office to raise the question of how many dollars are we really talking about, how much does an electron cost for computer usage, how much does it cost to use a facsimile machine when it is domestic.

"We are not talking about the 'everyone does it' argument," Coffin continued. "What we have discovered is not a wholesale appropriation of state resources. We have seen activity being done, periodically, to advance the office, and we have seen some to advance the campaign. The sum does not add up to very much . . . again, it leaves everyone in this state open to wondering why *this* constitutional officer is being singled out. If you had proceeded to convict, you can bet your boss and every other state constitutional officer will start seeing complaints. This [case] will be the measurement. This is a low bar. Were there discussions about that?"

"There was never a moment's thought to the fact that this would open up any kind of Pandora's box for state officials who were doing the right thing," Gardner said.

"This should not have been your bailiwick anyway," Coffin said. "You are not the political arm of the attorney general's office. If I were the attorney general, I would have thought, *Wait a minute, I live in a glass house, too.*"

By now, the tone was growing decidedly negative—it wasn't that the senators felt like defending Kathy as much as it was that they realized that almost anyone in politics might be targeted with similar complaints.

"I hope you think about this," said Senator Sandra Tiffany, a Las Vegas Republican, and a friend of Kathy. "My thought was, *Oh my God, this is a format for validating* [complaints of] *state employees.* I do not know what the future is going to hold for the rest of [our] politically elected officials. Did you consider the information they brought you as being stolen? I consider that stolen information." Tiffany meant the computer files taken by Jennifer and Jeannine from the controller's computer just before they quit. Tiffany said the data they had taken belonged to Kathy.

"My view is that that information should have never been on the state computer in the first place," Gardner replied. "I am not sure it can be stolen from a state computer. It should not have been there."

"We also heard that it was clear that some people wanted to thwart Controller Augustine's potential political ambitions," Tiffany continued. "Did you take that into consideration under this complaint?"

"There was nothing in the investigative reports or any of the evidence that indicated to me that there was an attempt or conspiracy to thwart Controller Augustine's ambitions," Gardner said.

"I hope you look . . . very seriously about motivation. It may seem minor to you. It seems major to somebody like me. If you are to spend twelve or fourteen years in political office and want to have other intentions . . . that, because you have an employee [who] is upset, they could use this as a tool now [to damage a political future] . . . You may or may not get another complaint like this again. It sure looks like it is punishment to me, not protection of the public."

After the beleaguered Gardner left the hearing room, the prosecution called a forensic computer specialist to explain how she had validated the computer data as having been on the state-owned computer. But under cross-examination, it appeared that the expert had no way of proving that the data hadn't first been on a private computer, then copied onto the state-owned computer for the purpose of incriminating Kathy.

Bit by bit, the case against Kathy was starting to unravel. Confident that the tide was flowing in the direction of the defense, Gentile asked the Senate to consider voting not guilty on all three articles of impeachment before even hearing the defense side of the case, just as a criminal defense lawyer might ask a judge for a directed verdict of acquittal. With that, the Senate adjourned for the day to consider the next move.

The next day, Majority Leader Raggio announced that he was going to vote to dismiss the first article of impeachment, the one that charged Kathy with employing Jennifer Normington to fill out the campaign finance statements. The legal opinion Reggio had asked for, the one that said it was permissible for state employees to complete the forms on state time, was decisive as far as he was concerned, along with the fact that Jennifer admitted that she'd quit her former job at the hotel/casino to go into "politics."

But, Raggio said, he wasn't ready to dismiss Articles 2 and 3, about the use and knowing use of the computer and other state facilities—the Legislature's legal opinion didn't go that far.

With that, the Senate voted 11–9 to dismiss the first article of impeachment, with one senator absent and not voting. It voted 15–5 not to dismiss the second article, use of the state facilities; and by a wider margin, 16–4, voted not to dismiss the third article, the one about "knowingly" using the state facilities, namely, the computer, the office telephones and the fax machine.

The stage was now set for Kathy's defense.

"The defense rests," Arrascada said, succinctly. They had decided not to call a single witness, not even Kathy herself.

Now each side had a few minutes for summary. Greco reiterated the points that had been made in the impeachment and in the trial itself—that Kathy had forced employees to work on her campaign against their will by being mean, nasty and intimidating.

Gentile, for his part, tried to get the senators to focus on the precedent they might be setting.

"I suggest to you that if you return the verdict of guilty on the articles of impeachment, that are based upon having personal information on your computer in a state office, then you are going to have a new administrative agency that is going to be called the computer police," Gentile argued. "There's going to be monitoring, or there should be, if you are going to apply this fairly and equally to everybody in office. I ask you to think about that."

Once the Senate voted to convict for having personal information on state-owned computers, anyone could be thrown out of office and possibly indicted, Gentile suggested. The only reasonable alternative was to admit that Kathy had been the victim of as Gentile put it, "a political assassination," dismiss the remaining two articles, then go home for the winter.

Now the senators had their say. One of the most eloquent was Bob Coffin of Las Vegas—surprisingly so, because he was a persistent political enemy of Kathy.

"The public does not know the difference between impeachment and conviction," Coffin observed, after noting his own history of political differences with Kathy. "We have put the stain of impeachment on Controller Augustine for the rest of her life. That is no small punishment. Forever, she will always be the 'former state controller,' impeached in 2004 by the Nevada State Assembly. This will always be with her name. She is a young person who will spend the rest of her life with this impeachment hanging over her head. In the public's mind, it is the same as conviction.

"Now we are being asked to set a standard for future behavior for all constitutional officers, if we convict on any of these two articles. The evidence and the testimony are so picayune that in the closing arguments it was stressed by defense counsel that there would have to be computer police watching over us if we had a standard set by the conviction in this case.

"You are now setting the standard for any district attorney or any group of two or three citizens who do not like you, or the way you are running the [public] television board, to bring you up on an ethics complaint and get you kicked out. It is not that you misappropriated funds, not that you stole money, not that you were corrupt, but that you stopped and campaigned or discussed something not having to do with your job. A precedent is being set.

"I became a bit worried about my own sentiments when, starting late in the summer, people were calling for her resignation. They said she should go. She did something wrong. She admitted it. I saw an editorial where a high public official said she should resign. I do not think any of those officials had ever considered resigning. They would take great umbrage at being told to resign when they were doing the same thing in their own offices. They cannot meet the standards either.

"The mob grew larger. The newspapers . . . based upon evidence they had not seen, or if they had seen they had not investigated, or if they had investigated, they had not the talent to look at it closely, they said she should resign. They said, 'Convict her,' after she was impeached. The people who control public opinion in our state said, 'Convict.' I cannot think of one that did not say, 'Resign.' Several said, 'Convict her, convict her. *Burn the witch*.' That is easy to do. They can do that to any one of us.

"When you take someone who is a little unpopular and

you single them out in a crowd, as her own party appears to be deserting her, it is easy to take these positions. It is a win–win situation: 'My friends are going to like it. She will not like it, but it does not matter, because she is just one person I did not like anyway, and she will drift off into obscurity, getting a job somewhere.'

"I applaud my colleagues for having deliberated in a calm atmosphere," Coffin concluded, but not before bashing the newspapers again for rushing to judgment, for acting as an ink-wielding lynch mob. He intended to vote against the remaining articles. In the end, the Senate failed to reach a two-thirds majority on the second article, voting 11–10 to convict, three votes short. But it voted 14–7 in favor of conviction on the third, the "knowingly" article. Coffin voted against both; majority leader Raggio voted for conviction on the third count—his vote was the difference.

In the Senate gallery, temporarily suspended as controller, but watching as her former colleagues decided her fate, Kathy cried. Politics might make for strange bedfellows, but when it's your bosom buddy who throws you out, you really know where you stand.

Not long after this, the Senate met to consider Kathy's punishment. Even Greco, the special prosecutor, realized that one meager, narrowly approved article of impeachment was insufficient to warrant Kathy's removal from office. Instead, the Senate voted 20–0 to censure Kathy, but allow her to remain in office until the completion of her term in 2006.

After all, some reasoned: why pile on? Kathy Augustine was finished as a political figure in Nevada, there was no doubt of that.

Chapter 13

Even before these events were to reach their anticlimax in the Nevada State Senate, Chaz had been thinking of leaving Kathy. That the marriage had not gone well was obvious to Kathy's Las Vegas neighbor, John Tsitouras. As early as August 2004, Kathy had confessed to him that Chaz had lost interest in her.

"He says, 'You're not thin enough and you're not blond enough,'" Kathy told John, characterizing Chaz's criticism. Kathy was distraught, angry, chagrined, all at the same time. Even so, she continued to believe that she and Chaz could still make it as a couple.

But then Kathy was impeached. According to Chaz's own later account, he decided he couldn't leave Kathy at that point—it would be too devastating for her.

This was a hallmark of Chaz's character, one that would be consistently demonstrated over the next three years: in his description of reality, he was always the good guy, the hero, the one who put aside his own needs in order to take care of someone else. He might have *wanted* to leave Kathy, he might have been entitled to leave her, but he stood by her in her time of need, a martyr. And as the next two years unfolded before Kathy's untimely demise, Chaz was always the one who did the right thing, no matter the abuse from Kathy. But the more Chaz suffered, or seemed to suffer, the more power he took from his wife.

By Christmastime of 2004, with the impeachment finally

concluded, Kathy and Chaz were visiting Phil and Mary Alfano in Turlock, California. One night Kathy approached her brother, and again brought up the trust she had created earlier in the year.

"Chaz is not to get a penny," Kathy told Phil, and from this Phil concluded that Kathy and Chaz's marriage was not going well. That was when Phil learned that at some point that fall, Chaz had virtually emptied the joint bank account he shared with Kathy—for what purpose, Kathy didn't say. But Kathy had been so angry at this maneuver that she had thrown Chaz out—a classic clothes-on-the-sidewalk separation. But then Kathy had relented, and Chaz had returned. Still, Phil knew that Kathy's eyes had been opened—when it came to money, Chaz could not be trusted.

Then, early in the New Year, Kathy learned that if Chaz could not be trusted with money, he could not be trusted with love, either.

The exact nature of the relationship between Chaz and Linda Ramirez was never fully explained by anyone, including Chaz and Linda. But judging from the evidence, they both seemed more caught up with the idea of flirting than actually having a physical relationship. Perhaps the thrill was in the pose, not the act.

Linda was a 21-year-old admitting clerk at South Meadows. She knew some Tagalog, the language of the Philippines, as did Chaz, from his marriage to Lorelei. Soon they began chatting each other up, with Chaz using Linda as a repository for his complaints about Kathy. Somehow, Kathy discovered that Chaz and Linda were exchanging florid emails. Chaz was smart enough to zap most of his emails to Linda, but Linda's emails to Chaz persisted on the Higgs–Augustine personal computer. At one point, Linda sent an email to Chaz asking if he still slept with his wife.

"It has been a long time," Chaz replied.

What happened next is obscure, but Linda was officially

reprimanded for using the hospital's email system for personal communications, and Chaz was placed on probation for the same misbehavior. Not long after this, Linda lost her job at the hospital, and there were those in the South Meadows emergency room who were convinced that Kathy had used her political clout to get her fired, a belief that Chaz did nothing to dispel.

At some point after the first of the year, Kathy brought Chaz to the South Meadows ER when he had a severe allergic reaction. According to Phil Alfano, Chaz had an allergy to nuts—"everything but peanuts," Phil said. Chaz's own medical records seem to indicate that the allergy was actually to thyroid medication, notorious for unwanted side-effects. In any event, the reaction caused Chaz to go into anaphylactic shock, similar to the reaction people who are allergic to bees get when they're stung. Untreated, it can be fatal, as the central nervous system shuts down, and it becomes difficult, sometimes impossible to breathe. Chaz was treated with some sort of drug; later Phil discovered a vial of epinephrine and a syringe at the Otter Way house, which he concluded was something Chaz kept on hand in case he had another allergic reaction.

Chaz's brief visit as a patient to the South Meadows ER had another consequence, however: it gave some of the nurses there a chance to meet Kathy in person. Most were not impressed.

"She was talking about herself and some project," the nurse Cindy Baker recalled. "I told her, 'We're not here for you, we're here for Chaz. He's not doing too good right now. He's not breathing well.'" The ER people formed the impression that in her own mind, Kathy was the star of the Augustine–Higgs solar system, while Chaz was just an asteroid along for the ride.

In the wider world, too, people were reacting to Kathy. Despite her impeachment and the censure, Kathy continued to attend political functions on a frequent basis. For Kathy, seeing and being seen were vital to her own sense of herself. But by early 2005, most people involved with politics didn't want to be seen with Kathy. Certainly, no one wanted to have their picture taken with the disgraced controller. Sometimes she and Chaz would show up at a political dinner, and find seats at a table. Whereupon everyone at the table would get up and find new places to sit.

Kathy tried to smile through the ostracism, but it was killing her inside. It made Chaz angry to see the politicians treat her that way, and it only reinforced his contempt for them, and for the practice of politics generally. He told Kathy she should just forget about politics, if that's the way people were going to act. Sometimes she would agree with him, but she couldn't resist being involved; for her, it was like a drug.

So the Odd Couple kept attending political dinners, fundraisers, parties, charitable events, making the rounds of seeing and being seen, while Kathy smiled on, trying to pretend she wasn't dying inside. Chaz usually sat by himself, glum, saying very little to anyone, and looking as if he would rather be almost anywhere else. Once, one of Kathy's longtime supporters, in real life the editor of an automotive magazine, struck up a conversation with Chaz about cars.

"He came alive," the editor recalled, and she realized that Chaz could care less about campaigns and elections, but was wild about carburetors and cam shafts. The editor thought that Chaz must be very good in bed for Kathy to have retained an attraction to him—he certainly knew nothing about politics, and didn't bother to hide his disinterest.

A revealing window on Chaz and Kathy's relationship during this period was later provided by Mike Higgs, Chaz's identical twin brother. For some reason, Kathy kept in email contact with Mike, who had just been called to active duty as a platoon leader of a maintenance company in Iraq.

"I was kind of a marriage counselor," Mike said, as if he didn't have enough to deal with in a country enmeshed in a sectarian civil war. As early as April of 2004, he said, Kathy sent him emails saying that Chaz wanted out of the marriage. At one point, Kathy told Mike, Chaz had told her he was "unhappy with the chemistry between us and that he'd never been sexually attracted to me.

"He told me he wasn't happy the day we got married," Kathy wrote Mike. "Quite a blow."

Abuse could go two ways, it appeared.

As the impeachment investigation ramped up in the summer of 2004, Mike recalled, Kathy became increasingly irritable and "stressed out." From what he could tell from thousands of miles away, the marriage "turned bad."

"Kathy was under a lot of pressure. She took it out on Chaz," Mike said. He advised Kathy to "stick it out," that the marriage was worth saving, even though Chaz kept saying he wanted a divorce.

By 2005, after the end of the impeachment proceedings, Kathy's insistence on attending political functions caused even more trouble in the marriage, Mike said. The repudiation made Kathy hyper-critical, especially of Chaz.

"She was being tossed aside by her own political party, and that caused her to treat Chaz worse."

Chaz told his brother he still wanted to divorce Kathy, but now he felt trapped—he couldn't leave Kathy, not while she was being ostracized by all her one-time political friends. But Chaz was clear about one thing, according to Mike. He hated politics and politicians, but much to his surprise, he found he was married to one!

"He was unhappy with this new lifestyle," Mike said. "Attending all the political events and fund-raisers, he felt like a fish out of water . . . he thought they looked down on him, and he felt inferior." Chaz might not have been a political scientist, but he knew when people were sniggering at him and Kathy.

Chaz was particularly sensitive to sotto voce criticism that he was nothing more than "Kathy's arm candy," Mike said, and especially to speculation that he was only after Kathy's money.

"Chaz suggested she do something to squash [sic] the rumors that he was only there for the money." That was when Kathy had created the trust, Mike said.

Things got so bad between his brother and Kathy, Mike said, that Chaz finally was able to convince her that her political career was the source of all their problems. According to Mike, Kathy agreed to quit politics altogether to save the marriage.

But then, as 2005 turned into 2006, Kathy reneged on her promise, Mike said.

She decided to run for the office of Nevada state treasurer.

Chapter 14

**IMPEACHED NEVADA CONTROLLER TO RUN FOR TREA-
SURER'S OFFICE**, the *Reno Gazette-Journal* headlined on
January 28. "Augustine, term-limited from seeking another
four years in her current post . . . said she has 'unfavor-
ables' to overcome. But she added that she has been hon-
ored for her work as controller, and polls show she has
strong name recognition." Being the only state official
ever to be impeached was one way to get political name
familiarity, it appeared.

Kathy's decision to try again for public office angered
Chaz, according to Mike Higgs, as well as several of Chaz's
co-workers in the South Meadows ER. It was after Kathy
declared her candidacy that other nurses noticed Chaz complaining about Kathy even more bitterly, as well as more
frequently. Once, angry at some demand of Kathy's, Chaz
snarled, told her he was busy and hung up the telephone.

"If I didn't have a daughter in Las Vegas, I'd kill her and
throw her body down a mine shaft," Chaz growled. People
laughed.

Kathy was irritating others besides her husband. By 2006,
most ER workers had had contact with her, usually by telephone, and almost all of it was negative. On some days,
Kathy called the ER to talk to Chaz five or six times.

"It was becoming disruptive," one nurse said later.

During one such telephone encounter, Cindy Baker tried
to explain that Chaz was too busy right then to talk to Kathy.

"It wasn't pleasant," Cindy recalled. Kathy lost her temper when Cindy put her on hold. Kathy hung up, called back, and told Cindy, "I can have your job by the end of the day."

Another nurse recalled asking Chaz if he needed any help with a particular task he'd been assigned.

"Yeah," Chaz said, "you can get rid of my wife for me." The same nurse recalled Chaz complaining about Kathy on a constant basis. When other nurses would ask what the problem was, Chaz would simply shrug.

"She's just a bitch," he said.

One nurse who particularly aroused Kathy's ire was Tina Carbone, who was Chaz's supervisor in the emergency room. In fact, Tina had hired Chaz, and was responsible for scheduling ER nurses. The schedule was always a sore point with Kathy, especially when Chaz was put on the night shift, which made it impossible for him to accompany her to political events.

Soon Kathy was calling Tina to complain about Chaz's schedule, and, apparently, throwing her weight around as an important state official. Tina thought Kathy was harassing her, by writing letters to the hospital administration to complain, even accosting her in the parking lot, demanding Chaz's paycheck. Just why Kathy would be demanding Chaz's paycheck was never made clear, but Kathy may have believed that Chaz was using some of his pay to chase after other women, and wanted to get it before Chaz could spend it.

"I was afraid I was going to lose my job," Tina said, of Kathy's interference. "I wanted it to stop." She filed a complaint about Kathy's behavior with the state's Commission on Ethics, the same people who had brought Kathy down in 2004. Nothing seemed to help.

Eventually Tina and other managers in the emergency room became concerned about Chaz's mental health. He seemed to be obsessed with his anger at his wife, they thought, and it was starting to affect his work. They suspected that Chaz was abusing drugs and alcohol to escape.

Finally Tina asked him: "Chaz, why don't you just go?"

"I can't right now," Chaz said. Tina didn't get it—what was keeping Chaz from leaving the marriage if he was so unhappy? It wasn't like he hadn't done it before. Tina even offered to rent him a room in her house, but he declined the offer. Still, it made Chaz feel good to know that others felt bad for him.

Unbeknownst to either Kathy or Chaz's supervisors in the ER, Chaz had resumed his email communications with Linda Ramirez near the end of 2005. In a message sent in early November, Chaz seemed to beg for an intimate relationship with Linda.

"I have to tell you that I have missed you every day since I last saw you," Chaz wrote, referring to Linda's firing earlier in the year.

> I want you to understand that what I am dealing with in the other person, is incredible. It has been a nightmare. I am planning on leaving every day. I am looking for a place to live. There is so much I want to tell you. I did what I did with us to protect you from her. I did not want to, I had to. Please write me at [here Chaz gave a new email address]. It is secret email. Miss you . . .

A month later:

> First, I want to say that I miss you, I have missed you every day and thought of you every day since we last spoke . . . You touched my heart and I want to be with you. I have never let go of the hope of being with you again . . . I feel so much for you, I want to give you the world.
>
> True feelings, true caring, true love only comes around once in a lifetime.

Let me say that the other party in this is very vindictive and has a lot of power. She is incredibly controlling, and wants to control everything in her life. She lost control of me when you came along and has not regained it since. She has made my life a living hell in the past by manipulation and threats . . .

Chaz apologized again for Linda's firing—it appears that Chaz had earlier fingered Linda as his illicit email correspondent in order to placate Kathy and save his own job.

I wanted only to protect you, so that is the only reason things happened like they did, it was out of protection for you. I was willing to sacrifice myself so they would not hurt you any more . . . But after that I was so hurt from loosing [sic] you that I made a pact with myself that I would live every day making her life a living hell. I live every day manipulating her and driving her crazy. It is working, as she wants to kick me out at the beginning of the year.

I hate this woman, and I will make her break . . . it's my quest in life to drive this bitch crazy, and it is working, she is loosing [sic] her mind. I don't care anymore what she tries to do to me, I was scared before, but not anymore.

I am already gone, I left here when I lost you, I am only a shell here. I know all of this may sound severe or even a little off . . . I will be free and I will be with you. That is what I want. You have my heart . . .

Although the cliché quotient of these communications was high, it wasn't just that Chaz was a bullshitter, as Phil Alfano would later decide. The fact was, when Chaz wrote these words, he really believed them—it was his way of pleasing Linda Ramirez, assuring her that she was special.

Being seen as someone who could make someone else feel special was vital to Chaz's sense of himself. The fact that he'd used much the same language with other women, even Kathy, didn't make him inconsistant, in his own mind; it was the way he saw himself—heroic and romantic.

An unconsciously self-revelatory aspect of these emails was the martyrdom: "I was willing to sacrifice myself so they wouldn't hurt you any more." If anything, the sacrifice was Linda's, who lost her job, not Chaz's. But flipping it around allowed Chaz to portray himself they way he wanted Linda to see him, as the good guy.

Finally, there was the characterization of "the other party," "the other person," "this woman." Not only did Chaz not use Kathy's name—as if Linda didn't know who she was!—but Kathy became progressively more demonic: "very vindictive," "incredibly controlling," "made my life a living hell." It was as if Kathy was all-powerful, and that he, Chaz, was impotent, at least until he decided to poison her life the same way she had poisoned his . . .

Which raises the question posed so frequently by Tina Carbone and others: Why didn't Chaz just leave? He'd already been divorced three times, so it wasn't as if he didn't know how to do it. Later, Chaz would claim that the reason he didn't leave Kathy months or years earlier was that he felt compassion for her—that having been attacked in the political arena, Kathy needed his love for her, even if it was driving him nuts, and causing him to spew vitriolic hatred of her wherever he went. Again, the portrait of himself put forward by Chaz was as the saint, the martyr, the one with compassion, who endured "the bitch."

The unlikeliness of this explanation struck almost everyone who later gave any thought to the circumstances surrounding Kathy's death. There had to be another reason, many thought, why Chaz continued to stay with Kathy, even while complaining about her incessantly. In fact, Chaz actually seemed to revel in his abject suffering. Others pointed to the phrase in his email to Linda Ramirez: "I don't care anymore what she tries to do to me, I was scared before, but not anymore."

Why would Chaz have been "scared" of Kathy? What could she do to him? Some conjectured that Kathy's hold over Chaz began the day Chuck Augustine died. Some suggested Kathy knew where the corpus delicti [literally, "the body of the crime"] was buried, when it came to that fortuitous event, which happened to save Kathy from a difficult divorce, while also making her comparatively rich. That Chaz Higgs had been one of Chuck Augustine's nurses just before he died escaped no one's attention.

Chapter 15

Phil Alfano was not surprised when Kathy told him she was going to run for Nevada state treasurer. When Chaz later contended that Kathy had promised him that she would leave politics for good, Phil knew Chaz was lying. There was no way that Kathy would ever get out of politics—it was her whole life. But Phil doubted Kathy could succeed in any election campaign.

"I think Kathy told me in February or March that she was running for treasurer, and I told her I thought it was a bad idea. And she said, 'Well, I want to get my name back, and I think I'd do a real good job.' And I said, 'I'm not disputing that, Kathy. [But] I know people, and all they're going to remember is that you were impeached. They're not going to remember that you were acquitted.'"

But Phil was wrong about one thing: it wasn't the same old Kathy, the person whose ambition had seemed so palpable before. This Kathy was more relaxed, Phil thought, not nearly as brittle as the candidate for controller in 2002. It was as if, having gone through the crucible of the impeachment —and perhaps having heard what her subordinates really thought of her—Kathy realized she had nothing to lose, and reached the sort of freedom that comes with having no expectations. Perhaps she'd even come to realize that what was really important in life could never be validated in a ballot box. Phil thought his sister seemed happier than she had in quite a while—all except for her marriage with Chaz.

In April of 2006, Phil and his wife planned a short trip to Rome for Easter week. At the last minute, Kathy and Chaz decided to join them.

The couples planned to meet at a hotel in San Francisco, then fly to Rome the next day, Good Friday.

"We were packing our bags," Phil recalled, "when my wife got a call from Kathy, and I could tell something was wrong."

"Here, take the phone, something's going on," Mary told her husband.

Phil took the telephone. It was Kathy, crying, almost hysterical, certainly very upset.

"Please," Kathy told him, "please talk to Chaz, he's trying to kill us. He's trying to kill both of us."

Phil was flabbergasted.

"What's going on? Where are you? What's happening?" he demanded. He gathered that they were driving over the Sierras from Reno.

"He's going to send us over the side of the mountain," Kathy said—Chaz was driving maniacally, speeding in the BMW, and Kathy thought he intended to kill them both.

Phil could hear Chaz in the background, yelling.

"No, no, everything's fine," Chaz yelled.

Phil had never heard Kathy sound like that before: scared, almost panicked.

"And she's telling him to 'Pull over, pull over.' I'm saying, 'What do you want me to do? Where are you?' And she says, 'There's nothing you can do. I don't think we're going to come,' and 'I'll try talking to you later.' "

Kathy hung up. Phil didn't know what to make of it. Mary Alfano tried calling Kathy back several times, but no one answered.

After several hours, they were able to reach Kathy.

"Is everything okay?" Phil asked.

"Everything's okay now," Kathy said, "and we'll meet you there."

That night at the hotel, Chaz approached Phil.

"Hey, I'm sorry," he said, "we were just having a bad argument."

"Oh, okay," Phil said. But later he asked Kathy.

Kathy wouldn't look him in the eye.

"Yeah," Kathy said, "everything's fine." But Phil could tell it wasn't. Kathy's behavior reminded him of the time years before when she'd told him not to tell their parents about her abusive boyfriend.

Whatever the problem was, Kathy soon seemed to recover her equilibrium. The flight to Italy turned out to be something of a fiasco, in that the plane they had hoped to take to Rome was full, so they had to go to Milan instead, which meant taking a train to Rome, an unexpected diversion on the tight schedule.

"It was a crazy trip getting there," Phil said, "but Kathy was taking it all in stride. She seemed to be having a great time. We went to Mass on Easter Sunday at the Vatican. Afterward, she said, 'All right, what's the plan? What are we going to do?'

"And I said, 'Kathy, I *have* no plan, I'm on vacation, I don't need an itinerary, you know.' And she just kind of laughed, and we just wandered from one end of Rome to the other, and she went down the Spanish Steps, and was running around in high heels." Kathy had no health problems as far as Phil could see. That became significant only a few months later when Chaz claimed that Kathy had been feeling weak for much of the previous year, ever since the impeachment.

"In fact, he had trouble keeping up with her," Phil said. Whatever had caused the argument seemed to have been disposed of, Phil thought. For most of the trip, Kathy and Chaz seemed to be getting along well.

They went to Pompeii near the end of the week on a packaged tour, and were taken to dinner in a restaurant by the tour operators.

"We ordered a bottle of wine," Phil recalled. "Kathy and I didn't have any, but my wife and Chaz did. It was a small bottle. I remember the name of it, the translation in English was, 'Tears of an Angel.' And I poured a glass for Mary and I poured a glass for Chaz. There was a little bit left, and we were talking and having a good time, and I went to pour some more for Chaz and Kathy said, 'No, he doesn't need any more.' "

Phil put the bottle down without pouring a second glass for Chaz.

"I didn't think much about it," Phil said. "Toward the end of the meal it was still there, and I went to pour it in his glass and this time she grabbed my hand. And she said, 'No, I *told* you, he doesn't need any. He gets mean when he drinks.' "

Kathy looked at Chaz.

"You know you're on medication," she said. "You're not supposed to be drinking."

Chaz meekly acquiesced to Kathy's order.

On May 12, 2006, Kathy officially filed her candidacy for the office of state treasurer. After filing the candidate forms at the Nevada Secretary of State's office, Kathy and several supporters had lunch at a restaurant in Carson City. Chaz was there, and the others present later said he seemed as cheerful as any of them at Kathy's return to the political wars. If he was disappointed that Kathy had broken her supposed promise to quit politics, he didn't show it. That led some to later suggest that Kathy had never made any such a promise to Chaz, that he was making it up.

John Tsitouras, for one, was sure that Kathy would never have told that to Chaz. "That girl lived for politics," he said later. "She never would have said that."

Still, after having been the only person in the history of the state of Nevada to be impeached, Kathy had to be a serious underdog. Who would vote for someone with her notoriety?

"The message I need to resonate with the voters," Kathy told a reporter for the *Reno Gazette-Journal*, "is my stellar record of financial excellence." Then she added: "Nobody in my state office is working on my campaign."

Kathy had two opponents in the Republican primary, Mark DeStefano, a Las Vegas financial consultant, and Joe Pitts, a retired Henderson, Nevada, firefighter. DeStefano was in some ways as controversial as Kathy. Two years earlier he had been removed from the ballot when it was determined that he didn't actually live in the district he was seeking to represent for the state university's board of regents. The elected university board was traditionally an entry-level election contest for statewide politics in Nevada.

Despite his baggage, it was soon evident that DeStefano was the preferred choice of the Republican Party bosses. The party's chairman proposed a rule banning general election endorsement of any candidate who had been impeached and convicted. That meant Kathy Augustine, the one and only candidate in the history of the state to have been impeached and convicted.

DeStefano soon called on Kathy to quit the treasurer's race.

"I told her there would be no personal attacks," DeStefano said, "but that I will have to explain the facts—she was fined, censured and impeached, and . . . she is unelectable." However politely couched, Kathy could only take that as a threat to smear her.

The following week at the Republican state convention, Kathy came out swinging. Approving a rule to prevent her from having the Republican Party's support in the general election was wrong, she said.

"If ethics are of a primary concern when backing

candidates," she asked, "then why would the party embrace a candidate for state treasurer who committed perjury . . . in order to seek public office?" Kathy was referring to DeStefano's residency imbroglio when he'd been removed from the ballot.

Kathy's plea did no good. The delegates voted 71–48 to deny her support in the general election if she won the party's nomination for treasurer.

"It is very upsetting to me," Kathy said, "that the people in this room, when I have stood by and supported every one of your [party] organizations, that because of an unfortunate circumstance, you would turn your backs on me." But still Kathy wouldn't quit, which caused some in the Republican Party to admire her grit. The "hick little state" remark seemed forgotten, at least temporarily. The Republican Party was given a choice between one candidate who had been impeached, one who had been publicly branded a liar, and a cranky old retired firefighter, as their nominee for the chief custodian of the state's money.

By June of 2006, DeStefano was ahead of Kathy in politics' most important measure—he was pulling in many large campaign contributions, sometimes as much as $20,000 each. Kathy had barely managed to collect $10,000—total.

Late that June, Kathy's cousin hosted a campaign fundraiser aboard his yacht in Marina del Rey, California. Phil was one of the few who attended.

"The turnout wasn't very good," he recalled, "and I thought, *Uh oh, Kathy's not going to be happy*. But she couldn't have cared less."

Kathy's cousin apologized for the low attendance.

"Don't worry about it," Kathy told him. She and Phil enjoyed reminiscing over old family stories with the cousin.

"She was having a great old time," Phil said. "Happy as could be."

Chaz was also there.

"He was drinking very, very heavily," Phil said. "The only

drinks were wine, but he was pounding them good. One of Kathy's friends from the airline industry was there. She had known Chuck as well. They started talking about Chuck and what a great guy he was, and she was quoting something that Chuck had said one time, and they were laughing. And I could see Chaz's demeanor change . . . and he became very, very withdrawn . . . but when Kathy left, she had a smile on her face, she was teasing my dad." The old Kathy would have been upset about the failure of the fund-raiser; but the new Kathy had gotten the real value from it: the love of her family and friends.

Later, Phil learned that just before the event, Chaz had been at his brother Tony Alfano's house.

"I guess he said something to my sister-in-law," Phil recalled, "to the effect that, 'Kathy's such a bitch.' He was saying some pretty derogatory things about her. My sister-in-law and Kathy weren't the best of friends. But even my sister-in-law was put off by what he was saying. And she said, 'Kathy's my sister-in-law, don't say those sorts of things.' She was upset."

Why would Chaz say bad things about Kathy to Kathy's sister-in-law? Because he knew that Kathy and the sister-in-law didn't get along, and expected that the sister-in-law would join him. But instead, the sister-in-law turned on Chaz—like all the Alfanos, they would defend each other to the death.

But then, Chaz was not an Alfano, and never would be.

Chapter 16

Kathy and Chaz spent the Fourth of July of 2006, a Tuesday, at a friend's house near Lake Tahoe. At one point, the friend asked Kathy about Dallas—had she heard from her daughter, and what was she up to?

But Kathy said that she and her daughter hadn't been speaking to each other for the past few months. If the friend really wanted to know about Dallas, Kathy said, she should ask Chaz: Chaz and Dallas had been emailing each other quite a lot lately, Kathy said.

The following day, Chaz reported to work at Carson Tahoe hospital in Carson City. He'd been hired as a part-time nurse at this hospital the previous May, and was being trained. He had quit South Meadows in June because he was tired of all the hassle between the South Meadows staff and his wife, he said later. Carson Tahoe would be a fresh start for everyone.

On Friday, July 7, Chaz was in the dual intensive care/cardiac unit with another nurse, Kim Ramey. Ramey was a specialist in patients with heart problems. She was showing Chaz the ropes—where the supplies were, the equipment, how to take care of the patients—when Chaz's cell phone rang.

It was Kathy.

Kathy had just discovered that Chaz had opened his own, separate bank account. How she discovered this was a mystery; but on this Friday, Kathy was angry at Chaz. They began to argue. Chaz cut her off.

"I will fucking talk to you when I get home," Chaz told Kathy. Apparently Kathy resisted this. "I *said*, I will fucking talk to you when I get home." He hung up.

"What was that all about?" Ramey asked.

"I can't fucking believe it," Chaz told her. "She found out I opened an account at Wells Fargo. I can't believe she found out."

Ramey said it sounded like Chaz was having problems with his marriage. Chaz agreed. His wife was "high profile," he said, a VIP, running for state treasurer. He hated it.

"She's a fucking stalker," he added. "I'm looking for an apartment because she's a fucking stalker. She's a bitch. She's a psycho."

Ramey told Chaz she knew all about bad marriages— she'd been in one herself, in Virginia, and the divorce had been a nightmarish experience. In fact it was still going on, she said.

Ramey was a "traveler"—that is, a nurse who moved from hospital to hospital, around the country, on a contract basis. She had no interest in Nevada politics, and didn't know Kathy Augustine from Saint Augustine. Chaz's description of his stalker wife as "high profile" meant nothing to her.

At some point during this conversation, Ramey noticed a copy of the *Gazette-Journal*, on a desk. The paper had a story about a murder case involving a wealthy Reno businessman, Darren Mack. Mack had been accused of stabbing his estranged wife to death, then shooting the judge in his divorce case with a high-powered rifle—through a courthouse window, no less. He'd then fled to Mexico, where he'd called the Washoe County District Attorney, a long-time acquaintance, and admitted his guilt. The case had electrified Reno because of Mack's prominence, and the bizarre circumstances.

Ramey said something about Mack's anger over his divorce, that the difficulties in disentangling from his wife must have had sent him over the edge. (In fact, Mack later initially pleaded not guilty by reason of insanity, although by early November 2007 he agreed to plead guilty to the first-degree murder, withdrawing his insanity claim. Still later Mack would attempt to withdraw his guilty plea and ask for a new trial.)

Chaz smirked, according to Ramey.

"He did it all wrong," Chaz said, of Mack. "If you want to get rid of someone, you just hit 'em with a little 'succs'—because they can't trace it at a post-mortem."

Chaz made a motion as if he were administering an injection.

When Chaz had used the word *succs*, Kim Ramey knew exactly what he meant. What nurse didn't? Succinylcholine—pronounced "suck-sin-ell-KO-leen"—was a standard drug available to ER workers throughout the country. A powerful muscle relaxant, it was created as a more reliable form of the South American natural paralytic curare. A shot of "succs" paralyzed every voluntary muscle in the body for a short period of time. Its primary use was to relax the throat muscles when attempting to intubate a patient—that is, to insert a plastic sleeve down the throat of someone to make sure they get enough oxygen in an emergency situation. The drug was mostly used on patients who were not breathing, although it had some auxiliary use when a patient had broken bones and was thrashing around too severely to permit a doctor to stabilize the breaks.

The most significant thing about succinylcholine, however, was that it paralyzed the lungs. In fact, if someone didn't ventilate the patient—give them oxygen by "bagging"—within a matter of a few minutes, the patient would suffer brain damage from the lack of oxygen, and soon suffocate. It was, by all accounts, a horrible way to die—conscious

Kathy Alfano Augustine, as a young student at John F. Kennedy High School, in La Palma, California. In part because of the school's namesake tradition, Kathy became interested in politics at an early age.

Photo courtesy of Phil Alfano

After two earlier marriages ended in divorce, Kathy married Chuck Augustine, a pilot for Delta Airlines. The marriage seemed to work well for both, at least up until the time that Kathy's political career began to take off. *Photo courtesy of Phil Alfano*

Kathy and Chaz seemed very happy while on an Alaskan cruise in the spring of 2004, but cracks in the marriage were already beginning to appear. At the same time, Kathy was under investigation by the Nevada Attorney General for illegally compelling state workers to work on her reelection campaign in 2002. *Photo courtesy of Phil Alfano*

Kathy and Chuck bought this luxurious Las Vegas house in the early 1990s. Previously it had belonged to legendary Las Vegas bookmaker/casino operator Mel Exber. *Photo courtesy of Carlton Smith*

The emergency room entrance at Washoe Medical Center's South Meadows facility, where Chaz was employed as an ER nurse. On the morning of July 8, 2006, Kathy was brought to this same facility after suffering what was first thought to be a heart attack. *Photo courtesy of Carlton Smith*

Jeannine Coward, left, and Kathy on the steps of the U.S. Capitol in 2001, before Jeannine initiated the Nevada Attorney General's investigation of Kathy. Jeannine would recall that after this picture was taken, Kathy berated her for her attire. The two women had a fractious relationship during Kathy's first term as Nevada State Controller.

Photo courtesy of Jeannine Coward

The Washoe County Courthouse, where the trial of Chaz Higgs was held in June of 2006. The old building, recently restored, is said by some to be haunted by the ghosts of those who were once hanged outside its doors in the 19th century.

Photo courtesy of Carlton Smith

Chaz Higgs at the start of his trial for murder in June 2006.

Marilyn Newton photo, courtesy of the Reno Gazette-Journal

The star witness against Chaz, acute care nurse Kim Ramey. Ramey testified that Chaz had told her the best way to murder someone was to inject them with succinylcholine. The next morning, Kathy was found comatose in bed.

Marilyn Newton photo, courtesy of the Reno Gazette-Journal

Chaz Higgs makes a point during his cross-examination. A bandage is visible on his right wrist after Chaz's second suicide attempt two days earlier.
Marilyn Newton photo, courtesy of the Reno Gazette-Journal

Dr. Bill Anderson, Washoe County chief toxicologist, with a tandem liquid chromatograph/mass spectrometer. A similar machine was used by the FBI to find succinylcholine in Kathy's system.

Photo courtesy of Carlton Smith

Chaz Higgs' lawyer David Houston after the verdict. Houston told reporters he believed Chaz was unfairly convicted.

Photo courtesy of Carlton Smith

Washoe County Deputy District Attorney Tom Barb after the verdict. "They never laid a glove on us," he said of Chaz's defense.

Photo courtesy of Carlton Smith

Kathy's mother, Kay Alfano, being interviewed by a reporter after the verdict.

Photo courtesy of Carlton Smith

Kathy's brother and executor, Phil Alfano, speaking to reporters after the verdict.
Photo courtesy of Carlton Smith

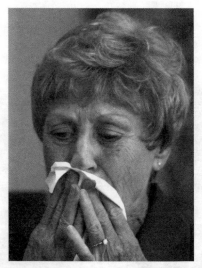

Chaz's mother, Shirley Higgs, broke down while testifying during Chaz's sentencing hearing, imploring the jury to give Chaz "some hope" by permitting him a possible future parole. The jury, apparently moved by the emotion, agreed that Chaz should be eligible for parole, the least possible sentence for the crime of murder in Nevada.

Marilyn Newton photo, courtesy of the Reno Gazette-Journal

Kathy Alfano in the last year of her life.

Photo courtesy of Phil Alfano

but helpless, slowly fading out, desperate for air, but unable to breathe.

Finally, because the drug passed through the human body very quickly—within ten minutes, some said—it was almost impossible to detect at a later autopsy. In short, it was the perfect poison.

Ramey said later she was shocked at Chaz's remark. She said she felt goosebumps on her arm, Chaz's demeanor was so cold.

"We're supposed to save lives, not take them," she said.

Later that evening, as Ramey was ending her shift in the ICU, she mentioned to Chaz that her "traveler" contract was up in four days. She and her boyfriend, also a nurse, intended to leave Nevada once their contracts expired. She invited Chaz to join her and some of her fellow nurses for a going-away party that night.

Chaz declined. He had to go home to see his wife, he said.

The next day was July 8.

The Test

Chapter 17

By Tuesday, July 11, Phil Alfano was convinced that Chaz Higgs had somehow caused his sister's coma. She lay in the Washoe Main ICU, by now unblinking, without even the leg twitch of Sunday, seemingly more dead than alive. The day had begun with a particularly distasteful bit of unpleasantness, when Phil was approached by the neurologist who had been monitoring Kathy.

"I heard that you want to withdraw life support," the neurologist said. "I think we should do another EEG."

"I don't know where you heard that," Phil told him, "but that's exactly what we want, another EEG. We want to make sure that there's no improvement in brain activity." Phil thought Chaz had told the neurologist that the family wanted to withdraw life support without another test—that he was inclined to pull the plug.

A struggle had already been brewing over who had the legal authority to withdraw life support. Chaz kept insisting that Kathy had named him, but he couldn't produce any document to support that notion. That morning, Phil called Kathy's lawyer, Mike Melarkey, who faxed a copy of the appropriate paperwork to the hospital. The document showed that Kathy's father, Phil Sr., had the authority, with Chaz as the first alternate in case Phil Sr. couldn't act.

Phil called Dallas, who was with Chaz, to tell her this. But Dallas told him that she and Chaz had found copies of the paperwork the night before. *That's odd*, Phil thought. *If*

Chaz knew he didn't have the authority to withdraw life support last night, why did he tell the neurologist this morning that it had already been decided?

The neurologist ran the new scan.

The news was bad—not only had Kathy not improved, she was getting worse.

AUGUSTINE UNCONSCIOUS IN HOSPITAL, reported the *Reno Gazette-Journal* that same Tuesday morning. The newspaper quoted Chaz Higgs from the press conference of the day before:

"I went to try to wake her, and I couldn't get her to wake up," he said.

The newspaper report and an earlier television newscast unnerved Kim Ramey. Chaz's casual remark about Darren Mack and the "hit with 'succs'" remarks echoed ominously through her mind from Monday night into Tuesday morning. It seemed like one and one was two: Chaz had said that Mack had "done it all wrong," that he should have used succinylcholine if he'd wanted to get rid of someone. Then, the very next day, Chaz's wife had gone down with what appeared to be a massive heart attack.

To Ramey, the explanation seemed reasonably clear. The chances were, she realized, that her one-day partner in the Carson Tahoe intensive care unit had done exactly what he'd prescribed: he'd "hit" his wife with a shot of "succs," and that was why she was in a coma. Ramey could still see Chaz's hands mimicking an injection.

What to do? Ramey was torn. What if she was wrong? She would be responsible for causing a lot of trouble for someone who was innocent. On the other hand, what if she'd reported Chaz for what he'd said, on Friday night? Might Kathy Augustine still be alive and unharmed? It was a torment for Ramey.

She talked to her boyfriend and another co-worker. She should call the police and report what Chaz had said, both told her. Still Ramey hesitated. Ramey's boyfriend and co-worker decided to act for her. They told Ramey's story about Chaz to Dr. Richard Seher, a heart specialist at Carson Tahoe. Seher approached Ramey in an anteroom in the hospital Tuesday morning. He noticed that she was trembling.

"You could tell by looking at her she was very emotional," Seher said later. He could also tell she didn't want to talk to him. He insisted that she tell him what Chaz had said the previous Friday. Reluctantly, Ramey complied.

"I know what he did," Ramey told Seher. "He said Darren Mack was stupid, he should have used succinylcholine." Ramey explained the circumstances of the conversation—Kathy's call, Chaz's anger.

"You have to call the police," Seher told her when she'd finished. When Ramey was still uncertain, Seher tried to impress her with the importance of what she knew.

"This isn't a traffic violation, this is a real crime," he said.

Ramey finally agreed to call the police. She went to a telephone. When she returned to the anteroom, Ramey told Seher she'd left a voicemail message with the police department.

"No, no, no," Seher told her. "Get back in there, get a live person."

It would have done little good. The days of the kindly old desk sergeant at police headquarters were long past, if he ever existed outside 1930s moviemakers' imaginations. Today's modern police departments are compartmentalized and usually automated. Another call would simply have routed Ramey back to the same voicemail robot that had taken her first message.

Seher decided to take action himself. He called Dr. Richard Ganchan, a cardiologist treating Kathy at Washoe Main, and told him what Ramey had said.

"God," Ganchan swore. He interrupted his hospital rounds and went to a telephone. He called the hospital's pathology lab, and repeated Seher's story to the doctor there. The pathologist called the South Meadows lab and ordered the samples from "Sarah Lambert" sent to the Washoe Main lab immediately. When they arrived a short time later, the pathologist ordered the urine and some of the blood frozen to help preserve them.

Ramey's first telephone call to the Reno police, at 11:20 in the morning, had been routinely transferred by the police operator to the department's Robbery–Homicide unit. By the time someone listened to her voicemail in the afternoon, the Alfano family and Chaz had already decided to withdraw life support for Kathy. One by one, the machines were switched off. Phil and the others were in the room, holding Kathy's hands as she clung precariously to life.

At 3:20 that afternoon, Reno police Detective Dave Jenkins returned Ramey's telephone call.

Ramey told Jenkins that she had worked with Kathy Augustine's husband, Chaz Higgs, at the Carson Tahoe hospital the previous Friday, and that Chaz was extremely angry at his wife, filled with hatred, in fact. She told Jenkins about Chaz's remark about Darren Mack's "stupidity," and how the smart way to get rid of someone was to "hit them with a little 'succs,'" meaning succinylcholine.

"What's that?" Jenkins asked. Ramey explained that succinylcholine was a powerful muscle relaxant—so powerful it could suffocate a person if it wasn't used properly. And, she added, it moved through the system so fast that it was practically impossible to detect at an autopsy—just as Chaz had said.

Ramey told Jenkins she hadn't taken Chaz's rant all that seriously at the time—she thought it was just another person in an unhappy marriage spouting off. But when she heard that Kathy Augustine had collapsed in her own bed just hours after Chaz's remark about succinylcholine, she was pretty sure that Chaz had tried to kill his wife.

Jenkins thanked Ramey for her information and hung up.

At first he didn't know what to think. He'd never heard of succinylcholine, and he had no way of knowing if Ramey was just trying to stir up trouble for Chaz.

There's only one way to find out, Jenkins thought. So he and his partner, Scott Hopkins, drove to Washoe Main, a few blocks away.

By this time, Mark Taylor—Kathy's loyal aide at the controller's office, who often handled the news media for her—had come to the hospital, where he encountered Dallas Augustine in the waiting room near the intensive care unit. Taylor looked up and saw two men in suits and ties come into the ICU.

"Those guys are cops," Taylor remarked to Dallas. It didn't seem out of place, to Taylor, that the police would come to find out what was going on, with a high-ranking state official in a coma. Dallas didn't say anything.

In the ICU, Jenkins encountered a nurse he knew, Lynn Shabi. Kathy had just been removed from life support. Shabi told Jenkins that Kathy's death was imminent.

"I got this phone call," Jenkins told Shabi, and recounted Ramey's story about succinylcholine. "Is this credible or not?"

Shabi turned pale.

"Oh my God," she said. "That fits, because what we have seen so far is not typical of a heart attack." Shabi told Jenkins that all the tests for heart attack had turned up negative, including the angiogram. At that point, Shabi didn't know of Dr. Seher's earlier conversation with Dr. Ganchan, or that Ganchan had asked that the blood and urine samples for "Sarah Lambert" be preserved.

Jenkins asked Shabi about Chaz. She said she thought Chaz had been acting odd ever since Kathy had arrived at the Washoe Main ICU—"aloof, distant, removed," were the words she used. He had recently left the hospital and it appeared that no one knew where he was.

Jenkins and Hopkins went back to the police station, where Jenkins began making telephone calls. One was to the Washoe County District Attorney's office. He spoke to Deputy District Attorney Tom Barb, and explained the circumstances of Ramey's suspicion. He related Shabi's belief that poisoning by succinylcholine was a viable possibility. At the least, he said, they were dealing with a case of suspicious death, if not a murder. He called the Washoe County Coroner's Office, and told Ramey's story to officials there. He asked them to declare Kathy's looming death an official coroner's case. Such a declaration would mean a mandatory autopsy.

Kathy Augustine died at 4:35 P.M. on Tuesday afternoon. She was surrounded by her family.

"We were there, at her bedside," Phil said. "Chaz was there as well. And Dallas, and my brother, and my mom and dad. We kind of took turns holding her hand, and standing by the bedside.

"Chaz was very— It was interesting to hear other people describe his demeanor. He was very—clinical, I guess is the way I would describe it. He would tell us, 'Okay, they're going to put a morphine drip in her, and she's not going [to] feel any pain.' And it was bizarre. It was bizarre."

At some point around the time she died, Chaz slipped off Kathy's wedding ring, and put it in his pants pocket. Tony Alfano watched him do this.

"And I know he didn't even buy the damn thing, my sister did!" Phil commented later.

The ring later turned up missing. Phil believed Chaz later sold it at a pawn shop for cash.

Shortly after Kathy died, Washoe County Coroner's Investigator Steve Woods arrived at the hospital. He approached Dallas and Chaz, and told them that the coroner had decided to perform an autopsy, so he was taking custody of the body.

Inside the ICU room, Woods took a number of photographs of Kathy's remains. Then he summoned the people from the funeral home, who had arrived at the family's request, and instructed them to put Kathy's remains in a plastic body bag, and take it to the county morgue, where it would be refrigerated pending the autopsy the next day.

"Mr. Higgs appeared to be very cool, very calm over the situation," Woods said later.

That evening, the Alfano family and Chaz held another press conference, this one at the hospital. Mark Taylor from the controller's office helped organize it. Dallas at first did not want to participate. But just before it was to start, she turned to Taylor.

"Write me something," she commanded. It appeared that some of Kathy's imperiousness had been inherited by Dallas. Bemused, Taylor scribbled some lines for Kathy's daughter to deliver at the press conference.

Chaz blamed stress from the impeachment and the recent campaign for Kathy's collapse.

"The one thing that really impressed me about Kathy, besides being a great wife, was that she was very passionate about serving the people who elected her," Chaz said. "She was incredibly passionate about that. She always did the right thing. She never did what the so-called good old boys wanted her to do . . . that's the one thing I would say. I would like her to be remembered for that."

When it was her turn, Dallas extolled her mother with Taylor's ghost-written lines.

"She was a great leader, mother, daughter, wife and friend, who will be greatly missed," Dallas said. "She will always be remembered for her strong commitment to her work, family, friends and causes. Please remember her that way."

Later that evening, Coroner's Investigator Woods returned to the hospital to pick up the frozen biological samples, including the urine. No one knew it at the time, but those samples would turn out to be the definitive, crucial evidence in charging Chaz Higgs with the murder of Kathy Augustine. And at the same time, the samples would raise another possibility: that Chaz Higgs had not only poisoned his wife, he'd earlier done the same thing to none other than Chuck Augustine.

Chapter 18

The Alfanos were somber as they returned to the Reno Hilton Tuesday night. There were at least two more things to do before they could leave for Las Vegas, where Kathy's funeral was to take place on Saturday, July 15. One, they had to meet with the lawyer Mike Melarkey about Kathy's trust. Since Phil Jr. was the trust executor, and Dallas was the beneficiary, both had to find out what to do next. And after that, someone had to go to the controller's office in Carson City to pack up Kathy's personal effects, a melancholy task indeed.

Dallas, meanwhile, returned to the Otter Way house with Chaz. The Alfanos hadn't seen much of her outside the hospital since Saturday. But Phil, for one, got the impression that Kathy's daughter was using the occasion of her mother's death to cast off years of resentment, and to demonstrate her freedom from Kathy's rules.

"She'd been spending all her time with Chaz," Phil said later. "It was very unusual, for a couple of reasons. One, I don't think she had met Chaz in person more than half a dozen times, and that's being generous—it was probably fewer than that." In fact, Phil recalled that when Dallas first met Chaz, probably in November of 2003, she had said, "I don't like him. I think he's gay."

Of course, Chaz was not gay. But Dallas' perception was evidence of his ability to seem to be what others, particularly women, wanted to see in him—his ability to be a "player," as Kim Ramey later put it, meaning someone who could pose, or play a role, someone adept at pretending, proficient at the emotional con.

Second, Phil said, Dallas had told him that she and Chaz and Jessie had stayed up until early in the morning, drinking in the Otter Way house.

"Boy, would my mom be pissed," Dallas told Phil. "I'm using the expensive dishes and ashtrays, and I'm smoking in the house."

On Wednesday morning, the Alfanos, Dallas and Chaz all assembled at Mike Melarkey's office.

"This was where things really started getting strange," Phil said later. Melarkey took them through the terms of the trust, and explained what Phil's responsibilities were. He suggested that Phil cancel all of Kathy's credit cards, and make arrangements to pay off the balances; it turned out the balances were about $45,000, a rather large sum. Because the trust included the real estate as well as around $150,000 in a money market account, along with Chuck Augustine's $4,600 monthly annuity, there were enough assets to pay the bills. With Kathy's death, of course, the Delta pension payments would stop. That still left Dallas, as the trust beneficiary, with substantial cash assets, real estate worth around $500,000 net of the mortgages, the $4,600 monthly annuity, and around $100,000 in precious stones—Kathy loved jewelry.

Phil would eventually sell the Otter Way house for about twice what Kathy paid for it. Melarkey's wife, a real estate agent, handled the transaction. The property would be purchased by one of Melarkey's associates. As for the Las Vegas house, Kathy had turned down an offer of $625,000 for it earlier in the year—as John Tsitouras recalled, Kathy wanted $650,000 instead.

"She got greedy," Tsitouras said.

Now in Melarkey's office, the immediate sale prospects of the Maria Elena house looked less promising, as the real estate market had softened. (Eventually, the house would be deeded by Kathy's trust—Phil, actually—to Dallas. Dallas in turn would deed the property to herself and her girlfriend, Jessie, as joint owners.)

With the financial matters settled, the Alfanos began to leave the office. That was when Dallas stopped Phil.

"Uncle Phil, I'd like to talk to you," Dallas said.

"Sure," Phil said. He asked Melarkey if they could use the conference room they'd just left. Melarkey agreed.

Phil entered the room with Dallas, and Chaz started to go in, too. Kay Alfano stopped him.

"No, Chaz," Kay said, "she wants to talk to him privately."

Chaz looked at Dallas, didn't say anything, and turned around. Phil closed the door behind him. Dallas looked at Phil.

"Uncle Phil, I think Chaz may have had something to do with my mother's death," Dallas said.

"Dallas, I'm kind of relieved to hear you say that," Phil told her, "because your grandmother and I were thinking the same thing."

That morning, Dr. Ellen Clark conducted an autopsy of Kathy's remains. In attendance were Deputy District Attorney Barb and Detective Jenkins. Watching a pathologist disassemble a former human being was one of the most disagreeable duties of being in law enforcement, yet both Jenkins and Barb knew it was an important part of their jobs.

Clark paid particularly close attention to the heart. She could find no evidence of heart attack. There was, however, substantial evidence, in the brain and elsewhere, of prolonged oxygen deprivation. Clark listed the proximate or immediate cause of death as cardiopulmonary failure—failure of the heart and lungs, the exact reason for which was not clear.

On Kathy's left buttock, Clark found two intriguing marks—"punctate wounds," as she described them in her report, meaning trauma that had apparently been inflicted by a needle. Clark could find nothing in the hospital record showing that Kathy had received any injections in her left buttock. Clark had a technician take close-up photographs of the wounds. There appeared to be two separate marks, one very slight, the other rather bigger, almost 3/4 of an inch deep, with a very narrow track. These both looked like injection marks to Clark.

Clark excised the area, and preserved the tissue by setting it aside for later freezing.

As Clark wrapped up the autopsy, she, Barb and Jenkins talked about Kim Ramey's report of Chaz's remark about succinylcholine, and the fact that it was almost impossible to detect in an autopsy.

"Well," Barb said, "succinylcholine's a poison, and that'll kill you."

"That'll kill you," Clark agreed.

Jenkins left the coroner's office and prepared a search warrant for the house on Otter Way.

He went to the house with his warrant the same afternoon. Later he did not recall that Dallas was present when he arrived, but she must have been there earlier, at least, to give someone the key to get in. It appears that Dallas left Reno while the police were searching the house.

Apart from a substantial amount of medical refuse left over from the paramedics' valiant effort to revive Kathy— Jenkins and his associates found this in the trash—the most interesting thing discovered was a black nylon backpack that belonged to Chaz. Inside it, Jenkins discovered a vial of etomidate, a muscle relaxant often used in emergency rooms— usually a "companion drug" to succinylcholine. In fact, Jenkins would later learn that both etomidate and succinylcholine were stored right next to one another in something called a rapid sequence intubation kit, a small, sealed plastic box kept in every ER and ICU's crash cart. It seemed possible to Jenkins that someone who had taken succinylcholine from one of those kits might have taken etomidate as well, reasoning that both drugs would later be replaced by the hospital's pharmacy, no questions asked, since they were often used together.

Meanwhile, Phil and his parents had driven to Carson City, and were busy removing all of Kathy's personal items from the controller's office, among them scores of photos of Kathy with various dignitaries, including President Bush. Around 2 in the afternoon, Dallas arrived. She said the police had come to the Otter Way house with a search warrant, and were going through the house right then. If Phil had had his suspicions about Chaz before this, Dallas' news absolutely confirmed them: now it wasn't just him, the police were suspicious too.

Dallas told her uncle that she'd removed two pistols from the house—both guns that had belonged to Chuck Augustine. She'd put them in her trunk, she said. And one more thing, she added: a neighbor on Other Way had told Dallas that if anything ever happened to Kathy, the police should investigate . . . Chaz.

With that, Dallas left, heading for Las Vegas. Phil tried to get her to take some of Kathy's office belongings with her, but she said she didn't have enough room in her car. Eventually Phil had to rent a storage locker for the things from the office, as well as possessions in the Otter Way house.

That evening, Phil drove his parents back over the mountain to Sacramento, where they boarded a plane back to southern California. Phil drove back to Turlock and fell into bed, utterly exhausted.

Chapter 19

Even as the Alfanos were cleaning out Kathy's office in Carson City, speculation about her death was flying around the capital, in Reno, and all the way to southern California.

The origin of the rumors wasn't clear, but by Wednesday afternoon, in the aftermath of the search warrant, there were any number of people who knew that the police were suspicious of Chaz Higgs.

There were, first of all, the nurses in three hospitals: in fact, Jenkins had specifically asked at least one nurse at Washoe Main about the properties of succinylcholine. There were friends of Chaz at South Meadows, where Kathy had been taken after her collapse; within a matter of hours, details of the case of "Sarah Lambert" were the subject of gossip around the South Meadows facility, along with increased speculation about Chaz's possible involvement. And there were other nurses, friends of Kim Ramey at Carson Tahoe hospital, who knew what Ramey suspected, and knew that she'd talked to the police.

There were people in the Washoe County Coroner's office, which had custody of the body; and there were a number of doctors at the three hospitals who also knew. Keeping an investigation secret under those conditions was virtually impossible.

The speculation quickly made its way to the news media. While the newspapers until then had been filled with politicians' paeans to Kathy, and regrets about "the stress" of political campaigning, some thought there had to be more to the story.

By late Wednesday, rumors about the police investigation, the search warrant and succinylcholine had made their way to Ed Vogel, a Carson City reporter for the *Las Vegas Review-Journal*. Vogel began asking people at Carson Tahoe hospital about Chaz, and about succinylcholine. No one there would give him any details, but Vogel, normally a political reporter, knew a non-denial denial when he heard one. He began to research succinylcholine—like Jenkins, he'd never heard of it before, but based on what people were saying, it seemed entirely possible that Kathy Augustine had *not* died of a heart attack, but was instead poisoned by none other than her husband, Chaz Higgs. And when Vogel heard that Higgs had also been Chuck Augustine's nurse in Las Vegas shortly before he died, he knew he was on to something interesting.

Greg Augustine first heard about his former step-mother's death from his sister-in-law, Heather, who lived in the Las Vegas area. It took Greg about half a second to suspect that Chaz Higgs was somehow responsible for Kathy's demise, and possibly his father's. That afternoon he called the Reno Police Department and was connected with Detective Jenkins.

"Did you know," Greg began, "that Chaz Higgs was one of the nurses on my father's case?"

Jenkins wanted to know who Greg's father was, and when Greg told him Chuck Augustine, Jenkins saw immediately what Greg was suggesting. While Jenkins had no evidence to indicate that Chaz was involved in the death of Kathy's former husband, he had to consider all the possibilities.

Later that day, discussions were held between the Reno Police Department and the state's Bureau of Investigation, an arm of the state attorney general's office. Within a day or so after that, a parallel investigation was launched in Las Vegas, focused on Chaz Higgs, his employment at Sunrise Hospital in that city, and his background. Inevitably, that investigation would focus on Chaz Higgs' two former wives, who were both now residents of Clark County, Nevada. Eventually one would tell investigators that her former husband had a penchant for keeping powerful drugs at home, and periodically injecting her with what he said was vitamin B-12.

Phil Alfano and his family arose before dawn the following morning, July 13, packed up their car and headed for Las Vegas. He had no idea he would soon be living a scene from a Fellini movie.

The plan was to rendezvous with Dallas at the Maria Elena house that afternoon, and wait for Phil Sr. and Kay the following day. Then all would attend Kathy's funeral on Saturday. Phil Jr. had no idea where Chaz was, and didn't much care. He knew that Kay had asked Chaz to stay at a Las Vegas hotel with any of his own family members who might come to Las Vegas for the funeral. Kay had told Chaz that the Alfanos wanted to stay at the Maria Elena house with Dallas, and there was no room for him.

It was pretty clear to Chaz that the Alfanos were shoving him out of the family nest—not that he'd ever been a welcome member. Kay Alfano did not explain her antipathy, but Phil Jr. knew that Kathy had often complained, before she died, that Chaz was seeing other women behind her back. Under the circumstances, Kay could hardly stand to look at Chaz, and in the present climate of suspicion—with police even serving a search warrant, yet—that went double.

In this atmosphere of deepening hostility, Phil, Mary and their three daughters drove into Las Vegas late in the morning of Thursday, July 13. All the way across central California and into Nevada, both Phil and Mary's cellphones kept ringing—different people from California and Nevada kept calling them, expressing shock, as well as suspicion of Chaz. When they got to Las Vegas just before noon, Mary

Alfano called Dallas on her cellphone to ask if she needed any help with the funeral arrangements.

No, Dallas said, everything had been taken care of. Then she said, "We're going to run some errands, and we'll meet you at the house." Neither Phil nor Mary was sure what Dallas meant by "we."

Phil went to Kathy's bank to make sure that no one was trying to raid her bank accounts before he could establish his authority as the trust's executor. Because Kathy's cause of death hadn't yet been officially determined, he had no death certificate. He had to present a letter from the Washoe County Coroner's Office attesting to Kathy's death to pay her outstanding bills, including the two mortgages. While he was doing that, Mary took the three Alfano daughters to lunch. Afterward, she called Dallas again.

Dallas was still running errands, Mary told Phil.

"You know," she said, "I think Chaz is with her."

We certainly wanted to keep him away from Dallas," Phil said later. After Dallas had voiced suspicion of Chaz the previous morning, and after the police had served a search warrant, almost all the Alfanos had the darkest doubts about Chaz.

"I was afraid," Phil said. "If this guy murdered her mother, would he do something to her? Or what? What's going on with this guy? I didn't know what to think."

Phil was especially puzzled by Dallas. After voicing her concern about Chaz the previous morning, why was Dallas apparently out and about with him?

Until then, Phil had believed that Chaz was going to book a room at a hotel.

"That's where my mom had left it with him." But here was Dallas, cruising Las Vegas with Chaz.

By 2:30, Dallas still hadn't shown up at the Maria Elena house, so Phil, Mary and the girls went over to visit the

Tsitourases. They waited for almost three hours—still no
Dallas. At that point John, who had keys to the house, agreed
to let them in. Soon Phil and Kathy's cousin Ross Simmons
arrived, and then Nancy Vinnick.

By then, all had been exchanging stories about Chaz.
Ross, who lived in Las Vegas, arrived on his Harley, wearing
his leathers. He told of having called Kathy on her cellphone around 9:30 on Saturday morning, at the same time
Kathy was in intensive care at Washoe Main. Chaz had answered. Ross told Chaz that someone in Las Vegas wanted
her to give him a call about the treasurer's race. Chaz said
he'd take the message, but neglected to tell Ross that Kathy
was in a coma. The next day, Ross told Phil, Chaz told him
that Kathy had had a heart attack, and that he'd found her
slumped in a chair in the living room. That was completely
at variance with the story Chaz had told the Alfanos.

Mary called Dallas again.

"We're in the house waiting for you," Mary told her.

"What're you doing in the house?" Dallas demanded.
"Don't go into my bedroom."

What was this about? Apparently Dallas had something
she wanted to keep secret, the Alfanos thought.

Mary wanted to go into the bedroom anyway, but Phil
said no—he wanted to respect Dallas' privacy.

Nancy Vinnick had been in the house the day before, with
Dallas' permission, to remove some financial records—she'd
been suspicious of Chaz from the day she'd heard about the
marriage, and had been one of the friends who suggested
Kathy form the trust.

"We were thinking Chaz was going to try to max out
Kathy's credit cards," Phil said later. While looking for the
records the previous day, Nancy had found Chaz's passport
in a bathroom drawer. Now the Alfanos and Nancy wanted to
see if the passport was still there. If it was missing, that might
mean that Chaz was on the run.

The passport was still there.

Dallas turned up about 5:30, and sure enough, Chaz was with her, along with Jessie.

The Alfanos were in the family room at the wet bar, the same place where Greg had been serving drinks after Chuck Augustine's death almost three years before.

"They came in the main doorway," Phil recalled, "laughing and giggling." The Alfanos could hear bottles clinking inside the sacks the trio brought in.

Uh-oh, Phil thought. He didn't want to make Chaz aware that the family was suspicious of him, but he wanted to get him out of the house, especially before Phil Sr. and Kay showed up the following day. But Phil realized right away that Dallas and Chaz had spent the afternoon drinking. He decided the friendly approach would be best, followed by a man-to-man talk.

"So I got up and went in the kitchen and, you know, 'How are things going?' and that sort of thing. They had several bottles of wine, I think some liquor with them, and some food they were putting in the refrigerator." Dallas introduced Jessie, whom Phil and Mary hadn't actually met while in Reno—Jessie had never come to the hospital in the days before Kathy's death. Then Phil motioned to Chaz.

"Hey, Chaz, can I talk to you for a minute?"

They went into the living room.

Dallas went into the family room, behind the bar. According to Mary, she headed straight for a rare collector's bottle of whiskey—probably one of Chuck Augustine's.

"My mom would never open this, but it's mine now," Dallas said, and she cracked it open and poured herself a drink. Then she showed Mary an expensive Armani suit she'd bought that day, using Kathy's credit card.

In the living room, Phil came right to the point.

"I know my mom talked to you about staying in the home here," he said, "and I just think it would be a good

idea, like you agreed, if you and your family stay somewhere else."

"What—what are you talking about? Why?"

Phil wanted to keep this as low-key as he could.

"Well, Chaz, look— I'm just trying to keep the peace
here, and my mom knows about the extra-marital affairs."

Chaz denied that he'd been seeing other women behind
Kathy's back.

"That never happened," he said. "It's not true."

Phil didn't want to give Chaz the idea that the family
was suspicious of him. He hoped to ease Chaz out of the
house by raising Kay's unhappiness over the fidelity allegations. He tried to seem reasonable.

"Look, I don't know if it happened or not," he said,
equably. "I don't know what went on with you and my sister. I just know my sister is dead, so anything she told my
mother is now the gospel truth. You know how it is. I just
think it would be better for everybody if you stayed somewhere else."

Phil saw at once that he'd hit the wrong note. He could
see it in Chaz's eyes—he'd seen it before with school kids
after a fight, the feeling of insult, gathering of rage. He
could also smell the booze on Chaz's breath. *Boy, is he lit*,
Phil thought.

"Look, Chaz—" Phil started, but Chaz blew.

"This is bullshit, this is *my* house!"

"Chaz, that's not really the issue here."

"This is *my* house!"

"Well, Chaz, if you want to get technical about it, it's
not. You were at the attorney's office, this is *Dallas'* house."

Dallas came in, her drink in her hand.

"What's going on?" she asked.

"I'm just asking Chaz to stay with his parents, so your
grandmother and grandfather can stay here."

"This is bullshit, this is *my* house!" Dallas said, echoing
Chaz. Phil guessed that Dallas and Chaz had discussed this

topic that afternoon, between drinks, and had prepared ahead of time for this confrontation.

Chaz went back to the kitchen. Dallas followed.

Phil heard the sliding door from the kitchen open, and seconds later he heard a loud crash. He went into the kitchen, looked out the window and saw that Dallas had thrown her glass down on the pavement of the patio and smashed it into tiny fragments.

Jessie came up behind Dallas, trying to console her. Dallas was on her knees, screaming something, bobbing up and down in a paroxysm of rage and grief.

Phil turned to see Chaz, sitting at the kitchen table.

"This is bullshit, this is fuckin' bullshit," Chaz said. "I don't know why people are accusing me of these things."

Ross came in to see what all the commotion was about. Nancy Vinnick, upstairs and fearing imminent violence, was dialing the police on her cellphone.

Chaz got up from the table.

"Maybe I should just fuckin' leave," Chaz said. He went to the front door, opened it and left, slamming the door behind him as hard as he could.

Phil could heard him bellowing outside.

"I want you people to know, I loved that fuckin' woman, I *loved* that fuckin' woman," Chaz was shouting. Mary looked at Phil, her eyes big.

Ross followed Chaz outside.

"You're in no condition to drive," Ross told him.

Chaz ignored him and got into the BMW.

Just then Jessie came rushing into the kitchen.

"Are you fuckin' satisfied?" Jessie demanded. "He just shot himself."

Phil, Mary and Nancy Vinnick just looked at one another. They had no idea of what Jessie was talking about. Then Mary got it.

"No," she said, "that was just the front door."

Police were now turning the corner onto Maria Elena.

The news media were giving chase. Mary and the girls went next door to the Tsitourases'.

The police, seeing a Harley and motorcycle leathers, immediately arrested Ross.

Phil went out to explain to the police.

Once they got all the players straight, the police unhandcuffed Ross. Dallas told them she didn't want any of the Alfanos to stay there, not even her grandparents. The police told Phil he'd have to leave.

"Trust me," Phil said, "we're not staying around here." Phil told the police about the guns Dallas had taken out of the house in Reno, as well as a third gun, a 9 mm semiautomatic that Chaz owned. Just to be safe, the police confiscated all the guns.

Over at the Tsitourases', Phil started calling hotels to find rooms. He called his parents to tell them he'd have to make hotel reservations for them, too, but didn't explain. He didn't want them upset when they drove to Las Vegas the following day.

For John Tsitouras it was déjà vu. Three years earlier, it had been Kathy kicking the Augustines out just before a funeral. Today it was Kathy's daughter Dallas who was kicking the Alfanos out. Kathy might be gone, but her spirit lived on, in her daughter.

Chapter 20

Back in Carson City, *Review-Journal* reporter Ed Vogel was making substantial headway on his story. That afternoon, he got confirmation that the Reno police were investigating Kathy's death.

"There wasn't evidence of long-term heart disease," Reno Deputy Police Chief Jim Johns told Vogel, when asked why the police were involved. Another officer, Steve Frady, said that the investigation wasn't based on any crime, and that "no one has been identified as a suspect or person of interest." That wasn't true—Jenkins' search warrant the previous day had specified that the search was for evidence of the "crime of furnishing/administering a controlled substance," the supporting affidavit named Kathy Augustine as the victim of "an attempt to kill her," and made note of the fact that Kathy had been found comatose by her husband, Chaz Higgs, in their home.

Given the circumstances, that Chaz was at least "a person of interest" was obvious to Vogel and every other reporter in Nevada who was working on the story.

Vogel still couldn't nail down the succinylcholine angle, but by late that afternoon, the rumor about "succs" was widespread. Vogel called Greg Augustine, and learned that Greg, too, had heard about "succs." Greg told Vogel he was suspicious of his father's death three years earlier.

"He was getting better, and then suddenly his organs

failed," Greg said. "There was never an autopsy. His body should be exhumed."

That evening around 7:30 Vogel tracked down Chaz at the Maria Elena house in Las Vegas. Chaz vehemently denied having anything to do with Kathy's death.

"I loved this woman who died," he told Vogel. "And now there's all this shit coming up. It's just crazy for people to assume I had something to do with it. *I* asked for the autopsy. I want to clear it up. My wife was a healthy fifty-year-old woman who dropped dead. I want to find out what happened. People don't know what went on in our home. She was frazzled and stressed out."

The next morning, Chaz tried to kill himself.

As the story was later pieced together, it appeared that Dallas had heard some sort of "thump" in a bathroom of the Maria Elena house shortly after 10 on Friday morning. She forced her way into the room, whose door had been tied shut with a necktie. There she found Chaz in the bathtub, blood oozing from both his wrists. Dallas called for help. Soon the fire department, paramedics and police were wailing their way to Maria Elena Drive, followed in short order, once more, by the Las Vegas news media.

Inside the house, paramedics Nathan Sorenson and Michael Fredericks found Chaz with a two-inch cut on his left wrist from a razor blade, and a smaller cut on his right wrist. He seemed flat, lethargic. Both medics could smell alcohol on his breath, and Chaz told them he'd taken three Vicodins, washing them down with most of a bottle of wine, before using the razor blade. The cuts didn't seem to be life-threatening—the paramedics estimated he'd lost only 300 cubic centimeters of blood, a little more than a cup. Chaz told them he'd tried to kill himself, "to be with my wife."

Roused by the wail of the sirens, John Tsitouras watched Chaz being put into an ambulance. By that time the television cameras had also reached the scene. In two days,

Maria Elena Drive had seen more excitement than in the previous thirty years. John called Phil Alfano to tell him what had happened.

Phil and Mary were on their way to the funeral home, with Phil Sr. and Kay. Phil wanted to make sure that Dallas had properly taken care of the arrangements as she'd said she had—after the scene the previous day, and the obvious fact that Dallas and Chaz had been drinking, he wasn't leaving anything to chance. He'd filled his parents in on the events, and explained why they would be staying in a hotel. Kay already knew some of what had happened. Phil said later that Dallas and Chaz had called her to assert that it was her house, and that she could choose who to allow to stay there. It was not a pleasant conversation, with Chaz reiterating that he "loved that fuckin' woman."

"Hey," John now told Phil, "I want you to know, they're wheeling Chaz out on a stretcher. I think he may have overdosed, or done something." Phil called Detective Jenkins in Reno, and told him what had happened.

Jenkins called the Las Vegas police, who had by then taken possession of a number of handwritten notes left by Chaz, most of them written in the early morning hours.

Chaz had addressed one of these to the news media.

"Media," he began, "this is the story."

Chaz claimed that State Treasurer Brian Krolicki and his predecessor, Bob Seale, both had interests in an Atlanta investment firm, and that they had placed some of the state's money there. The arrangement, Chaz asserted, was threatened by Kathy's decision to run for state treasurer, and that was why the Republican Party bigwigs wanted Kathy's opponent, Mark DeStefano, to win:

> Isn't it interesting that eight years ago, when Kathy became controller, Bob Seale told her, "You are going to fuck it all up." What was she going to fuck up, perhaps some money deals in Atlanta?

Chaz said he and Kathy had been investigating the situation before her death. That assertion came as a surprise to those who knew Kathy—the idea that Chaz was assisting her in anything political, given his distaste for politics, seemed absurd.

But in his note, Chaz was blaming Krolicki, Seale and DeStefano for Kathy's death:

> *Thank you, Brian Krolichy [sic] and Bob Seale for pushing this so much just to make a few dollars, that my wife's career was ruined by you and she drove herself to the grave, just to prove that she was right . . .*
>
> *Does the story come together now? I am truly looking forward to seeing these gentlemen in the afterlife so we can have a few words. Thank you for taking my wife away from me.*

Chaz's sarcasm was evident.

In another note, headed "A few passing remarks," Chaz lashed out at Phil Jr. and Kay:

> *Dear Phil, fuck you. It is amazing to me how all of a sudden Kathy is important to you when you wanted to ostracize her before.*
>
> *Dear Kay, amazing what Kathy told you about our marriage. Did you ever think to ask me or anyone else what really happened, or get another opinion? There was a lot going on that you do not know.*
>
> *I want to be buried beside my wife so we can hold hands in the sunshine . . .*

The following day, Saturday, more than 200 people assembled at the Guardian Angel Cathedral in Las Vegas for Kathy's funeral, including a number of ranking state officials. All the harsh words said about Kathy in the past were forgotten. Kathy was extolled as hard-working and tenacious, a star of the political firmament.

John Tsitouras looked around the sanctuary and saw the Alfanos, Dallas and Chaz, who had apparently gotten a haircut from the day before, because the permed curls were gone. Then John realized it wasn't Chaz at all, but Mike Higgs, his identical twin—until that day John hadn't realized that Chaz was one of a pair. Chaz was still in the hospital and so missed the funeral of the woman he claimed to love.

Afterward, Kathy's casket was taken to Paradise Memorial Gardens for interment. She was laid to rest less than one hundred feet from the grave of Chuck Augustine. When Dotty Tsitouras tried to express her condolences to the girl who had grown up next door Dallas was rude to her, and John guessed Dallas was mad at the Tsitourases for letting Phil and Mary use their telephone two days before. Or maybe she was mad at John, who told the news reporters who had besieged the neighborhood two days running that he was suspicious of Chaz. Dallas seemed to be the only one in the family still standing by him.

Dallas' curt dismissal of Dotty saddened John, and made him mad at Chaz.

"I never did trust the sonofabitch," he said later. "He destroyed the entire family."

While Kathy was being buried, Chaz remained under psychiatric care at Monte Vista Hospital. Asked why he had been admitted to the psychiatric hospital—a standard initial evaluation question—Chaz first said, "Because I needed a break," then added, "because I tried to kill myself last night." The treating psychiatrist, Dr. Adekunle Ajayi, summarized his condition on admittance:

> *He has been feeling depressed and hopeless since his third wife of two years suffered a massive heart*

attack . . . and subsequently died on July 11, 2006.
The patient wrote several suicides [sic] notes . . . one
to the media, who, he stated, had been unfairly crit-
icizing his deceased wife. He then drank a whole
bottle of wine and overdosed on three tablets of Vi-
codin . . . then attempted suicide by cutting both
wrists with a razor blade . . .

He stated that he had not expected to live after his
suicide attempt and his goal was to join his deceased
wife in death.

Ajayi noted Chaz's history of hypothyroidism, and its
possible connection to depression. He declined to make an
assessment of any potential personality disorder, such as
sociopathy, now usually termed "anti-social personality
disorder." And in fact, Chaz did not seem to have a key background factor for sociopathy: an early and pervasive pattern
of childhood and juvenile misconduct in which the rights of
others were consistently violated. In some other ways, however, Chaz's background contained some of the remaining
criteria: deceitfulness, impulsivity, irritability, recklessness,
financial irresponsibility, and blaming others for things that
happened.

Later, a psychologist hired by his defense lawyers would
give Chaz a number of tests designed to measure his capacity for anti-social personality disorder. The tests showed
that whatever else he might have been, Chaz was not a sociopath. In other words, he had a conscience and was capable of feeling guilt. In fact, some said he was *too* capable of
feeling guilt, which was why he so often tried to escape
commitment.

Asked for a self-assessment during his treatment, Chaz
said that his greatest strength was being "hard-working" and
going "beyond and above helping people." His greatest weakness was his lack of tolerance for "lazy, whiney people." He

rated his own self-esteem as "low." He denied a history of excessive drinking or drug use.

By Tuesday, July 18, Chaz was ready to be discharged from the hospital. Ajayi met with Shirley and Mike Higgs, who said they planned to take him back to North Carolina with them, where Chaz planned to live with his mother. Chaz seemed in good shape to Ajayi, who would write later:

> He was neatly groomed, calm and coherent. He reported a fair appetite and improvement in his mood. His affect was brighter and he was smiling appropriately. He denied any thoughts of harming himself and regretted his suicide attempt while he was intoxicated with alcohol . . .

Despite Dr. Ajayi's description of Chaz's suicide attempt as "near-fatal," others weren't quite so convinced.

One was Reno Police Lieutenant Jon Catalano.

"Is this a real attempt or was this an attention-getter? We don't know that. If I was a critical care nurse, I might choose something else," Catalano told the *Gazette-Journal*. It seemed strange to Catalano that a critical care nurse couldn't find his own major blood vessels with a razor blade.

As for Kathy's death, Catalano said that the failure of the autopsy to pinpoint a heart ailment as the definitive cause of death was troubling. He could refute rumors that Kathy had been poisoned with pills of some sort, he said.

"We just don't have any indicators on the cause of death. And that's somewhat significant. But there were no pills in her stomach and nothing else that would indicate any type of poisoning or intoxication. I am hoping that when we get the toxicology report back that it will answer some of the questions."

That was just what Dr. William Anderson of the Washoe County Sheriff's Office's Crime Lab was hoping, too.

Chapter 21

Not long after Kathy's inconclusive autopsy, the coroner's office delivered the blood and urine taken from her body on the morning of her collapse to Dr. Anderson, the crime lab's chief toxicologist. At that point, Anderson had at least two advantages over reporters like Ed Vogel who were trying to figure out what was going on with Chaz Higgs and Kathy Augustine. For one thing, Anderson knew of Kim Ramey's suggestion that Chaz had poisoned Kathy with succinyl-choline.

Second, he had a brand new piece of equipment to look for it—a liquid chromatograph/tandem mass spectrometer, a sophisticated (and expensive) piece of machinery that represented the state of the art in identifying chemical substances. The equipment had just been unpacked from its manufacturer's crate, and had never been used before in Washoe County.

Anderson looked at the samples of frozen urine, blood and injection site tissue that had come from the coroner's office, and he looked at the shiny new LC/MS, as it was called. But because the machine was new and its operation hadn't yet been certified by validation tests, Anderson didn't want to use it. Questions might be raised as to the machine's reliability, or even the lab's ability to conduct the tests—after all, poisoning by succinylcholine was hardly routine. In fact, as far as Anderson could tell, there had never been a case where succinylcholine itself had been identified as a poisoning agent, for the simple reason that it so rapidly passed through the body. How often was a potential victim brought to a hospital in time to recover indisputable chemical evidence of the poison? It had never happened before, as far as Anderson knew.

"I didn't want to use it on this case for the very first time," he said later. So Anderson checked around and soon learned there were only two laboratories in the country with experience in identifying succinylcholine from biological samples for forensic purposes: National Medical Services, a private outfit in Willow Grove, Pennsylvania, and the Federal Bureau of Investigation Laboratory in Quantico, Virginia.

As it turned out, both labs had a checkered history with regard to succinylcholine.

Succinylcholine is the artificial result of the combining of two compounds, succinic acid and choline, both of which are found naturally in the human body. Without the two separate compounds, life could not exist. When put together outside the body in a manufacturing process and then injected into the body, however, death is the inevitable result unless precautions are taken.

Both succinic acid and choline are found in plants and animals, and are usually ingested through food. Succinic acid plays an important role in nerve chemistry. It also has a long history as a medicine. Once called "spirit of amber," after its ancient derivation from stone-hardened pine sap resin, it has been used by humans for thousands of years as a nerve and muscle tonic, often to reduce rheumatic aches. It is chemically related to citric acid, found in most fruits.

Choline is also found in many ordinary foods, including egg yolks, soy and liver products. It plays an important roll in maintaining cellular integrity, principally by reinforcing the walls of cells.

When combined artificially, the two compounds form one compound, succinylcholine. Succinylcholine mimics the actions of curare, the paralytic agent used on South American poison darts and arrows. As a paralytic agent, the compound is considered a "depolarizing neuromuscular blocker." In essence, it prevents electrical connections in voluntarily controlled muscles such as the limbs and diaphragm by stopping willful contractions, such as breathing. It has no effect on muscles governed by the central nervous system, such as the heart. As a result, although air intake stops, the heart continues to pump. It is not anesthetic or sleep-inducing—full consciousness is retained, but the recipient is unable to move or speak.

To have an effect, succinylcholine must be injected—oral ingestion doesn't work, because the stomach's acids almost immediately render it harmless. In emergency rooms, "succs" is almost always injected intravenously because of its rapid action—it usually takes effect on the body's musculature within thirty seconds. It can also be injected directly into muscle tissue, although that route may take several minutes before paralysis occurs. Most frequently it is used to facilitate the insertion of a breathing tube, although it may sometimes be used to immobilize a patient so that broken bones can be set. It should never be used without administering oxygen, because the drug prevents a patient from breathing.

Once inside the bloodstream, an enzyme known as "pseudocholinesterase" quickly breaks succinylcholine down into its metabolite, "succinylmonocholine," known colloquially as "mono." "Mono" itself then breaks down, over a longer period of time, back into choline and succinic acid, although some residue of "mono" remains. Generally, unless repeated injections of "succs" are given, the paralytic effects last only two to three minutes, significantly wearing off within ten to thirty minutes. Sequential dosage of succinylcholine is not recommended because of two deleterious side-effects: the possibility of "hyperkalemia," or overheating of the body, and atrial fibrillation—heart seizure.

As a controlled substance, succinylcholine is almost exclusively confined to hospital settings, although in some places it may be in the possession of emergency medical personnel faced with the necessity of rapid intubation in the field. In theory, as a controlled substance, the supply of succinylcholine requires close monitoring by medical authorities because of its potential lethality. In actual practice, as Detective Jenkins was to discover, controls over the substance were fairly lax at both South Meadows and Carson Tahoe hospital in the summer of 2006. Nor was this unusual for any hospital—when "succs" was needed, no one had time to fill out any forms in triplicate. So most medical establishments across the country had relatively loose access procedures for it.

"It's on the crash cart, it's in the [ICU] refrigerator," Jenkins said later. "There's some in every surgical unit in the hospital, essentially on every ward, and the consensus of all the nurses that I spoke to was . . . that as a nurse, if they had some nefarious criminal intent, they would have very little difficulty secreting succinylcholine out of the hospital."

In other words, anyone with free access to a wide variety of hospital areas could easily pocket a vial of succinylcholine and walk away with it, with no one the wiser.

The fact that succinylcholine so quickly metabolizes to succinylmonocholine, and then largely to choline and succinic acid, makes it extremely difficult to detect, as Chaz had observed, according to Kim Ramey. While it can be detected in controlled experiments, its discovery in a poisoned person is virtually impossible for the simple reason that by the time the victim receives medical attention, the compound has completely disappeared, leaving only succinylmonocholine as evidence of its passage.

Thus, for years, the discovery of "mono" at an autopsy was considered by pathologists to be proof positive that someone had been poisoned by succinylcholine. But even the discovery of "mono" was rare—unless a pathologist had reason to look for it, it was not a subject of routine toxicological testing.

Still, there was one rather notorious case in which succinylcholine played a prominent role in criminal prosecution for murder. This was the two murder trials of Florida physician Carl Coppolino, an anesthesiologist, in the mid-1960s. Coppolino was charged with using "succs" to poison the husband of his lover in New Jersey in 1963, and two years later, his own wife in Florida.

Defended by the flamboyant lawyer F. Lee Bailey, Coppolino was acquitted of the murder of his lover's husband in 1966, but convicted of the murder of his wife in another trial the following year. The conviction turned on the discovery of abnormal levels of succinic acid, then thought to be evidence of succinylcholine poisoning, in the brain tissue of Coppolino's wife. Allegations were raised that the toxicologists had fabricated their findings of abnormal succinic acid. Coppolino served 12 years in prison before being paroled in 1979, still denying guilt. Bailey later recounted the details of Coppolino's two trials in *The Defense Never Rests* (Stein & Day, 1971). Coincidentally, Washoe County Deputy Prosecutor Tom Barb, who had been present at Kathy's autopsy along with Jenkins, had read Bailey's book when he was a Marine back in the early 1970s—it even influenced his decision to become a lawyer. That was why he already knew that succinylcholine was a potentially deadly poison.

A case similar to the Coppolino allegations, also in Florida, involved another physician, Dr. William Sybers, who was accused of using succinylcholine to murder his wife in 1991 in Panama City. As it happened, Sybers was the official medical examiner for the area around Panama City, on the Gulf Coast about two hours east of Pensacola. So another pathologist was brought in to examine the body of Syber's deceased wife, which had already been embalmed.

Five months later, this doctor issued a death certificate asserting that Syber's wife had died of "sudden unexpected death due to undetermined natural causes." Two weeks after that, he issued an amended certificate, leaving out the word "natural."

The death of Sybers' wife proved so controversial in Florida that a criminal investigation was undertaken, eventually resulting in Sybers' indictment for first-degree murder in 1997. The indictment claimed that Sybers had injected his wife with an unknown substance.

After a series of legal maneuvers and appeals, the state of Florida asserted that Sybers had killed his wife by an injection of succinylcholine. The state put on evidence from Dr. Kevin Ballard, an M.D. with a Ph.D. in pharmacology. Ballard was director of research and development of National Medical Services, the Pennsylvania laboratory. He had devised a process in which solid tissue samples from organs such as the liver, brain or kidneys could be liquefied, run through a liquid chromatograph/tandem mass spectrometer, and evaluated for the presence of foreign chemicals. The process of liquefaction and its use in the machine was a trade secret, Ballard said.

Ballard testified that using his secret process he had discovered levels of "mono" in tissue samples taken from Sybers' wife, and that from this, he concluded that Sybers' wife had originally been poisoned with "succs."

But Ballard's method of proving that succinylmonocholine was in the tissue samples was controversial. For the proof, he took specimens of the same type of tissue from other sources, then "spiked" them with succinylmonocholine. When these "control" samples were put through the LC/MS, they showed that the machine could detect "mono." When the "questioned samples"—that is, the tissue from Mrs. Sybers—were put through the machine, the spectrographic profile between the two was the same. Ergo, "mono" was present in Mrs. Syber's tissues.

Ballard admitted that there might be another possible reason for the "mono"—perhaps it had come from the embalming process—but he thought the chance of this was highly unlikely.

Another criticism: Ballard had not validated his test procedure with other, similar samples from other victims. Ballard said that was impossible—Mrs. Sybers' samples were virtually unique, as far as possible poisoning by succinylcholine, for the obvious reason: one couldn't inject a living person with succinylcholine, watch them die, then test their tissue for "mono."

Ballard sent some of the Sybers samples to the FBI Lab in Quantico, disclosing his secret process. There, an FBI toxicologist, Marc LeBeau, performed similar tests. LeBeau also found "mono" in Mrs. Sybers' tissues. Then LeBeau took samples of embalmed tissue from other cadavers, and tested them—this time, no "mono." He took more unrelated embalmed tissues, and spiked them with "mono." Sometimes the machine found it, sometimes it didn't—it depended on the type of tissue and a variety of other factors.

Some critics pointed out that no one knew whether "mono" was naturally found in at least trace amounts in embalmed bodies, or even if succinic acid and choline could somehow combine after death to account for "mono."

At length, after a protracted court hearing, a Florida judge ruled that Ballard's process was scientifically valid despite the criticisms.

Sybers' trial took place in 2001, with the prosecutors permitted to use Ballard's testimony. At that juncture, Sybers' defense introduced its own experts, one of them H. Chip Walls, a toxicology expert from the University of Miami, who criticized the Pennsylvania lab for its procedures, particularly what appeared to be sloppy control over who had the samples at any given time—it was possible that Mrs. Syber's samples had been inadvertently contaminated while at the Pennsylvania lab.

Moreover, Walls and the other defense experts testified that, depending on the type of embalming fluid used, "succs" would degrade either quite rapidly, or possibly stabilize as "mono." In any case, it was highly unlikely that any "mono," let alone "succs," could be found after more than two years had passed since the embalming. Even tissues that had been frozen were unlikely to produce positive results after two years, they said.

Despite this testimony, Sybers was found guilty. He appealed the verdict, and in early 2003, it was reversed—the testimony from Ballard and LeBeau was held to be "novel" scientific testimony, not generally accepted by other scientists, and was therefore admitted in error.

The net result was to throw the entire question of "mono" as proof of "succs" into confusion. Was "mono" a result of embalming? Was it part of a natural decomposition process after death? No one could say for sure. But one thing was clear—the existence of "mono" could no longer be used to prove the previous existence of "succs." The Sybers case had established reasonable doubt.

But the situation with Kathy Augustine was different. Where the Sybers case involved tissue samples from a person who was deceased *and* embalmed, the samples taken from Kathy had been obtained while she was still alive, if barely. In her situation there was no embalming, there wasn't even any natural decomposition. Her samples had been collected four days before she actually died. Kathy's case seemed unique—the only situation in which biological evidence had been taken within minutes of the alleged poisoning. That meant there was a chance that "succs" itself might be found in her samples, not just "mono."

And if that were the case, there was no way in the world that succinylcholine could have gotten into her system except by deliberate injection, since succinylcholine was not a natural substance.

Anderson made his decision: he would send Kathy's samples to the FBI at Quantico for the bureau's analysis. He packed the frozen urine, the supposed injection site tissue and the blood in dry ice, and air-couriered it to Virginia by United Parcel Service. Then he waited for the results.

And waited.

And waited.

Chapter 22

Chaz's attempt to kill himself removed the last sliver of doubt from Phil Alfano, Jr.'s mind. Chaz had killed Kathy, Phil was sure of it. To him, it was almost as good as a signed confession. Dallas, however, saw things differently. She thought there was no way Chaz could have killed Kathy— the suspicions were unfair, she said. Exactly why Dallas would flip-flop on Chaz's culpability after she'd told her uncle of her suspicions was a mystery to the Alfanos. But then, Dallas had always marched to her own beat.

Although he'd told the psychiatrist he intended to return to North Carolina with his mother and brother, Chaz didn't leave right away. Instead he stayed at the Maria Elena house throughout much of the rest of the month and into early August.

On the following Tuesday, when Phil was barraged with reporters' questions about the Reno Police Department's investigation, he took pains to say that he wasn't speaking for either Dallas or Chaz. The inference of a split in the family was unmistakable.

"While our family hopes and prays she died of natural causes," Phil said, "we are extremely grateful an investigation has been launched, and we have the utmost confidence in the Washoe County Coroner's Office, the Reno Police Department and the special state investigative team conducting the investigation. Our family requests that anyone with any information that could assist investigators with this task, please come forward."

Two days later, Phil was pulling into the parking lot of his school in Modesto when his cell phone rang. The caller's area code was unfamiliar to Phil. He answered the call. It was Chaz, using his brother Mike's cell phone.

"Why did you change the locks on the house?" Chaz demanded. He meant the house in Reno, on Otter Way.

"Well, it's not your house, Chaz," Phil told him. "I'll be more than happy to meet you up there with the sheriff if you want to get your belongings out."

Chaz hung up. A few weeks later Dallas called Phil and asked him to meet Chaz in Reno so he could retrieve his clothes and other personal effects. By then, Phil had gone through the house, sorting things: Kathy's possessions in one group, Chaz's in another. In doing this, Phil discovered what appeared to be a drawing by Chaz—he recognized the style from similar sketches he'd seen in the past. This drawing, on a Southwest Airlines note pad, showed a stick figure wielding a dripping syringe standing over another stick figure, this one supine with its eyes marked by two Xs, as in a cartoon representation of someone who'd been knocked out, or was dead. Phil took the drawing, and later compared it to one he knew Chaz had made—this one of a woman with a large head of hair, labeled "The Controlla," and a second figure, a grinning man with a punkish haircut labeled "Nurse Ratchit" [sic]. Both drawings were by the same hand, Phil concluded.

Two weeks later, Phil and Tony went to Las Vegas. Phil had discovered that Kathy had a safe deposit box in a bank there. He wanted to get into it in case Kathy had left anything in writing about Chaz. Kathy also had about $100,000 in jewelry that Phil wanted to give to Dallas. When they reached Las Vegas, they saw that the *Sun* had published a long background report on Chaz, headlined WHO IS CHAZ HIGGS?

"Do you believe this?" Phil asked Tony, handing him the

newspaper. But there it was in black and white—Chaz's three previous marriages, his bankruptcies, the allegations about womanizing, his abrupt retirement from the Navy, his impoverished existence at the time he met Kathy.

Phil was shocked by these details of Chaz's background. "I mean, I learned more about him from reading that article than I knew during the whole time that I knew him," he said later. But Chaz had always been reticent about his past.

The next morning, Phil, Tony and Dallas went to the bank. The bank refused to let them into the box. Eventually Phil obtained a court order requiring the bank to open it. To Phil's disappointment, there was nothing in it that incriminated Chaz.

That same week, an FBI toxicologist, Madeline Montgomery, was beginning a series of tests on the biological samples sent to her by Washoe County's Bill Anderson. The samples arrived at the FBI lab on Friday, July 21, still packed in dry ice. An FBI employee assigned to the Evidence Control Unit logged the shipment into the lab, and placed it in a refrigerator.

The following Tuesday afternoon, the contents of the package were inventoried: ten separate samples of blood and tissue, including the excised injection site. By the time Montgomery received it, it was no longer frozen. Montgomery put it in a freezer—she knew that heat had the effect of degrading both succinylcholine and succinylmonocholine.

What happened to the samples between July 25 and August 16 isn't clear, for the simple reason that Montgomery was not permitted by the FBI to answer any questions about her procedure, except under oath. She later referred any questions to the FBI's public affairs office. That office never responded to inquiries.

But Montgomery was clear about one thing—her task was to look for succinylcholine. She knew that much from conversations with the Washoe County Crime Lab.

On August 16, Montgomery retrieved the frozen urine sample from the lab's freezer, and conducted her first test on the urine, using the FBI's LC/MS equipment. She found succinylmonocholine. The following day, she tested for succinylcholine. But before the test could be completed, the power failed in the lab, ruining the test. The next day, August 18, Montgomery tried again, completed the test, and this time found succinylcholine.

Or did she? There wasn't any way to know for sure that the result was actually succinylcholine, although it looked like it should be, based on the molecular profile of the chemically similar "mono." To validate her analysis, Montgomery collected urine samples from fifteen people in her lab and "spiked" them with a supply of succinylcholine on hand in the lab. Those spectrographic profiles matched the one she'd found with Kathy's urine.

At some point during her testing process, Montgomery also tested two blood samples taken from Kathy on the morning of July 8. These proved to be negative for either succinylcholine or succinylmonocholine. Why the blood samples wouldn't have had at least some trace of "mono" was a puzzler—since "mono" took eight times longer to disappear from the system than "succs," it was reasonable to expect that at least some "mono" would be found in Kathy's blood. But there was none—perhaps the failure to freeze the blood was an explanation, but no one could say for sure.

Based on the established rate that "succs" metabolizes into "mono"—as a rule, after thirty minutes all but 10 percent of "succs" is usually transformed into "mono"—the presence of any succs at all in the urine was surprising. If the urine sample had been taken at 7:35 a.m., a little less than an hour after it had been theoretically administered, at least 90 percent of the "succs" should have been metabolized, that is, turned into "mono" by the time the sample was taken. But if that was the case, why were there still substantial amounts of "succs" still in Kathy's urine? No one knew.

On September 18, Montgomery liquefied tissue from the supposed injection site on Kathy's upper left buttock, and ran that through the LC/MS. She found no trace of either "succs" or "mono."

One week after that, Montgomery sent a report to the head of the Washoe Crime Lab, Don L. Means.

"Succinylcholine and succinylmonocholine . . . were identified in the [urine] sample," she reported. None of the other seven biological samples showed any trace of either substance.

Chapter 23

As the weeks passed after Kathy's funeral, Phil Jr. kept in touch with Detective Jenkins of the Reno Police Department. By this time, Phil had talked to Ed Vogel of the *Las Vegas Review-Journal*. Vogel told him of the rumors about succinylcholine. Phil asked Jenkins about this, and Jenkins admitted that the FBI was testing Kathy's samples, but wouldn't say why. The police suggested that the tests might take two weeks to complete, but as July turned into August, and August into September, there was no word from the FBI.

Phil called Jenkins several times, but all Jenkins could say was that there was no new information. Phil and Greg Augustine talked—for the first time in three years—and compared notes about Chaz and the chance that Kathy, and maybe Chuck, had both died from a syringe wielded by Chaz. Greg and Phil had at least one thing in common—they both loathed Chaz Higgs.

Where they parted company was over the issue of motive. Phil believed that Chaz had killed Kathy because he wanted her money. Greg believed that Chaz had killed her not only because he wanted the money, but because Kathy knew he had killed Chuck Augustine.

Chaz, meanwhile, was getting legal representation. This unfolded even while he was still in the psychiatric hospital after his suicide attempt. Over that weekend, Shirley

Higgs began searching the Internet for a lawyer for Chaz. She eventually ran across a site or a reference that linked to Alan Baum, a veteran criminal defense lawyer who had offices in Woodland Hills, California.

"His mother needed someone she could consult," Baum recalled later. "She was surfing the Internet and found something about me. She emailed me, and I called her back. We just chatted, like family."

Baum advised Shirley to go to Las Vegas. He agreed to represent Chaz for the purposes of inquiries from the news media or the police. By that point, Baum recalled, there were already suggestions that a criminal investigation of Kathy's death was underway.

Late in August, Baum called Detective Jenkins in Reno. He said that if Jenkins wanted to talk to Chaz, he'd try to make him available. According to Baum, Jenkins downplayed the importance of any investigation, saying, "I'm sure it will be nothing."

Baum and Jenkins were playing games with each other. By the time Baum contacted him, Jenkins knew that there was a credible allegation that Kathy had been poisoned with a dose of succinylcholine, and that the FBI had been asked to test for it. Given the circumstances—that Kathy had been found unconscious by Chaz, then revived by the paramedics, any injection of "succs" had to have occurred within five to eight minutes before the paramedics' arrival, around 6:40 at the latest. Much earlier, they would not have been able to revive her—she would have been dead. In Jenkins' mind, that meant only one person could have given her the "succs"—Chaz Higgs, the only other person present when Kathy had stopped breathing. So it wasn't "nothing." In Jenkins' imagination, he could see Chaz quietly panicking inside when Pratt brought Kathy back to life, something he'd never believed could happen after he'd poisoned her.

Baum was also fooling Jenkins. If Jenkins actually intended to arrest Chaz, Baum had no intention of allowing the detective to interview him. From his limited contact with Chaz so far, Baum knew it might be hard to restrain him from *wanting* to be interviewed by Jenkins, but as far as Baum could see, there was no advantage in it for Chaz.

Of course, Baum did not know as much as Jenkins about the case, and might not have known about the pending test for succinylcholine, but he knew that if anyone was a prime suspect, it had to be his client.

September 25, when Montgomery finally sent her report on the analysis of Kathy's samples to Washoe County, was a Monday. After discussion between the Washoe County District Attorney's office and the Reno police, a decision was made to seek an arrest warrant for Chaz Higgs. At the same time, Jenkins asked for a second warrant allowing the police to monitor the location of Chaz's cell phone. Within a day or so, the telephone company reported that Chaz had last used his cell phone in Tennessee, and from this, the police concluded that Chaz was driving east, headed toward his brother Mike's home in Hampton, Virginia.

Before obtaining the cellphone warrant, Jenkins had been keeping loose tabs on Chaz throughout July and August. He knew he couldn't press too tight—he had no probable cause.

"During this whole time," Jenkins said later, "we were mindful of the fact that although we had some suspicious circumstances, we didn't have the definitive cause of death, and we were waiting . . . we had to be very careful that we didn't prematurely go out and do irreparable damage to somebody."

If Kathy had in fact died of natural causes, Jenkins said, he would be guilty of having severely damaged Chaz's reputation by going too far, too fast.

But Jenkins was also aware of the fact that Chaz had not voluntarily come forward to talk to him. Jenkins and his partner thought that was unusual.

"In most instances where you have an investigation into a suspicious death, the spouse is very interested in knowing about the details," he said later. "In fact, Chaz was conspicuously absent, in what seemed to be his avoidance of contact with us . . . I found it certainly unusual that he hadn't called up to say, at least, 'Now, do I have this right, do you suspect that someone may have killed my *wife?*' There was no such communication."

As for Baum's earlier promise to produce Chaz for questioning if the police ever wanted to talk to him, Jenkins disagreed.

"Well, that's *not* what he said! That's not what he said," Jenkins said later. "That's what he *says* he said, but that's not what he said. Mr. Baum said that if at some point I wanted to talk to him, he would facilitate my *contacting* him. He never made any . . . suggestion that he would make him available to be interviewed, and basically, my spin on that call was, [Baum] was on a fishing expedition to try and determine what level of interest law enforcement had in his client."

So Jenkins never talked to Chaz before the FBI's report arrived. Instead, once they had their arrest warrant, he and Hopkins got on a plane just before midnight on September 29 and flew to Richmond, Virginia, arriving about 4:30 A.M. There they rented a car and drove to Hampton, not far from Norfolk.

After reaching Hampton, Jenkins and Hopkins met with the Hampton police and the FBI about 8:15. A covert surveillance of Mike's house was undertaken. It appeared that Chaz was no longer there. As they were mulling over what to do next, they began to get new reports on Chaz's location—Chaz had turned his cellphone on again, and every time he drove past a cellphone tower the number registered with the telephone company's wireless system. Back in Reno, another detective in contact with the phone company relayed Chaz's movements to Jenkins and Hopkins. Chaz appeared to be near Jacksonville, North Carolina, and his mother. He was driving the BMW that Kathy had paid $41,000 in cash for three years earlier.

Jenkins and Hopkins headed for Jacksonville. They received periodic updates from Reno as to Chaz's location.

But while the Reno detectives were driving south, Chaz was heading north, although that wasn't clear at first to Jenkins and Hopkins.

"They were giving us GPS coordinates—'He's here, he's here, he's here,' and we're about an hour behind him, trying to catch up. Every time he passed a cellphone tower, it pinged." But Chaz's telephone company had poor coverage in eastern North Carolina, so it was hard to pinpoint his exact location and direction.

"In some areas we would lose contact with him for an hour, and then our next reading would be eighty or ninety miles away, and we'd think, *Okay*, and we'd try to catch up to that," Jenkins said.

Late in the afternoon, though, they began receiving reports of a steady signal. It appeared that Chaz was heading back to Mike's house. Jenkins and Hopkins were about ninety minutes behind him.

Guessing that Chaz would go directly to his brother's, they called the Hampton police and the FBI and asked them to put Mike's house under surveillance again.

Sure enough, an hour or so later, Chaz pulled the BMW into Mike's driveway. At that point, FBI Agent Paul Gray, a Georgia native, stepped forward with his gun drawn. He ordered Chaz to put his hands on the steering wheel where Gray could see them.

"I kept tellin' him, put his hands on the steering wheel, and he just wouldn't do it," Gray said later, in his Southern drawl. "He finally moved his hands up there, but he was real close to bein' shot."

Once Chaz had been handcuffed, Gray searched the BMW. He found a large knife under the seat, and Chaz's black backpack on the floor in front. On the dashboard was a single sheet of paper listing Alan Baum's California telephone number. It seemed that Chaz had anticipated being arrested at any moment.

Inside the Hampton police station, Gray advised Chaz of his legal rights on arrest. Chaz invoked his right to speak with an attorney. Other than that, he said nothing. Baum had drilled his client well.

"We initially thought we could have an opportunity to talk with Mr. Higgs prior to placing him under arrest," Jenkins said later. But Jenkins and Hopkins were worried that with his previous attempt at suicide, Chaz might try something drastic. As a result, they decided not to ask him any questions. Chaz called Baum in California.

After some conversation with the defense lawyer, Chaz gave the telephone to Jenkins. Baum told Jenkins that Chaz didn't want to make any statements. Jenkins asked Baum if Chaz was going to oppose extradition back to Nevada. Baum told Jenkins he wasn't sure, but that once he knew, he'd let Jenkins know.

At about the same time, Phil Alfano called Jenkins. Jenkins had told Phil before leaving Reno that the FBI had found succinylcholine, and that they'd decided to arrest Chaz. He asked Phil to keep it quiet—they didn't want to spook Chaz before they could apprehend him. But by Friday afternoon, Phil still hadn't heard anything, so he decided to try to reach Jenkins on his cellphone.

"It's funny you should call," Jenkins told him. "We just arrested him."

"I couldn't have been off the phone for more than two minutes when it started ringing again," Phil said later. Reporters were calling Phil for his reaction. How they found out so fast was a mystery to him.

Phil called Dallas. Dallas had begun to reconsider her

earlier defense of Chaz. She'd asked Phil to tell her if he heard any news. But Dallas didn't answer, so Phil left a message, telling her that Chaz had been arrested.

Jenkins and Hopkins flew back to Nevada. Over the next few days Baum, in conversation with Shirley Higgs, agreed to represent Chaz in a criminal trial in Reno. Chaz soon waived extradition, and a week later, Jenkins and Hopkins returned to North Carolina to escort Chaz back to Reno. Once he arrived, Chaz was placed in the Washoe County jail to await his trial.

The trip back to Reno, as Jenkins recalled it, was long— there were two layovers. But all the way back to Truckee Meadows, Chaz said almost nothing. Even if the authorities in Nevada thought they had the right man for the death of their state controller, they were still going to have to prove it beyond a reasonable doubt.

Chapter 24

A little more than a week after Chaz's return to Reno, workers at Paradise Memorial Gardens in Las Vegas removed the earth covering the grave of Chuck Augustine. A large tripod with a pulley system extracted the oversized coffin, which was then put on a flatbed truck and driven to the Clark County morgue. Three years after he'd tried to interest someone—anyone—in conducting an autopsy of his father's remains, Greg Augustine had finally succeeded.

The fact that Chuck's former nurse at Sunrise Hospital, the subsequent husband of Kathy Augustine, had been arrested and charged with using succinylcholine to kill her had tipped the balance. Clark County Coroner P. Michael Murphy wasn't sure what was going on with Chaz Higgs and the two dead Augustines, but with Kathy in the ground not 100 feet away from her third husband—treated at Sunrise Hospital by her fourth husband, no less—Murphy wanted to find out once and for all if there was more to the story.

By that point in early October of 2006, after Chaz's arrest, political circles in Nevada were rife with idle chatter. Scores of people who had seen Kathy at political gatherings in Nevada between 2003 and her death recalled having seen Chaz as her escort—the Odd Couple, as most remembered them. Chaz was recalled as glum and uncommunicative, disinterested. The permed, bleached hair, the earrings were recounted—not the sort of appearance that the Republican Women's Club stalwarts were used to see-ing in their members' husbands. Some even recalled him appearing at political events wearing a tee-shirt.

The obvious variance between mainstream Kathy and her Stanley Kowalski–type husband soon led to more specu-lation, especially after Chuck's casket was exhumed. In the absence of any facts, it wasn't long before some began to speculate as Greg Augustine had—that the marriage be-tween Kathy and Chaz was a pact made in hell, some sort of *Double Indemnity* reenactment, in which Kathy had traded a murder of her estranged, stroke-disabled husband for a slice of the pie. And when the guilt had gotten too large, the thieves had fallen out, just as Fred MacMurray and Barbara Stanwyck had reached the paranoid end of their own affair. Only Chaz had hit first, with his weapon of choice—succinylcholine.

Tom Barb, who would eventually prosecute Chaz for Kathy's murder in Reno, was well aware of all the talk, even as he prepared to bring Chaz to trial for one murder, not two.

"You know what?" he said later. "I don't know what it is, or what it was, but I think for some reason in his mind, he had to get rid of her. I don't know what that reason is, I could speculate for days about that, but for some reason he believed, he perceived her as some sort of threat to him, that divorce wouldn't cure. And so he had to get rid of her. But what that is, I don't know."

Still, the fact is, there wasn't a shred of hard evidence to suggest that Chaz had anything to do with Chuck Augustine's death.

After disinterment of Chuck's remains, Clark County Coroner Murphy's experts conducted an autopsy, and found nothing to indicate anything different from the original cause of death—cardiopulmonary collapse resulting from Chuck's horrific stroke in August of 2003. Still, after Montgomery's findings of succinylcholine in the FBI Lab, Murphy didn't want to take any chances. He had samples of Chuck's remains sent to National Medical Services in Pennsylvania. He didn't want the FBI to conduct the tests, he said later, in case someone later claimed that the FBI was predisposed to finding "succs" in order to validate the tests they had already conducted on Kathy's samples. However, the FBI wouldn't have taken the samples anyway—after the Sybers case, they would no longer analyze tissue that had been embalmed.

Murphy and Clark County District Attorney Roger consulted with the eminent pathologist Michael Baden of New York. Baden said that if succinylcholine had been administered intravenously, there was almost no chance of finding it three years later. But if Chuck had been given a shot of "succs" intramuscularly, it was possible remnants might still be found in Chuck's tissues.

As Murphy recalled, Chuck's remains were in remarkably good condition—well-embalmed, and in a quality casket. So the samples were sent on to the Pennsylvania lab for testing.

Meanwhile, detectives from the Las Vegas Metropolitan Police began trying to pin down Chaz's whereabouts in the days and hours before Chuck's death on August 19, 2003. They discovered that Chaz wasn't on duty at Sunrise Hospital either the day Chuck died, or the day before. If Chaz had poisoned Chuck with "succs," there was no way to prove it.

As for Chaz himself, when he was eventually interviewed by a television magazine program, *48 Hours*, he insisted that it was "crazy" to believe he'd had anything to do with Chuck's death. Anyone who thought that was "insane," he said. "It's completely outlandish."

Or was it? What wasn't reported at the time was that the Pennsylvania lab's testing showed that Chuck Augustine had measurable levels of succinylmonocholine in his tissues—"mono," in other words. Was this the result of embalming or natural decomposition? No one could say for sure, not now, not after the Sybers case.

As Murphy later explained to Greg Augustine, that meant

no one could say definitely that Chuck *hadn't* been poisoned with succinylcholine—only that there wasn't any evidence of it.

"You can never say never," Murphy said.

As for Greg, he remained convinced that his father had been poisoned by Chaz Higgs.

"I think he was killed," Greg said later. "I think Kathy got Chaz to do it. I think they did it so they could go away happily ever after."

That Kathy and Chaz did not "go away happily ever after" was due to their guilty secret, Greg believed, a monstrous truth that eventually led Chaz to kill Kathy to keep her quiet, an act that brought him finally before the bar of justice in the Biggest Little City in the World.

Chaz on Trial

Chapter 25

The lack of definitive findings by the lab in Pennsylvania benefited Chaz. In March of 2007, after almost six months in the county jail, he was released on $250,000 bail, pending trial. Shirley Higgs moved to Reno to stay with her son as he awaited his moment of truth.

By this point Shirley and the rest of the Higgs family had banded together to pay Alan Baum to represent Chaz. Up until Chaz's arrest, Baum had only agreed to act as his attorney for purposes of the news media and any inquiries from the police. Once Chaz was arrested, Baum and the Higgs family had to make new arrangements. That was one reason Baum was unable to tell Jenkins immediately whether he would oppose extradition from North Carolina. Only when the financial arrangements were in place was Baum able to formally represent Chaz on the criminal charges.

But Baum had another problem: he wasn't licensed to practice law in Nevada. To do that, he needed a lawyer licensed by the state to act as his co-counsel, someone to vouch for him in the Nevada courts. Baum began interviewing Nevada lawyers. There were a number who were interested in the case, because of all the publicity it had generated so far, and would continue to generate: for lawyers, publicity is good advertising. After some time he selected David R. Houston, a well-known Reno defense lawyer, to serve with him.

Houston was 44 years old, blond-haired, blue-eyed. He

was well-known in the Reno courts, and respected for his aggressive defense of the accused. At first, Houston believed that Baum would do the lion's share of the work defending Chaz, and that he would only be there holding Baum's coat, so to speak. But as the case unfolded at the end of 2006 and into early 2007, Houston found himself shouldering more and more of the load. Eventually, there would be some resentment between Chaz's two lawyers over each other's style and level of commitment.

For his part, Baum realized very early that the Nevada courts saw him as an interloper, a hired gun from the Big City. Where judges might be willing to give Houston a little slack because he was a known commodity, Baum understood that no one was going to give *him* any breaks.

As Baum and Houston saw the case against Chaz, the whole thing rested on the FBI's identification of succinylcholine in Kathy's urine. If they could break that linchpin, the case would collapse. That meant attacking Montgomery's identification of "succs."

Baum soon became familiar with the Sybers case, the reef upon which previous succinylcholine cases had foundered. He made contact with H. Chip Walls, the Florida toxicologist whose testimony had been so devastating to Sybers' prosecutors, and enlisted him as an expert witness. Baum was confident that Walls could prove that the FBI's Montgomery had erroneously found "succs" where there was none in Kathy's urine.

In addition, the defense took aim at several other parts of the prosecution's case. For one, they wanted to attack Jenkins' search warrant, the one served at the Otter Way house. They intended to show that the warrant was invalid because Jenkins had failed to establish probable cause—Jenkins' omission of Kim Ramey's name as his informant meant that no judge could reasonably believe that a crime had been committed. Without Ramey's name and her qualifications, no judge should have reasonably approved such a warrant.

In that way, Baum and Houston hoped to get the vial of eto-midate, the companion drug to "succs" that had been seized by Jenkins, thrown out. Even Jenkins admitted that the dis-covery of the etomidate had convinced him of the truth of Kim Ramey's information.

The defense also wanted to convince Chaz's judge to throw out the case based on the fact that the FBI's Mont-gomery had destroyed evidence—the tissue from the sup-posed injection site. In testing the tissue, Montgomery had had to liquefy it. That test eliminated the opportunity for the defense to examine the injection site tissue to see whether there was proof that the injection had occurred after Kathy had been hospitalized—if so, that would tend to eliminate Chaz as the source of any "succs."

But the heart of the defense was its argument that Mont-gomery's testing procedure was flawed. For that, Baum was sure he had the ideal witness in Dr. Walls.

Walls was technical director of the forensic toxicol-ogy laboratory at the University of Miami School of Medicine's Department of Pathology. He had over three de-cades' experience in the detection and analysis of drugs. His testimony had helped sink the prosecution of Dr. Sybers, and was probably more responsible than any other person for the finding that mere "mono" was insufficient to prove that succinylcholine had been used as a murder weapon. In short, many considered him to be the leading expert in the country on poisoning by succinylcholine.

But in order to attack the FBI's conclusion that "succs" had been found in Kathy's urine, Walls needed to know ex-actly what Madeline Montgomery had done in performing her analysis. This proved to be difficult information to get.

As early as December of 2006, Chaz's prosecutors from the Washoe County District Attorney's office had wanted to put Montgomery on the witness stand to testify that she had found "succs." Baum had successfully prevented her testimony when he noted that Montgomery had not turned over any notes she had taken during the testing process. Without the notes, Baum argued, there was no way the defense could intelligently cross-examine Montgomery. He'd wanted Montgomery's notes to give to Walls, so Walls could brief him on the questions he should ask. But Montgomery steadfastly refused to turn over her notes to the prosecutor for forwarding to the defense under the rules of discovery.

"The FBI's policy, or the laboratory's policy," Montgomery told the judge during Chaz's preliminary hearing, "is that we will turn over the notes after we receive a written discovery order, and it is reviewed by our counsel at the laboratory. Or unless it is told to me by a judge."

Prosecutor Barb said he'd tried to get the notes, but the FBI wouldn't even turn them over to him.

After some additional discussion, the judge in Chaz's preliminary hearing ordered Montgomery to turn any notes she had with her over to the defense. After a short recess, Montgomery provided a stack of paper "three or four inches thick," according to Baum. There was simply no way the defense could read and understand the notes in time to cross-examine Montgomery that day, he said. At that point, Barb, the prosecutor, withdrew Montgomery as a witness. It didn't matter for purposes of binding Chaz over for trial—the judge still found probable cause to believe that Chaz had committed the crime of murder, based on other evidence, primarily the testimony of the nurses Kim Ramey and Marlene Swanbeck, and medical examiner Ellen Clark. But the dispute over Montgomery's testing methodology wasn't over.

After this hearing, Baum had turned the stack of paper over to Walls. All through the spring, Walls tried to make sense of what Montgomery had done to reach the conclusion that "succs" had been found in Kathy's urine. In the end, Walls concluded that he still didn't have enough information—he had no way to determine how Montgomery had validated her results. According to Houston, Walls was puzzled as to the lack of "mono" in the blood samples. He also thought that the ratio of "succs" to "mono" in the urine itself was reversed—that there was too much "succs," and not enough "mono," given the supposed time of injection.

Baum and Houston asked for additional paperwork from the FBI Lab. This was not forthcoming, or at least not in a readable form. Walls contended that pages of Montgomery's documents that had been faxed to him were unreadable. There were more bureaucratic delays inside the FBI's hierarchy. At length, facing a trial that was set to begin on June 18, 2007, Baum and Houston asked for a continuance. They wanted more time to get the paper to give Walls more time to analyze Montgomery's work. The defense contended that Walls had reviewed Montgomery's records and found them to be "incomplete and inadequate for his purposes as an expert witness . . . Our expert has indicated to us, while he possesses a conclusion, he does not possess the methodology or testing regimen utilized to reach the conclusion."

Without the additional information, Houston told the court, Walls couldn't replicate Montgomery's results— something that was necessary to establish her findings as proven science under legal standards.

"At this point, defense counsel is in the position of receiving a questionable conclusion from the FBI with little backup documentation to learn exactly how the FBI reached this rather disputed conclusion," Houston argued. "It is clear this case is based upon the FBI conclusion, and the FBI conclusion alone."

The defense wanted a quantitative analysis of the "succs" and "mono" in the urine—a mere "qualitative" analysis, simply showing the presence of the substances, was insufficient when the amounts found might reveal flaws in the testing procedure.

The prosecution objected to a continuance, saying that a

quantitative analysis wasn't necessary—if there was any "succs" at all in the urine, that proved the case, they said. And if Walls hadn't been able to understand Montgomery's method almost five months after getting her initial notes, it was too late now to ask for a delay—he should have made that clear much earlier.

After listening to both sides, Nevada District Court Judge Steven R. Kosach rejected the continuance.

If Walls didn't trust Montgomery's methodology, Kosach said, he could simply get up on the witness stand and say that: "Why doesn't he just come in and testify, 'Based on my scientific knowledge, experience, skill, expertise, I don't trust the validity of the stuff I got from the FBI, and therefore, I cannot conclude that there's succinylcholine in the system'?"

But Walls soon explained the dilemma to Baum and Houston: if Prosecutor Barb were to ask him if the FBI had detected "succs" in the urine, he'd have to say yes, based on the readings from the LC/MS. If someone asked him how Montgomery reached her conclusion, he'd have to say he didn't know. And if anyone asked him how it got into Kathy's urine in the first place, he'd have to say he had no idea.

Chapter 26

Chaz's trial began as scheduled on June 18. Before proceeding to jury selection, though, Houston and Baum tried again to get Madeline Montgomery's critical testimony thrown out. Any time the government wanted to use scientific evidence to prove its case, Baum argued in a preliminary motion, the burden was on the government to prove its reliability. The prosecution couldn't do that in *State of Nevada* vs. *Chaz Higgs*, he said.

Prosecutor Barb said he would show that Montgomery's findings *were* reliable. He called Dr. William Anderson, the Washoe County toxicologist

"Do you have any opinion of the trustworthiness of the FBI's procedure?" Barb asked.

"I have no problem with it, either with the finding of succinylmonocholine or succinylcholine," Anderson said.

Houston tried to get Anderson to admit that Montgomery had made up her testing procedures as she went along, "on the fly," as Houston put it, since there had never been a case before with real-world samples of "succs" found in a victim. But Anderson said he was satisfied that Montgomery's methodology was sound.

Houston now called Walls to the witness stand.

"Are you aware of any valid procedure to test for the presence of succinylcholine?"

"There is no validation standard for tests for succinylcholine."

Walls said that without knowing exactly how Montgomery conducted her tests—and particularly the control samples of urine taken from the lab volunteers—he could not be sure that the test of Kathy's urine had not produced a false positive, possibly a contamination from one of the "spiked" samples used to validate the LC/MS "profile."

Barb's cross-examination was quite short, and to the point.

"Would you agree that the FBI Lab found succinylcholine in the urine sample taken from Kathy Augustine?"

"Yes," Walls said. Given the limited information he had about the FBI's testing procedure, he would have to agree that the LC/MS had detected "succs" in Kathy's urine.

And with that statement, Walls had blown Chaz Higgs' defense right out of the courtroom. As Baum put it later, there was no way they could put their star witness on during the trial if he was going to say that "succs" had been found in Kathy's urine. That was the whole ballgame.

In addition to the complexity of the scientific evidence—overcoming any juror's natural inclination to tune out complicated testimony about liquid chromatography/tandem mass spectrometry, control samples, validation runs and the like, and instead simply accept the technical mumbo jumbo as proven—the defense had a far more human problem.

They had to demonstrate that Chaz and Kathy really *did* love each other. That meant walking a fine line—portraying Kathy as mean enough to justify Chaz's desire to leave the marriage, but not so mean that Chaz would be driven to kill her. The defense also had to show that while Chaz had said bad things about his wife, he really didn't mean them, that in fact, he was the long-suffering, loyal partner in a marriage that wasn't as bad as Chaz's own words seemed to say it was.

To achieve that tricky balance, there had to be someone else to blame. Baum and Houston focused on Kathy's impeachment, and put the onus on the politicians for Kathy's treatment of her husband. But even then, they had to contend, Chaz's solution to the marital strife was leaving the marriage, not murder.

The prosecution had a different problem: why would Chaz, by all accounts an intelligent, seemingly rational adult, choose to kill Kathy rather than just walk out? After all, he'd divorced three times before, and there were no children to be concerned about. Because Chaz wasn't a beneficiary of Kathy's trust, he couldn't be said to have killed her for money. As for Chuck Augustine's death, the Clark County Coroner's finding that there was no proof of foul play took that motive off the board, as well. The only motive the prosecution could ascribe to Chaz was simple hate. The question was whether jurors would believe that Chaz hated Kathy so much he was willing to murder her.

It took the better part of a day to pick a jury. Four men and eight women were selected within eight hours, despite the pervasive publicity the case had received in the Reno area, and throughout Nevada, for that matter.

The case was to be tried in the historic Washoe County Courthouse. In its time, the building had seen many things, including over 30,000 divorces granted when Reno was considered the divorce capital of the country back in the 1920s and 1930s—when newly freed wives made a ritual of tossing their gold bands into the river to declare their manumission. It had also seen its share of lurid murder trials, and was said to be haunted by the souls of those who had been condemned to death within its walls, then later hung just outside its doors.

Just a long toss of the wedding ring from the Truckee River a few steps to the north, the courthouse was first erected in brick in 1871, then rebuilt in Classical Revival style in 1911 with a fanciful copper dome, and restored in 2002. With its 19th-century ceilings and wooden pews for the gallery, going into Department 7 of the courthouse was like stepping back into the era of the Scopes trial.

Opening for the prosecution was Deputy District Attorney Christopher Hicks, a tall, blond, young up-and-comer for the Washoe prosecutor's office. With Higgs and Hicks, Baum and Barb, the sounds of the names in the acoustically challenged old courtroom could sometimes be confused.

Hicks began summary of the case by explaining what succinylcholine was, what it was usually used for, and how it affected the body—total paralysis of voluntarily controlled muscles.

"They cannot move, they cannot breathe," he said of patients given the substance. "Without assistance, they will suffer brain damage."

He recounted nurse Kim Ramey's version of the conversation she'd had with Chaz on July 7—how Darren Mack had done it "all wrong," that he should have "hit" with "a little 'succs.'"

"The very next morning, Mr. Higgs' wife, Kathy Augustine, was found not breathing. What was found in her system was 'succs.' Chaz Higgs hated his wife. He desperately wanted to leave her, but couldn't. Two hospitals had very little controls in place on 'succs' to prevent its improper usage."

Hicks went on to name the witnesses who would be called and to summarize their expected testimony—Ramey, the nurses at South Meadows, the doctors, the paramedics, Madeline Montgomery, the medical examiner Ellen Clark, and Detective Jenkins.

"You'll hear from many of Chaz Higgs' co-workers that he commonly called Kathy Augustine many nasty names, talked often about leaving her, or even getting rid of her.

"Chaz Higgs is a calculated murderer who used his trade to accomplish his goal—to get rid of his wife," Hicks concluded.

Houston gave the opening statement for the defense.

"This case is much more complex than the state would like you to believe," he said. "It's very important to establish the entire context of the relationship between Chaz Higgs and Kathy Augustine, and not snatch bits and pieces, as was done a moment ago. The remarks attributed to Mr. Higgs by the state are not sinister, but understandable when placed in context."

The context began, Houston continued, when Chuck Augustine died in Las Vegas, and Chaz met Kathy.

"There existed a chemistry between them—it may have been unsightly to some, who might have thought they were going too fast, but they married in September of 2003 in Hawaii—this was not a planned event. When they returned from Hawaii, they faced criticism, but they didn't care, they were in love.

"Chaz Higgs was not aware that the person he had married was an important person in Nevada. That lesson would come, but slowly over the years. But at the start, Chaz Higgs was the happiest he'd ever been in his life . . . but that changed in 2004. They were notified by the Nevada Attorney General that there was an investigation underway to make a case against Kathy Augustine for improprieties, of misuse of her office.

"This investigation, which eventually led to Kathy Augustine's impeachment, began in early 2004. The wonderful atmosphere between Kathy Augustine and Chaz Higgs became strained. Mr. Higgs learned that this small world they had created for themselves was not impenetrable. As the impeachment unfolded, the mind-set of Kathy Augustine was not as pleasant as it had been when they first met. Eventually, Chaz Higgs realized he couldn't live this kind of lifestyle, with Kathy Augustine's obsession with the political environment. After the impeachment, Kathy Augustine was very depressed—this thing that had been so important in her life was taken away from her, her political career, her public reputation . . . She became obsessed with politics, and getting her reputation back.

"You will learn that Chaz Higgs couldn't live this kind of lifestyle; he wanted a divorce. They agreed to separate after the impeachment was finished. He would become a travel nurse, and come visit her from time to time. But Chaz and Kathy didn't separate after the impeachment; he couldn't bring himself to leave her when she was down. Even in bad times, when you want out the door, sometimes you know you have to stick it out. Chaz Higgs stuck it out. 'I can't leave her right now,' he told people, when they asked why he just didn't get out of the marriage.

"Chaz Higgs believed it was over, although by 2005, they faced a mass of legal bills; some other things began to happen. For one thing, Kathy Augustine was as devoted to the political world as you could possibly imagine. Although Kathy had told Chaz that she would get out of politics after the impeachment . . . she changed her mind. Kathy advised him that she intended to run for state treasurer. Chaz was not happy with this decision.

"By 2006, Chaz Higgs had decided once and for all to leave the marriage. He got his own bank account and began to look for his own apartment. Then Kathy Augustine was found unconscious and not breathing on the morning of July eighth, 2006, and the life of the woman Chaz Higgs had loved, but could no longer live with, was over.

"There was absolutely no motive that would cause a human being to take the life of another human being . . . There was no motive. In April of 2004, Kathy Augustine signed a will and living trust for the transfer of assets to her daughter Dallas on her death. Chaz was aware of this, he had discussed it with Kathy. As a nurse, Chaz made about the same amount of money as Kathy.

"On the evening of July 7, Chaz Higgs left his shift at the

hospital, talked with Kathy, and explained why he was establishing his own bank account, and getting his own apartment. Kathy told him she wasn't feeling well, that she wanted to get some sleep, that they'd talk more in the morning.

"The next morning, Chaz awoke first, went into the garage. When he came back into the bedroom, he became alarmed at Kathy's breathing. He opened the blinds, he could see something was wrong. He immediately began CPR. He called 911, REMSA. He wanted to save his wife. Why would he call before she was irretrievably lost? Why would he call the paramedics? Ask yourselves that question."

The jury would hear that Chaz had been unemotional throughout Kathy's ordeal in the hospital before her death. But the jury needed to know the other part of the story—that Chaz, as a trained professional, wasn't given to emotional outbursts in medical crises. In fact, as a combat medic—Houston said that Chaz had served with Navy SEAL units in combat in the gulf—Chaz had long before learned to keep his feelings in check.

The real cause of Kathy's death was sudden, unexpected heart failure due to natural causes, Houston told the jury.

"Not every death is a homicide; not every heart attack is obvious. The possible causes of heart failure are too numerous to mention. You will learn . . . there is evidence that heart failure caused the death of Kathy Augustine. Chaz Higgs asked for an autopsy. He knew that his wife had a mitral valve problem with her heart. Mitral valve prolapse with regurgitation.

"Dr. Anton Sohn, a professor of pathology at the University of Nevada, Reno, will testify, in stark contrast to the state's opening, that it is most likely that Kathy Augustine died of heart failure caused by this defect in her heart."

The jurors would also hear about "a defect" in Kathy's upper left buttock, Houston said, and the state would contend that it was the mark left behind by a needle.

"But you will hear that no one can say for sure what that defect was, or where it came from, or when it was made. And if the state can't prove those things, the state's case will collapse. The evidence will in fact prove diametrically the opposite—that Chaz Higgs could not have murdered his wife with succinylcholine.

"Do not be misled by the cherry-picking of statements or circumstances. The state's case will not survive beyond the testimony of the defense pathologist."

The prosecution's first witness was Kim Ramey. July 7, 2006, she said, was "a day from hell." The Carson Tahoe hospital had a combined ICU and critical cardiac care unit, and Ramey's job was to "float" between the two. There were several patients, including one in isolation. That meant Ramey had to put on a new gown, gloves and mask every time she attended the patient. As a result she'd begun to ask Chaz, who had been assigned to her for training, to get various supplies and equipment, thereby minimizing the changes. She had begun talking conversationally with Chaz.

"Did he ever mention his wife?"

"Yes."

"What did he say about her?"

"He said she was a filthy bitch, that she was a stalker."

"Did you form an impression of Mr. Higgs?"

"Yes."

"What was that?"

"That he was a player. I shared personal information with him. I told him I was going back to Virginia. He had this anger, you could tell he had this anger."

"Did he mention any topics that made him angry?"

"He was angry about the divorce, angry about his wife."

"What did he say about the divorce when it first came up?"

" 'Oh, I'm getting a divorce, too.' "

Ramey said she'd told Chaz that she and her boyfriend were going back to Virginia the following week.

"So you wanted to let him know you had a boyfriend?"

"Yes."

"He told you who his wife was?"

"Yes."

"What did he say?"

"He said she was high-profile. Kathy Augustine. State controller. She was running for state treasurer. He didn't like it. 'She's a fucking stalker. I'm looking for an apartment because she's a fucking stalker. She's a bitch. She's a psycho.' "

"Did he indicate that he loved his wife, in any way?"

"Not that I saw."

"It was his wife on the phone?"

"Yes. I assumed it was his wife."

"What did he say to her over the telephone, if you can recall?"

"He said, 'I will fucking talk to you when I get home . . . I said, I will fucking talk to you when I get home.' I said, 'What was that all about?' He said, 'I can't fucking believe it, she found out I opened an account at Wells Fargo. I can't believe she found out.' "

Ramey said she'd told Higgs that the same thing had happened to her, and explained a bit about her own divorce.

Hicks asked her if the subject of Darren Mack had then come up. Ramey said it had, there was an article that day in the newspaper about Mack.

Hicks asked what she knew about Darren Mack.

"He had been in and out of court. He shot the judge, killed his wife, fled to Mexico."

"What did Mr. Higgs say about Darren Mack?"

"He said that the guy did it wrong. 'If you want to get rid of someone, you just hit 'em with a little 'succs'—because they can't trace it at a post-mortem.' "

Ramey said Higgs illustrated this simultaneously by making a motion with his hand as if administering an injection.

"What was your reaction to that?"

"The hair raised on my arm. I had a physical response, goosebumps."

"Where did this conversation take place?"

"At the nursing station." Ramey said she was sitting on the edge of the table, just before she headed for the medication room.

Ramey said she told Chaz he shouldn't hold so much anger. Then she invited him to a going-away party for her and her boyfriend to be held that night. But Chaz declined.

"He said, 'I'm just going to go home and tell her' " about the divorce.

"A couple of days later, did you tell anyone what Mr. Higgs had said to you?"

"I was off Saturday. On Sunday I saw in the paper, the headlines, that Kathy Augustine was comatose in the hospital." Actually, this must have been Tuesday, not Sunday; there was no newspaper report of Kathy's collapse until that day.

"What was your response?"

"I had the same bodily feeling I'd had before. My gut, my intuition was that he had done something to her."

"Did you call the police?"

"I believe it was July eleventh—not that day, not the day after, [but] on July eleven."

"Can you explain why you didn't call right away?"

"I had four shifts left. I've had lawyers up to here. I work so hard for twenty-one-and-a-half years, and— You have no idea how much I despise lawyers. I didn't want to deal with any more lawyers. I was hoping he'd be arrested and I'd be off the hook."

This was a day from hell?" Baum asked Ramey, when he began his cross-examination.

"It was a normal day for me."

"You previously described it as a day from hell."

"Okay, it was a day from hell."

"Working in the ICU is stressful, agreed?"

"Stressful," Ramey nodded.

Baum asked Ramey about the rapid sequence intubation kit, commonly called an RSI kit, the sealed box that contained, among other things, succinylcholine and etomidate.

"Now the red tab that's on the RSI box, you saw it on the box that day? You have to break it to use it?" Baum wanted Ramey to testify that the seal on the box hadn't been broken—in other words, Chaz couldn't have taken "succs" from the crash cart in the Carson Tahoe ICU that day. But Ramey didn't cooperate.

"I don't remember."

"Did you need to use the RSI kit?"

"No."

"Who takes the inventory once the red tab is broken?"

"The pharmacy."

"Someone could take the whole box, and the pharmacy would replace it?"

Ramey agreed, someone could have taken the whole kit, although that disappearance should have been noted on the hospital's drug restocking inventory.

"Did you ever ask Mr. Higgs to get anything from the refrigerator?" More "succs" was kept in the unit's refrigerator.

"No."

"When during the day did you and Mr. Higgs first have a conversation about your divorce problem?"

"Not about the problem, just about the divorce."

"You said you thought he was a player. You thought he was hitting on you?"

"Within five to fifteen minutes, I thought he was a player. I'm usually pretty accurate, I can tell what's going on. We deal as nurses with all of them. No, I didn't think he was hitting on me. I think he was a player."

"What did he say to you?"

"He said his divorce was going to be easy—it would only take seven weeks. He wanted to explain who his wife was."

"After the phone call—does he confirm that was his wife?"

"He told me multiple things. Lots of things. He said he was getting a divorce, but I found out later he hadn't even filed. His credibility as the day went on wasn't getting higher."

"This conversation about Darren Mack, was this before the phone call from Kathy Augustine?"

"Yes."

"What started the conversation about Darren Mack?"

"I can't remember. Maybe the newspaper was open to the article. I think I said something like it was obvious to me that Darren Mack went off the deep end because of the divorce."

"The phone call from Kathy Augustine came in the afternoon?"

Ramey confirmed that it had.

"You were working twelve-and-a-half-hour shifts?"

"My shift ended at seven forty-five P.M."

"You invited him to a going-away party? And he responded, 'I'm going to fucking go home and tell her'?"

Ramey nodded.

"You said you had goosebumps when he supposedly said that about the 'succs'—why?"

"Nurses don't kill people, we save people."

"You were alarmed?"

"Not alarmed, but upset."

"You weren't alarmed at the time?"

"I should have called—I should've listened to my boyfriend. Hindsight is twenty/twenty."

Baum's cross-examination of Ramey accomplished very

little for the defense. Afterward, Houston expressed disappointment that Baum hadn't been more aggressive in trying to undercut Ramey's credibility. The main point remained unrefuted—Chaz had talked about using "succs" as a murder weapon just the day before Kathy had collapsed.

Chapter 27

Over the next week, the prosecution brought more than two dozen witnesses to the stand. Doctors Seher and Ganchan explained how they had ordered Kathy's urine and blood samples frozen after hearing Ramey's story. Lab personnel at South Meadows and Washoe Main established the chain of custody of Kathy's samples, necessary to show that no one could have tampered with them before the FBI's tests. Another doctor, Paul Mailander, an anesthesiologist, described the effects of succinylcholine on the human body—anyone dosed with succinylcholine could be fully conscious and feel pain, he said. But they'd be unable to move, speak, or even cry out.

The paramedics, Ben Pratt and Manny Fuentes, described going to the house on Otter Way and reviving Kathy. Pratt's testimony particularly damaged Chaz. He said that when he and Fuentes arrived at the Otter Way house, Kathy was lying on her back in bed. That indicated to Pratt that Chaz had *not* performed CPR, as he claimed he had to the 911 dispatcher—the best way to perform resuscitation was to place the victim on a hard surface, such as the floor. It was hard to believe that Chaz, a trained critical care nurse, didn't know that. Thus, he had lied from the beginning.

Nurse Marlene Swanbeck described taking Kathy's urine, Chaz's demeanor in the South Meadows ER the morning Kathy had been brought in, and the gift of the donuts with the request for his paycheck the following day. When asked if Kathy had been given succinylcholine by anyone in the ER, Swanbeck said no. It hadn't been necessary, because the paramedics had already intubated Kathy when they found her unconscious.

Other nurses testified that Chaz habitually criticized Kathy for her controlling, jealous nature, and that on more than one occasion wished that someone would "take care of" her. The remark about throwing Kathy's body down a mine shaft was told several times.

There was little the defense could do to blunt this portrait of Chaz as someone who despised his wife. Houston tried to bring out the fact that many in the ER did not like Kathy, that Kathy was considered arrogant, self-centered, vengeful and overall, a thorough disruption. But the net effect was to show Chaz as a chronic complainer, someone prone to exaggerating the baleful behavior of his wife.

Both Baum and Houston tried to establish that Chaz's criticism of Kathy was actually only light-hearted banter, typical gallows humor in the ER—sort of Youngmanesque: "Take my wife . . . please!" But while many nurses admitted that gallows humor was prevalent in the ER, no one really thought Chaz was joking about Kathy. They thought he was miserable in the marriage, and didn't understand why he just didn't walk out. This point was brought home as witnesses repeatedly testified that when they asked why Chaz just didn't leave Kathy, Chaz would only say that he couldn't— underscoring the unattractive image of him as someone who manipulated others to get their support, if not their pity.

Several other doctors testified, including Stanley Thompson, a cardiologist who had given Kathy the angiogram at Washoe Main on July 8. The prosecution played a DVD of the X-ray of Kathy's heart—literally a moving picture of her beating heart after she was stricken, but before she died. Thompson said the angiogram proved there was no blockage in any of Kathy's heart arteries. He identified areas of necrotic, or dead, tissue in the heart that he said could have been caused by a lack of oxygen after Kathy was stricken.

The defense tried to induce Thompson to acknowledge that Kathy's "mitral valve prolapse" could have caused a leak of blood into the mitral chamber of the heart, thus stimulating a heart arrhythmia and fibrillation.

"And arrhythmia can cause ventricular fibrillation? And ventricular fibrillation can lead to sudden cardiac death, can it not?" Baum asked.

"I've never seen that," Thompson said.

"Ever seen anyone hit by lightning?"

"I've had friends hit by lightning."

"Ever hear of coronary artery spasm?"

"It's been reported but never proved."

"It doesn't exist?"

"It exists, but if it causes death, it isn't known."

"So it's impossible?"

"It's unlikely, but you would have to have symptoms over the previous few months—chest pains, indigestion."

Baum suggested several other causes of sudden heart death not associated with arteriosclerosis, but Thompson said he found no evidence that any of those conditions were present when Kathy was stricken.

Barb moved quickly to cut down this avenue of speculation. He asked Thompson if Kathy's heart could have been restarted by the injection of epinephrine and atropine, and chest compressions, as Pratt had done, if she'd had an arrhythmia. No, Thompson said. If Kathy had had an arrhythmia, the paramedics' drugs would have had no effect. The fact that the paramedics hadn't used their electric defibrillation paddles, but got the heart started anyway, proved there was no arrhythmia, no fibrillation.

To make sure that the jury got the point that Kathy had not died from other natural causes, Barb called another Washoe Main doctor, Steve Mashour. Mashour said he'd examined Kathy before her death and found no evidence of a blood clot in her lungs, another possible explanation for her collapse. Mashour said he'd seen a report that morning that barbiturate had been found in Kathy's blood, but didn't believe it, based on her symptoms. He'd asked for a second test, and that one had come back negative for barbiturate.

Houston had been waiting for Mashour to take the stand—they'd already had a conversation in the days before the trial.

"Based on what you saw," Houston asked, "you can't rule out sudden cardiac death, correct?"

"Based on the information that I have, it's possible," Mashour said.

Houston asked if Mashour knew that the supposed means of introducing the "succs" into Kathy was by intramuscular injection in the left upper buttock area. Mashour said that was what he'd been told.

"And you've also advised that you feel it would be highly unlikely to be the cause of death in this case. Haven't you said that?"

"Based on the medication that is being suspected, that would be highly unlikely to be the cause of death, in my opinion."

What was this? Suddenly one of the doctors who had treated Kathy was saying it was "highly unlikely" that "succs" had caused her death.

"Okay," Houston said. "And the reason it would be highly unlikely that succinylcholine would be the cause of death is because you would have to administer so much, true?"

Mashour caviled a bit, saying he wasn't sure how much "succs" would be needed if the needle hadn't penetrated to the muscle of the buttock. In fact, he said, he didn't even know how much "succs" would be required to kill someone if the needle had actually hit the muscle. But the substance caused an intense burning sensation at the place it was administered, he said.

"Didn't we actually discuss the notion that it could be as high as—What was it?—eight hundred milligrams in order to achieve any effect whatsoever?"

"That's a very rough estimate . . . That's a ballpark guess, at best."

Houston pointed out that to get 800 milligrams of "succs" into someone, it would require four separate injections of ten cubic centimeters each. He held up a 10 cc syringe to show the jury. He produced a paper cup and began squirting the syringe's contents into the cup. It seemed to take a long time to empty.

Houston sat down, satisfied that he'd made the point that to kill Kathy with "succs," multiple shots over several minutes would have been required. The demonstration seemed to show it would have been difficult, maybe impossible, to give someone thrashing around in pain from the burning sensation sequential shots without damaging the surrounding tissue rather bloodily.

Barb wasn't going to let this go by.

"Is it your opinion, or is it Mr. Houston's opinion, that succinylcholine isn't the cause of death in this case?" he demanded.

"Well," Mashour said, "I think it's less likely that—"

Barb cut him off. "Doctor, has anybody told you that there was succinylcholine present in Ms. Augustine's urine after her death—or, excuse me, when she first came to the hospital?"

"When she first came to the hospital? I was not aware of that," Mashour admitted.

"Does that change your opinion?"

"Well, it would change my opinion."

But the core of the case against Chaz was presented by Madeline Montgomery.

From the outset of her testing, Montgomery said when she took the stand, she'd known what to look for—

succinylcholine. The people in Washoe County who had asked for the analysis were clear on that. Montgomery said she'd begun her testing by looking for succinylmonocholine, reasoning that "succs" might well have disappeared by the time her tests began. If she tested for "mono" and found none, she would know right away that there could be no "succs"—no "mono" meant there could be no "succs," and therefore, no reason to continue testing. The test for "mono" was positive.

But before she could test for "succs" itself in the urine, Montgomery said, she'd needed to find a way to prove it could be found. That required her to first obtain fifteen samples of other urine—from her colleagues in the lab—and first test those samples to show that none had "mono" in them. In other words, to demonstrate that "mono" did not naturally occur in a living human body.

Next, Montgomery took some of the volunteer urine samples and "spiked" them with a supply of succinylcholine on hand at the lab. After this, Montgomery put the "spiked" urine samples through the liquid chromatograph/tandem mass spectrometer machine, and established a profile for what urine would look like if it contained "succs."

Finally, Montgomery again put Kathy's urine through the LC/MS. The profiles matched that of the control urine that had been spiked. The result, Montgomery said, was that she had established the presence of "succs" in Kathy's urine.

When it was his turn, Houston tried to blunt this testimony by suggesting that Montgomery's testing process was flawed.

Wasn't it true, he asked, that Montgomery herself had discovered that "mono" could be found naturally in decomposing tissue?

Montgomery admitted it was possible.

"The science around succinylcholine is ever-evolving?"

"Absolutely. That's why I devised my own testing

protocol. I adapted our methodology for determining succinylmonocholine for succinylcholine."

"Has your procedure ever been published in a scientific journal? Has it been validated by peer review?"

"Our procedure has never been published, but it has been peer-reviewed by scientists in our laboratory."

If "mono" was a possible natural result of decomposition after death, Houston asked, wasn't it also possible that the body of a person who had technically died, then was revived, could have begun to produce it as part of the interrupted decomposition process?

Montgomery said she thought that was highly unlikely. As far as she knew, she said, "succinylmonocholine has never been found in a living person."

Houston next tried to suggest that Montgomery's testing procedure had generated a "false positive," that is, detection of "succs" or "mono" because of contamination from one of the control samples. The sensitivity of the LC/MS was such that even the tiniest amount of a chemical might throw the machine off, he said.

"Are you familiar with the term 'sticky molecule'?" he asked. But Montgomery said that in between tests she'd run "test blanks" with distilled water. This had had the effect of thoroughly cleaning the machine.

Houston tried to induce Montgomery to admit that the failure to find "succs" or "mono" in either the blood or the supposed injection site tissue indicated that the urine readings were the result of a "false positive," but Montgomery wouldn't go there. One reason the blood might not have produced readings for "mono," she said, was that it had not been continually frozen—enzymes in the blood between the time the sample was taken and the time it was tested could have reduced the "mono" to choline and succinic acid.

Without Walls to contradict her, there was little else the defense could do with Montgomery's testimony, so Houston finally released her as a witness. Barb chose not to ask her any new questions.

Near the end of the first week of trial, the judge permitted the defense to put on a witness out of order. Normally, defense witnesses are called only when the prosecution has finished its case, but Judge Kosach allowed Baum and Houston to call their first witness before the prosecution rested.

This was Dr. Anton Sohn, chairman of the University of Nevada School of Medicine's Pathology Department, and a former medical examiner for Washoe County. As medical examiner, the 71-year-old Sohn had worked for years with law enforcement in Washoe County, and was well-respected. He had testified many times in Washoe County courts, "90 percent of the time" for the prosecution. Over his nearly forty years in Reno, he had performed over 3,000 autopsies, many of them in connection with crimes.

But in this case he was being called by the defense.

Baum asked Sohn what he'd done to prepare for his testimony. Sohn said he'd reviewed the autopsy report, the hospital treatment records, Madeline Montgomery's toxicological findings, and Dr. Ellen Clark's testimony about the autopsy at Chaz's preliminary hearing.

"Oh?" Baum asked. "Do you know Dr. Clark?"

"I hired her," Sohn said.

Baum asked Sohn to evaluate his former employee's work in the Kathy Augustine case.

He had two problems with Dr. Clark's findings, Sohn said. For one, in her microscopic examination of Kathy's heart tissue, Clark had missed something important. A closer examination of the slides of the heart tissue, Sohn said, showed that Kathy had larger than normal heart muscle cells. This was a strong indication of cardiac hypertrophy, that is, an enlarged heart. Sohn said the enlarged heart was probably due to the "mitral valve prolapse," the heart murmur. The weakness in the heart meant that Kathy's heart had to work harder to pump blood, which was why the muscle cells were larger than normal. An enlarged heart could lead to "sudden cardiac death," Sohn agreed, but only because the heart had become susceptible to heart failure over time.

"It's important," Sohn said, "because with hypertrophy, it takes weeks or months to set in. It's not something that could happen overnight, or within four or five days."

"Dr. Clark made no mention of this?" Baum asked.

"No, she did not."

"Do you consider this a significant omission?"

"I do."

Baum showed Sohn three photographs taken of Kathy's buttock area during Clark's autopsy. He pointed to the "punctate area," the supposed injection site.

"Do you see that?" Baum asked.

"Yes, I do," Sohn said.

"When was that punctate mark made? Can you form an opinion as to the age of that mark?"

"Yes. My answer is that it's not more than twenty-four hours old. It's highly unlikely to have been given on July eighth." At the outside, he said, the wound could have occurred no more than forty-eight hours before Kathy's death on July 11. That made Sunday, July 9, the earliest possibility for the supposed injection.

Elaborating, Sohn called the punctuate area an "acute" injury—meaning it was fresh, inflicted just prior to death. He could tell by its color, between purple and bright red. The injury had occurred just before death and the autopsy, not eighty-one hours earlier. Had the FBI preserved the tissue rather than liquefy it for the "succs" test, he added, additional examination would have proved the age of the wound beyond any doubt.

This was the dynamite testimony that Houston had promised the jury in his opening, when he'd said that "The state's case will not survive beyond the testimony of the defense pathologist."

If the jury believed Sohn, the supposed injection could not have been inflicted by Chaz Higgs on Saturday morning just before Kathy collapsed. It had to have occurred much later, when Kathy was in the Washoe Main ICU. Ergo, the punctate wound had nothing to do with the case—*if* "succs" was really in Kathy's system, and if Sohn was right about the date of the wound, the compound had to have been introduced by some other means to the body.

Once the punctate wound was out of the equation, there was really only one other place Kathy could have been given the succinylcholine: the South Meadows emergency room, and then, only between 7:05 A.M., when she had arrived, and 7:35 A.M., when the urine was drawn, Houston suggested.

If Montgomery was right, and the urine did contain "succs," the window of opportunity for introduction of the succinylcholine had to have been between 6:40 and 7:35 on Saturday morning. Establishing that the wound had occurred well after Saturday morning seemed to narrow that even further, to between 7:05 and 7:35, when Chaz wasn't even present.

Houston was laying the groundwork for a later assertion that someone in the ER had given Kathy the fatal injection, perhaps by mistake, despite Marlene Swanbeck's assertion that no "succs" had been given. That is, if indeed the substance found by Montgomery *was* "succs." If it was, and Kathy had been given the "succs" in the ER, Chaz Higgs was off the hook.

And in fact, if the punctate area had occurred just before death, as Sohn insisted, "succs" couldn't even be the cause of death—because Kathy had been put on oxygen from the time of the paramedics' arrival. It had to be a heart attack.

Prosecutor Barb's job at this point was to undermine Sohn's credibility. It wasn't a task he relished, having known and worked with Sohn for so many years. But it had to be done.

Barb asked Sohn if he'd reviewed the records of Kathy's treatment in the hospital from July 8 to July 11. Although he'd earlier said he'd based his opinion in part by studying those records, Sohn now said he hadn't looked at them. Barb pointed out that the records did not reflect that Kathy had received any injections in the upper left buttock area while being treated before her death.

"She could have gotten a shot and it wasn't charted," Sohn said. "I've seen that happen plenty of times."

"You said you'd conducted more than three thousand autopsies," Barb reminded him. "How many cases out of those three thousand were 'sudden cardiac death'?"

"Maybe one hundred?" Sohn answered.

Barb asked Sohn to define the term, and Sohn said it was an electrical malfunction of the heart brought on by an arrhythmia or sometimes a blockage. Cardiac hypertrophy could be a factor in that, he said.

Barb asked if the records showed any evidence of an arrhythmia.

"There's no way to tell if there was an arrhythmia," Sohn said.

"Did you review the records of the paramedics?"

"No, I did not."

The implication was that Sohn was unaware that Kathy had been given atropine and epinephrine by Pratt, which meant that an arrhythmia could not have taken place—the drugs would not have worked, in that case. The only thing that could have re-started the heart was the defibrillator.

"Of the three thousand autopsies you've done, how many involved succinylcholine?"

"None," Sohn said.

"If you had been told that Kathy Augustine had succinylcholine in her system, would that change your opinion?"

"No, it would not."

"If over the last five years, Ms. Augustine had normal

blood pressure, would that eliminate a finding of an enlarged heart?"

"Yes," Sohn said.

"Did you review her medical records?"

"No."

When it was his turn again, Baum zeroed in on the prime question: "If the results from the FBI are wrong, could there be a different cause of death?"

Yes, Sohn said—sudden cardiac death.

Barb couldn't let that one pass.

If there had been succinylcholine found in Kathy's urine, didn't that mean someone had to have injected her with it?

Not necessarily, Sohn said. "Succinylcholine can occur naturally in the human body."

Barb was stunned by this.

"How do you know that?" he asked, seeming genuinely perplexed. All the testimony prior to that point had agreed that "succs" was an unnatural compound.

"Just from what I've read," Sohn said. "It's part of the decomposition process."

Barb challenged Sohn to cite any article in any reputable medical journal that proved that succinylcholine could be manufactured naturally inside the human body. Sohn admitted he couldn't name one. It appeared that Sohn had confused "succs" with "mono." That seriously undercut the value of his testimony for the defense.

Chapter 28

The following day, the prosecution moved to nail the lid shut on Sohn's testimony. They called Ellen Clark to the stand.

Barb showed Clark the photographs taken of the punctate area, and asked her to describe its coloration. The area was "blue, green, purple and red," Clark said. "It is consistent with a needle puncture."

She'd reviewed the hospital treatment records, Clark said, and while there were many needle marks on the body stemming from the care Kathy had received from the paramedics and the ICU, there were no notations reflecting any injections in the upper left buttock area.

"You heard Dr. Sohn testify?" Barb asked her.

"Yes," Clark said. But she disagreed with Sohn: there was no evidence of scarring or dysfunction of the mitral valve, only mild degeneration. In her opinion, there had been no "sudden cardiac death." The cause of death was evident from examination of Kathy's brain tissue—a massive amount of brain swelling indicated a constricted blood flow and a pronounced lack of oxygen.

What about the supposed injection site? Had she heard Sohn testify that it was "acute," inflicted no more than forty-eight hours before the autopsy?

The color didn't mean anything, Clark said. One couldn't determine the age of such a wound by the color alone. The fact that there was red only indicated that blood had seeped into the area at some point between the infliction and the autopsy. In her judgment, the mark could have been made more than three days prior to death—in other words, on Saturday.

Even if the punctate area had come later, Clark said, that didn't mean that Chaz hadn't injected Kathy some place else on her body that Saturday morning. A critical care nurse might be able to give an injection without her being able to find any evidence of it, she said.

It was true, Clark said, that she hadn't signed a final death certificate until October, after the FBI had completed its tests. But that was only because until the FBI did its work, Clark could find no clear reason for Kathy to have died.

"Did you form an opinion as to the cause of Kathy Augustine's death?" Barb asked.

"It is my opinion that Kathy Augustine died of succinylcholine poisoning," she said.

Baum tried to move Clark away from her opinion that the supposed "needle mark" was more than three days old.

"I am not specifically identifying it as a needle mark," Clark reminded him, referring to her description of it as a more generic "punctate wound." She was only "fifty-one percent sure it is a needle mark," she said.

"I did a very thorough examination of the body," she said. "There's nothing in the hospital records that show these punctate marks were by design, or the medical care provided."

Baum wanted to know if she'd inspected the tissue from the punctate area under a microscope before sending it to the crime lab, and thence to the FBI.

"I did not," she said. "I wanted to submit the tissue for a toxicological analysis."

Because previous testimony had indicated that intramuscular injection with succinylcholine caused the intense burning sensation at the injection site, Baum suggested that anyone repeatedly injected—as Houston's four separate shots of 10 cc's each suggested—would thrash around in considerable torment before the substance took effect. He wanted to know if Clark had noticed any tearing of the skin around the punctate wounds, as one might expect from a writhing victim. Clark said there was no apparent tearing of the skin.

If it hadn't been for the FBI's "succs" findings, Baum persisted, how would Clark have listed the cause of death?

An unexplained heart attack, Clark responded.

"If it isn't this poisoning, then," Baum said, "the most likely possibility would be the mitral valve prolapse causing the arrhythmia, the fibrillation, is that right?"

"I don't know if I'd agree with that," Clark said.

"You can't rule it out, though?"

"No," Clark said.

Having exhausted the science, and believing that they'd been able to establish an edge in the battle between Sohn and his one-time protégé, the prosecution returned to the matter of motive. They called Chaz's former Internet paramour, Linda Ramirez.

To that point, the police had only recovered the emails that Linda had sent to Chaz in early 2005—those that had been found in the South Meadows computer system. But as the trial neared its end, Linda had contacted the district attorney's office to tell them that Chaz had resumed email communication with her in late 2005, without Kathy's knowledge, and that these messages had continued right through August of 2006—even after Kathy's death. Linda gave copies of these emails from Chaz to the prosecution.

On Monday, June 25, Hicks put Linda on the witness stand, and used Chaz's emails to show that he had been flirting with Linda—well, electronically—even before Kathy's death, and then again after she died. These emails included Chaz's assertion that he wanted to get even with Kathy, to drive her crazy, to make "her life a living hell," as Chaz had put it in one of the emails.

Hicks read from some of Chaz's messages to Linda.

" 'I hate this woman, and I will make her break,' " Hicks read. " 'It's my quest in life to drive this bitch crazy, and it is working, she is losing her mind. I don't care anymore what she tries to do to me, I was scared before, but not anymore . . . I will be free and I will be with you. That is what I want. You have my heart . . . ' "

Did Chaz send those words to her?

Yes, Linda said.

Hicks read from another message, in which Chaz told her he was single—and that he wanted to spend time with her in San Diego. Had Chaz written that?

Yes, Linda said.

Had she known how Chaz had become single?

Yes, she said. She'd seen it on the Internet. Chaz had told her he wanted to move out of Nevada, "due to recent events."

When it was his turn, Baum simply asked Linda how old she was when she'd met Chaz at South Meadows.

Twenty-one, Linda said.

Wasn't Chaz just flirting with her, Baum asked—not being serious? Wasn't it true that they'd never had a physical relationship?

"I had no intention of seeing him while he was married," Linda said. "My understanding of it was that it was just flirting, it never became physical."

She'd only seen Chaz twice outside of the hospital, she said.

"Did he ever even kiss you?"

"There was one kiss—in a gas station," Linda said.

"Mr. Higgs broke it off with you because he didn't want to cause you any more problems, isn't that right?"

Linda said that was what Chaz had written to her in late 2005 to early 2006.

"At this point, you can see this is really going nowhere?"

Linda agreed.

"It's just a friendship?"

"Yes."

"Mr. Higgs never gave an invitation to you for a more intimate relationship, did he?"

"No."

"The only invitation was from you, which he never pursued, correct?"

"Yes."

Hicks counterattacked by reading from an email Chaz had sent to Linda on August 28, more than a month after Kathy had died.

"He wrote, 'I can make you the happiest woman on earth,' didn't he?"

"Yes."

"Does that sound like a 'friendship'?"

"No."

Baum tried again.

"You would agree that in July 2006, just before Kathy Augustine passed away, you were not in a love affair with Chaz Higgs?"

"No," Linda said, meaning she agreed—she was not in a love affair with Chaz Higgs when his wife suddenly collapsed and died.

Linda's testimony wrapped up the prosecution's case. Now the defense moved to "strike" or suppress all of the testimony about the urine tests, arguing that the state had failed to prove that Montgomery's science was both replicable as well as reliable. Not only that, they said, there were holes in the state's chain of custody on the urine—the state couldn't prove that someone hadn't tampered with it before the testing.

"Your Honor," Baum said, "it's the state's burden to establish the chain of custody, and the more witnesses they called, the more gaps became apparent." That was why the judge should simply throw out all testimony related to the urine tests, and instruct the jury to disregard it.

That was just poppycock, Barb said. The defense had failed to introduce one bit of evidence that the chain of custody was ever broken. Every sample was correctly labeled and logged, and there was no such break.

"That's all there is to it," he said.

Judge Kosach rejected the motion to strike.

Baum tried again—he wanted the judge to throw out the whole case. There was insufficient evidence to warrant continuation, let alone conviction, he said.

Not only was the science of succinylcholine testing wobbly, Baum said, but the court had heard evidence that the supposed injection could not have been the means by which the substance was introduced, *if* it was introduced, to Kathy Augustine's body.

That was an overstatement, Barb countered. Clark had testified that trying to guess the date of an injection by the mere color of its wound was impossible. Besides, she'd pointed out that she couldn't say for sure that Kathy hadn't been injected some place else on her body that she hadn't been able to find.

"A good critical care nurse could inject someone without leaving any mark," Barb said. "We've shown the motive—he hated her. He wanted out at any cost. He killed her."

Kosach denied that motion, too. Baum, the out-of-towner, was oh-for-almost everything he'd tried in Washoe County.

Now Baum and Houston had to put on a defense for Chaz, and without Walls to prop them up, it didn't look good.

Chapter 29

Chaz's first witness was his twin brother, Mike. Doubtless Shirley Higgs could tell them apart, but for the jury and almost everyone else in the courtroom, it was a case of seeing double: one Chaz at the defense table and another on the witness stand.

Mike said he first learned that Chaz and Kathy had married when he got a telephone call from his twin in late September of 2003. Curiously, this was a couple of weeks after Chaz had sent him an email saying that Kathy had just bought the BMW for Chaz to drive.

"Were you surprised they had gotten married?" Houston asked.

"Surprised? Yes I was. I thought it was fairly quick. I thought maybe they should have taken time to get to know each other first. But they were in love, like high school kids. I figured they knew what they were doing."

Mike said that, as far as he could tell from his home in North Carolina, Chaz and Kathy seemed very happy through the end of 2003.

"Did things begin to change in early January 2004?"

Mike missed his cue to blame the politicians.

"No," he said.

Houston tried again.

"Did you become aware of an investigation of Kathy Augustine in the early months of 2004?" He did, Mike said, getting it now.

He'd first heard of the impeachment investigation when he was in Iraq, Mike said. His National Guard unit had been activated, and he was sent to the Middle East. Once the investigation became the subject of the negotiations between Kathy's lawyer John Arrascada and the attorney general's office, he said, the marriage "went downhill, it turned bad."

"Why?" Houston asked.

"Kathy was under a lot of pressure," Mike said, "a lot of stress, and she took it out on Chaz."

As early as April of 2004, he said, Chaz had told him he wanted to get a divorce.

"I told him to stick with it, to give it time," Mike said. Kathy also emailed him with complaints. Mike said he encouraged both partners to stay together. One reason Chaz did not leave was that he felt he had to support Kathy during the impeachment and its aftermath. He felt it was his duty as a husband.

"In hindsight, when things really got bad, I should have told them to split," he said.

The major issue in the marriage, Mike said, was Kathy's obsession with her political career. Chaz "felt like a fish out of water in political circles," Mike said. He was particularly sensitive to insinuations that he was Kathy's "arm candy," as Mike put it, or suspicions that he was only after Kathy's money.

It was his brother who first suggested that Kathy form the trust, in order to "squash" that gossip, Mike said.

"Did it work?"

Mike shook his head, negatively.

When Kathy decided to run for state treasurer, Mike advised her it would damage her relationship with Chaz. At that point, he didn't think the marriage would last.

"Who wore the pants in the family?" Houston asked.

"Kathy," Mike said.

"Chaz was subservient to her?"

"Yes," he said.

Hicks tried to use his cross-examination to show that Mike really knew very little about Chaz's true feelings toward Kathy.

"You weren't in Reno on July eighth, 2006, were you?"

"No."

"You have no knowledge of what happened that day?"

"No."

"You said she wore the pants, she was very controlling?"

"Yes."

"You said that by April 2004, your brother wanted out of the marriage?"

"Yes."

"Did he ever file for divorce?"

"Not to my knowledge."

Chaz didn't go through with a divorce because he felt obligated to support Kathy through the impeachment?

That was true, Mike said.

Hicks turned to the emails Chaz had sent Linda Ramirez, and read excerpts from them, including Chaz's declaration that his "quest in life" was to "drive this bitch crazy."

"Does that sound like a dutiful husband?"

Mike shrugged.

"Do you still think he was a dutiful husband when he was trying to start a relationship with Linda Ramirez?"

"Yes, I do," Mike said.

Hicks read from some of the email Kathy had sent to Mike, including her lament that Chaz had told her he "had never been sexually attracted to me."

That was just the residue of Chaz's unhappiness with Kathy's political obsession, Mike said.

Had he ever talked to Chaz's co-workers in the ER about Chaz's habitual disparagement of his wife?

"No," Mike admitted.

"Did your brother ever tell you of his pact with himself to make every day of his wife's life a 'living hell'?"

"No."

Houston tried to soften the effect of Hicks' cross-examination by showing that Chaz's emails to Linda had been sent at a time when Kathy was angry and depressed because of her treatment at the hands of her former political friends.

"After she was impeached, her political party ostracized her," Mike said. "That was stressing Kathy." Chaz's emails to Linda were "not reflective of his true feelings."

"Have *you* ever made a pact with yourself to make somebody's life a living hell?" Hicks asked on redirect examination, when Houston was finished.

"No."

"Did you ever promise to drive someone crazy?"

No, Mike said.

When it was his turn again, Houston elected not to ask Mike any more questions.

For his next witness, Houston called Dr. Earl Nielsen, a Reno clinical psychologist. Nielsen was an expert in traumatic stress disorder—he had served his internship in a Palo Alto veterans' hospital that treated many combat cases from the war in Viet Nam. Nielsen was also an experienced witness, having testified well over 200 times in various courts as a forensic psychologist.

Nielsen said Houston had called him on June 19, 2007, the day after the trial started, to ask him if he would testify about the way different people handle grief and loss. He met with Chaz that day. Coincidentally, Nielsen had seen Chaz together with Kathy only a few weeks prior to her death, when they had appeared at a fund-raiser for a children's charity that Nielsen sponsored, so Chaz and Kathy weren't complete strangers to him. Following the June 19 session, Nielsen had met with Chaz three other times, and had given him a battery of five psychological tests.

"In general, do we all respond the same to the loss of a loved one?" Houston asked.

"Not at all," Nielsen said. "There are varied responses."

If a person had been trained to handle crises, would that make a difference in their behavior?

"That would absolutely be true," Nielsen said. Crisis training helps people not to take things personally, "so they can do the job as best they can without reference to emotions," he said.

That was especially true for Chaz, he added. "Mr. Higgs has had exceptional training to deal with the most extreme kinds of crises." Chaz's service as a Navy medic in the Middle East had profoundly influenced his behavior. "He's been trained, perhaps overtrained."

"Does that mean he doesn't care?"

"No. He is so well-trained that the rest of us don't see the grief in his response."

Chaz's behavior at the time of Kathy's collapse was actually quite typical of many veterans, Nielsen said. Military personnel are trained "not to think, just act. Those who react by impulse are better insulated from post-traumatic stress syndrome." When Chaz had picked the newspaper off the dashboard of the ambulance taking Kathy to Washoe Main and casually perused it, it was simply his way of distracting himself.

Chaz's "calm, professional behavior" while at the Otter Way house and at the two hospitals "is consistent with fifteen years of military training," Nielsen said. "When training is thorough and appropriate, we expect it to work."

Providing an explanation for Chaz's behavior on July 8 had been Houston's original intent in consulting Nielsen, but after meeting with Chaz, Nielsen told Houston that he might be able to provide the jurors with an answer to the central puzzle of Chaz: why he didn't just leave Kathy if he was so unhappy in the marriage. He'd just spent the weekend with Chaz and his mother, and had given Chaz the tests to see what they said about his personality.

Now Houston asked Nielsen if he had an explanation for Chaz's emails to Linda Ramirez. Nielsen said he did.

"One possibility is that he's a man who enters relationships with great romantic fantasy and great hope," Nielsen said. "But the weakness I observed with Mr. Higgs was—he does have trouble with the concept of commitment."

Chaz had begun his relationship with Kathy "wanting it to be perfect, but when he discovered it wasn't going to be perfect, he wanted out." Linda Ramirez was just a possible escape route for Chaz, and not the only one. "I'm not sure that Ms. Ramirez was the only person he considered an option."

The wellspring of Chaz's behavior, Nielsen suggested, was his idealistic ideas of how a marriage should work. Chaz wanted perfection. He expected it of himself and of Kathy. But when problems arose, Chaz essentially wanted to erase things and start over, to find someone else who could make his dreams come true.

"What's a 'hopeless romantic,' Doctor?" Houston asked.

"Someone who thinks romance will solve all their problems," Nielsen said.

Almost throughout the marriage, Nielsen said, Chaz was torn between wanting to leave, and wanting to stay. His desire for perfection told him to move on, but his view of himself as good, kind, helpful and supportive person compelled him to remain with Kathy.

Chaz's complaints about Kathy to Linda Ramirez and to his co-workers in the ER were pretty normal for a couple under stress, Nielsen said.

"What happens when a couple in an intimate relationship has a conflict, each person is liable to speak out to their 'support base,' " friends and family who are most likely to take your side in the dispute, Nielsen said.

"Sometimes we say things we don't act out on?"

"Most of us do that," Nielsen said.

When he sent Linda his emails, Chaz was exaggerating

his angry feelings toward Kathy, in part because he considered Linda sympathetic. "He considers Linda Ramirez to be a safe setting," not unlike his friends in the ER.

Houston asked about Chaz's suicide attempt, and his protestations of love for Kathy. Weren't the suicide notes reflective of his true feelings?

"It's more complex than that," Nielsen said. "It's not just love, it's also guilt. He created stress for Kathy by opposing her political career. He thinks he created stress for her," that resulted in her having a heart attack.

Barb thought this was all rubbish.

"Doctor, what's a sociopath?" he asked.

"Essentially, a person without a conscience, someone cold, calculating, manipulative. A person who always has their own best interest at heart."

"Does that sound like Mr. Higgs?"

"If you put all the pieces together, but it's a little bit out of context."

Nielsen was waiting for Barb to ask him about the "context" so he could explain the tests that seemed to show Chaz was not a sociopath, but Barb did not oblige.

"Did the defense tell you that Kathy Augustine had poison in her system?"

"No."

"Would that change your opinion?"

Not really, Nielsen said. He knew that that was what had been alleged. "I read the newspapers."

Barb suggested that Chaz's military training was seven years behind him. Didn't Nielsen think that it had worn off by now? Not really, Nielsen said, because after getting out of the Navy, Chaz had become a critical care nurse, so he was still in crisis situations.

"You don't think we should think ill of him for reading the newspaper while riding, lights and siren going, to Washoe Main?"

"No."

Barb rattled off examples of Chaz's behavior after Kathy's collapse, including the paycheck/donut incident. Chaz had also signed papers to get Kathy's state pension as her beneficiary—one day before she actually died, Barb pointed out.

"What does that do to your opinion of Mr. Higgs?"

Houston objected.

"What, I can't ask questions?" Barb retorted.

Kosach denied the objection, and Nielsen said his opinion would depend on what Chaz knew of Kathy's medical condition at the time.

"Was that a grief reaction?" Barb asked. "Would you go to find out how much you were going to gain after her death, and you'd call that a grief reaction?"

"Not necessarily," Nielsen said.

"He was conflicted about staying in the marriage?"

"Yes."

"He certainly knew how to get out if he wanted to. He'd been married three times before, hadn't he?"

"That's correct."

"He found out he couldn't control Kathy Augustine, so he searched for a twenty-one-year-old, isn't that correct?"

Nielsen said he felt he'd explained why Chaz had flirted with Linda by email. "He'd started a romantic relationship, but he hadn't crossed the physical boundary. He had not ignited the relationship to be an intimate one."

"It was just a fantasy?"

"It was a fantasy in his mind, it kept him safe."

"It's all about him, isn't it, Doctor? Isn't that the description of a sociopath?"

Houston wanted to rehabilitate Nielsen after Barb's cross-examination.

"Now, when you met with Mr. Higgs, did I say there was anything you couldn't talk about?"

"No," Nielsen said.

"Mr. Barb *suggested* that Mr. Higgs was a sociopath. Is Mr. Higgs a sociopath?"

"No," Nielsen said. "I tested him. I determined he is not a sociopath."

"Mr. Barb has cherry-picked things out of context?"

"Yes. The psychological testing does not confirm the diagnosis of sociopathy."

"Mr. Barb's theories are half-baked?"

Barb objected to Houston's characterization. Both sides were now getting a little punchy.

Barb asked if Nielsen was aware that the day before Kathy collapsed, Chaz had told another nurse that the smart way to get rid of someone was to "hit 'em with a little 'succs,'" and that later "succs" had been found in Kathy's system.

"That particular comment would make me highly suspicious," Nielsen admitted. "Assuming it was true that 'succs' was found. Which I don't know for a fact."

Houston had one more witness for the defense.

Chaz Higgs.

Chapter 30

Chaz took the witness stand just before 4 P.M. on Monday, June 25. Houston took Chaz through his upbringing in North Carolina, one of three sons of a career U.S. Marine. After getting out of high school, Chaz said, he'd joined the Navy and had become a hospital corpsman.

"Why was medicine so important to you?"

"I love helping people," Chaz said.

"You trained with the SEALs?"

"Yes."

"Was there a reason you didn't complete the training?"

"I broke my arm."

Houston asked Chaz where he had served.

"Bahrain, the United Arab Emirates. Saudi Arabia. Kuwait. Eritrea, Oman." He'd been at the Khobar Towers bombing, Chaz said.

How had he met Kathy Augustine?

"At Sunrise Hospital in Las Vegas. I was in the cardiac ICU. There was a patient there, Charles F. Augustine, her estranged husband."

"How long had they been estranged?"

"Five years."

After Chuck had died, Chaz said, Kathy had passed out "thank you" cards to the hospital staff, but had omitted him. Realizing her omission, Kathy had invited him to have a cup of coffee with her.

"Can you describe the beginning of that relationship?"

"We went out. We felt a real chemistry, that's what we had."

"Were you a little nervous over the quickness?"

"I was. But I decided to follow my heart."

His heart had led him to go with Kathy to Hawaii, Chaz said, where they were married.

"How soon was this after Mr. Augustine died?"

"Less than one month."

"Did she kill her husband?"

"No."

Houston did not ask whether Chaz had killed Chuck.

Chaz's family thought he was crazy to have married someone he only knew for a month. But he didn't care, he said—he was in love. Even snide remarks that he was Kathy's "arm candy" didn't bother him, at least at first.

He knew nothing about politics, and didn't at first realize that Kathy was one of only six government officials elected statewide in Nevada.

But as the weeks and months passed, Chaz came to realize how much Kathy's career as a politician meant to her.

"I personally didn't like it." He felt ill at ease around people who talked about politics and government incessantly.

"I never felt comfortable that Kathy wanted me there. I wanted to be there, but I never felt comfortable."

Then, in January of 2004, Kathy had thought she'd been selected to be the next U.S. treasurer. Then the state attorney general's people had come to interview her. A few days after that, the White House told her that she wouldn't be appointed.

"She was devastated," Chaz said. "She got closed off, angry. She came home like that—so cold, so hard, so scared, so defensive."

A few months later, Chaz said, he told Kathy he wanted a divorce. Kathy begged him not to divorce her, not while she was under investigation. Then came the impeachment, the trial, and the censure. By then it was January of 2005.

"And you reached out to Linda Ramirez?"

"Yes."

"Are you proud of the emails you sent to her?"

"No."

He'd sent the emails to Linda Ramirez because "I was hurt, I was mad," at Kathy for shutting him out in her anger over her political reversals. "I was lashing out. I was frustrated at the way she was treating me." And Kathy's bad relations with the ER staff made things worse. "They were like my family, I felt caught in the middle."

"Were you dishonest with Kathy?"

"I told her I was leaving."

"Was she upset about the fact that you were leaving?"

"Yes. She felt like I was abandoning her. She said, 'I need you right now.'" After losing out on the federal appointment, Kathy wanted him to stay and help her through the looming impeachment. And after the impeachment and trial, he couldn't leave, because Kathy was depressed.

"There were a lot of ups and downs, a lot of emotion," Chaz said. That was when he began the first flirtation with Linda, the one that Kathy had discovered. Kathy saw this as just one more betrayal, Chaz indicated.

"She felt others were out to ruin her?"

"Yes. Nobody wanted to touch her," Chaz said. "She was damaged goods. She would solicit invitations to political functions. People would tell her, 'You're not on the guest list.' It was so sad. She would cry, and say, 'I can't believe this is happening to me.' It was devastating. It made things worse."

That spring of 2005 was when he'd made Kathy promise to quit politics, Chaz said.

"Did that happen?"

"No."

Instead, the next year, 2006, Kathy decided to run for state treasurer to "reclaim her career."

"How did that make you feel?"

"I felt bad. The woman I loved was basically begging people. I told her, 'I can't watch you destroy yourself like this.'"

As her campaign got going, Chaz said, Kathy began receiving threats—some people didn't want her to get elected treasurer.

"She was getting a lot of threats against her life," Chaz said. "She was actually nervous that something might happen to her, to be honest." Chaz said there were "certain politicians" in Nevada who considered Kathy dangerous to their plans. That was why he'd written the note to the news media in Las Vegas.

Houston read a portion of the note and asked Chaz if he'd written it.

"Why did you want the media to know this?"

"Because I needed them to continue what Kathy was investigating."

In the end, he'd decided he just couldn't live with Kathy's obsession, Chaz said. That was why he'd decided to get his own apartment, his own bank account, and finally start the divorce.

"Did you know how you were going to end it?"

"I would get a divorce."

"Were you going to murder her?"

"No."

Houston turned to July 7, and the encounter with Kim Ramey. Ramey had eavesdropped on his conversation with Kathy about the bank account, and afterward pestered him with personal questions, he said. He didn't want to answer questions about Kathy from Ramey because he didn't want to get in trouble for taking personal calls at work, as he had at South Meadows.

He'd never used the word "fucking" when talking to Kathy, Chaz said. "I never said that."

It was Ramey who had brought up the Darren Mack situation, Chaz said. Ramey had gone "on and on and on" about her own divorce.

"I wasn't paying much attention to what she said about Darren Mack. I was reading my [hospital] orientation material."

"Did you say something about succinylcholine, that it couldn't be detected in a post-mortem?"

"I didn't know that," Chaz said.

"Did you tell Kim Ramey that Mack was stupid, that 'he should've hit her with a little "succs" '?"

"I never said it," Chaz insisted.

Nor had Ramey chided him for having so much anger, he said. "*She* seemed pretty angry, to me."

Ramey had invited him to have drinks with her when the shift was over, but Chaz had declined. Ramey tried to cajole him anyway, but Chaz said only that he wanted to go home.

"When you left the hospital that night, were you carrying any succinylcholine, any syringes?"

"No."

"Did you have any hidden at home?"

"No."

When he got to the Otter Way house, Chaz said, he told Kathy he wanted an amicable divorce. "I wanted to be friends," he said. Kathy was lying on the living room couch.

Chaz said Kathy wanted to talk about it in the morning—she said she didn't feel well, and she wanted to go to bed. She went to bed early, he said.

The next morning, he got up early, around 6. He decided to let Kathy sleep while he worked on his car in the garage. Around 6:30 he'd returned to the bedroom and opened the blinds. He saw Kathy unmoving, face down, in bed. He opened the blinds.

"What did you think at that time?"

"This doesn't look right," Chaz said. That was when he called 911.

"Why didn't you put her on the floor?"

"I didn't think of it. I just started CPR."

"Why were you outside when the paramedics came?"

"The house is hard to find." Then, after the firemen ran into the house, followed by the paramedics, he'd hung back in the doorway because he didn't want to get in their way. It wasn't because he didn't care that Kathy seemed to be dying.

"Did you wait to call 911 so you could be sure her heart was stopped and could never be started again?"

"No."

At South Meadows, and then at Washoe Main, he'd been in shock, Chaz said. He had "turmoil" inside.

"It was very hard, it was the most painful morning of my life. I blamed myself. I thought, *My God, all the strength she had in her life is gone.*"

He'd spent the night at the ICU talking to Kathy and holding her hand, he said.

Then, over the next three days, when it had become apparent that Kathy would not recover, the family decided to withdraw life support.

"It was the mutual decision of all parties," Chaz said.

Then, on Thursday, he'd gotten into the argument with Phil Alfano. He'd slammed the door, the police were called, and the Alfanos left. Chaz went back in the house and started drinking. He felt numb, he said.

"I passed out in a chair. Around two, I woke up and went upstairs." He drank some more, then wrote the notes.

"And then you cut your wrists?"

"I wanted to do it," he said. "I felt guilty for causing the stress."

"Is that why you tried to kill yourself?"

"I wanted to be with her."

"Why should we believe you?"

"Because I'm telling the truth."

"Why should we believe that you did not kill your wife?"

"Because I did not do it."

That ended Houston's direct examination of his client. It was just before 6 P.M. The next day, Barb would have his crack at the man he'd already labeled a "cold, calculating, manipulative" sociopath.

But then Chaz tried to kill himself again.

Chapter 31

Very early in the morning of the day after he'd testified, Chaz went into the kitchen of the apartment he shared with his care-taking mother Shirley and began cutting his wrists. Somehow, Shirley heard him fall to the floor. She went into the kitchen and found him bleeding. She dialed 911, and was connected to REMSA.

While the ambulance was speeding toward the apartment, the 911 dispatcher asked Shirley where the knife was. Shirley said she thought the knife was in the kitchen sink. Turning to Chaz, she asked if that was correct.

"It's in the sink," Chaz confirmed.

Later, some thought this conversation between mother and son bizarre. Shirley didn't seem panicked about Chaz's condition, and Chaz himself seemed to be quite coherent. That led Chaz's detractors—Phil Alfano among them—to believe that this was just another bogus suicide attempt by Chaz, another ploy to get sympathy.

But others—including prosecutor Barb—thought that Chaz was just frightened of being cross-examined the following morning. Slicing his wrists might have been one way to avoid that unpleasant prospect. Chaz was taken to the hospital.

When court convened later that morning, the prospect of a mistrial had become a possibility. Maybe that was why Chaz had cut himself—to force a mistrial. That would mean the whole proceeding would have to start over from scratch, with a new jury, a sort of do-over, as Greg Augustine might have called it. And it might mean more weeks or even months of freedom for Chaz.

Judge Kosach and the lawyers met for nearly an hour, discussing what to do next. The jury waited in their box, fidgeting. Finally Kosach emerged, and told the jury that Chaz had been "injured," as he put it. He had decided to temporarily suspend the trial.

Kosach now said he had a "doubt as to the defendant's competence," a legal declaration that allowed him to suspend matters until the doubt was resolved. But until that happened, Kosach was loath to release the jurors. Depending on how long it took to resolve the competency question, Kosach said, he wanted the jurors to check in with the court every day to see if the trial could be resumed. That might take "a week, two weeks," Kosach said.

After the jurors filed out, Barb moved to revoke Chaz's bail. He wanted Chaz jailed as soon as he was released from the hospital.

Houston protested this.

"It's not appropriate at this time," he said. "We don't know what happened or why it happened."

No soap, Kosach told Houston.

"I'm going to revoke the bail," he said. "I'm going to order Mr. Higgs be placed on a suicide watch [in jail]. This is the second time. Like they say, 'Do it to me once, shame on you. Do it to me twice, shame on me.'"

Afterward, Houston talked to assembled reporters in an impromptu news conference. Chaz had tried to kill himself around 3 A.M., he said. Shirley had found him and called the medics.

"He wanted to clear his name," Houston said, "and felt that's what he did with his testimony yesterday. He wanted to join his wife . . . he felt that he had finished his job on this earth, and decided to dispatch himself."

Asked about Chaz's condition, Houston said "he's certainly on the road to recovery."

Would it cause a mistrial?

"It's a problem," Houston said. "It's unrealistic at this point to suggest we should go forward with this trial. We're going to have to watch the situation to see how it develops."

Down the hall of the courthouse, Phil Alfano, Jr., was giving his own reaction to what had happened.

"He's a cold, calculating S.O.B., that's all there is to it," Phil said of his one-time brother-in-law. "This was just one more attempt to draw attention to himself. One more sign of sociopathy."

Chaz's main intent was to avoid Barb's cross-examination, Phil said. "He lied about a number of things yesterday. There was a lot of perjury going on."

Was the suicide attempt real?

"He knows how to kill himself," Phil growled. "If he wanted to, he'd be dead."

Chaz did seem to make a remarkable recovery. The following day, Wednesday, Houston told Judge Kosach that Chaz was competent to continue the trial.

"We discussed the case in detail," Houston said. "We also checked his competence with a psychologist. He's still connected to reality. He clearly understands the proceedings, he understands what's happening."

Prosecutor Barb told Kosach he was confident that Chaz's mental competence was not an issue, that no appeal could later be raised if the trial went forward.

Kosach said he accepted the defense assurance that Chaz was fit to resume. He had thought he might have to question Chaz in camera to be sure, but he was willing to go forward based on Houston's statements.

He ordered the jury to return to court the following day so the trial could go on.

Barb's cross-examination of Chaz began the next morning just after 9 A.M. He began by asking Chaz to tell the jury why the trial had been delayed. Two large white bandages were obvious around both of Chaz's wrists, so Barb knew he had to address the subject. He also wanted to establish that Chaz was indeed mentally competent to go on with the trial.

"You were injured recently, is that correct?" he asked. "That's what caused a delay of two days in this trial? You had injuries that were self-inflicted?"

"Yes, sir."

"Help us understand what was going on Tuesday night. You left a note? Where?"

"In the bathroom, on top of the vanity."

"You felt that you'd told your story and that was all you needed to do?"

"Yes, sir."

"Do you understand why people might think this was a sympathy ploy?"

"Yes."

"Do you understand that some people might also think that this showed consciousness of guilt?"

"Yes."

"Isn't this just one last attempt to control the process?"

Chaz looked confused. Barb tried it another way.

"Who is Chip Walls?"

"He's a scientist who worked on my case."

"He said the FBI found succinylcholine in your wife, didn't he?"

"I don't remember what he said."

Well, that was about as close as Barb could come to establishing that Chaz knew what was going on, and the legal peril he was in. Barb turned to his previously planned cross-examination. His objective was to show that Chaz frequently lied, or at the least, consistently shaded the truth in his own favor.

Over the next two hours, Barb took Chaz backward and forward through his story, trying to highlight his inconsistencies, trying as well to show that Chaz always tried to make himself look good when the facts indicated otherwise.

"You said that Kathy wasn't feeling well, that she went to bed early that night."

"Yes."

"What time was that?"

"She went to bed at nine P.M.," Chaz said.

Barb asked Chaz to draw a rough floor plan of the house. Chaz complied. The prosecutor asked about doors—were they all locked on the morning of July 8?

The door from the garage was unlocked, Chaz said, while the front door was locked.

"You went into the bedroom about six thirty?"

Yes, Chaz said. He wanted to talk to Kathy about the divorce.

"This was around six thirty?"

"Yes."

"Did you see any evidence that anyone else was in the house?"

No, Chaz said.

"Did you hear anyone else in the house?"

"No."

Barb now produced more emails, these sent by Chaz to women other than Linda Ramirez. All of them seemed to contain some sort of solicitation, or at least flirtation by Chaz. One was a posting in an on-line chat room for singles, sent less than a month after Kathy had died.

Why did he do that, so soon after the wife he said he loved had died?

"I was in a fog," Chaz said. "I was reaching out to some-one."

"Every time you come out of the fog, you remember you love Kathy?"

Chaz didn't answer.

Barb produced another email, to yet another woman.

"Did you tell her how much you love Kathy?" he asked.

"No."

"You didn't tell her. Is that why you wrote, 'You should run away with me'? Is that why you wrote, 'Oh, by the way, did I tell you I'm single again?' Is that why you said you wanted to meet someone who was 'hot, sexy, cool, nice'?"

Chaz said he'd decided he wanted to be a travel nurse, just like Kim Ramey.

"And it's your testimony that you had a loving relation-ship with your wife?"

"I did have, most of my marriage," Chaz said.

Barb decided he'd demonstrated Chaz's desire to be a playboy sufficiently. He turned to the events of the morning of Kathy's collapse.

"Okay," he said, "you found your wife on the bed. She's not breathing, no heartbeat, no pulse. You started CPR while she was still on the bed?"

"Yes, sir."

"Why didn't you roll her off the bed?"

"I don't know."

"You asked that she be taken to South Meadows. Was that so your 'family' at South Meadows wouldn't suspect you?"

"No."

Barb turned to Kim Ramey's testimony about the "succs."

"What's Kim Ramey's motive for making up a story like that?"

"I have no idea." Chaz said he didn't remember saying anything like what Ramey said he'd said about "succs."

"She was just lucky to pick 'succs'?"

Chaz said he still didn't remember any conversation with Ramey about succinylcholine.

"You could have cared less about Kathy's money, is that right?"

"Yes." He had no legal interest in either of the Augustine houses, he said.

The only thing he received from the marriage after Kathy's death, Chaz said, was the BMW.

"The one that cost forty-one thousand dollars?" Barb said. "She paid cash for it?"

"I helped pay for the insurance," Chaz said.

Barb turned to Chaz's claims that Kathy's obsession with her political career had ruined their marriage.

"Kathy loved politics?"

"She did, to a point," Chaz said.

"Where's the stress of doing something you love?"

Chaz didn't answer.

"She wanted to get out of politics, you say?"

"After she lost the job for U.S. treasurer, she did. I told her I wanted to get a divorce, so she said she'd quit politics."

That was when Kathy had started being mean?

Yes, Chaz said.

"Describe some of the horrors, the hardness that was there," Barb demanded.

Chaz said Kathy would yell at him for leaving the cap off the toothpaste.

"She would argue with me," he said. "She closed herself off, she was unemotional."

"You didn't want to live a life through her politics?"

"Yes."

"Wasn't your threat to divorce her just a threat so you could control her?"

"No."

"Did you play the divorce card every time you didn't get your way?"

"No."

"Why did she have to beg you not to divorce her, if you loved her?"

Chaz didn't answer.

Chaz had told Kathy in early 2006 that he thought she was "fat and disgusting," hadn't he? Barb demanded, drawing from one of the emails Kathy had sent to Mike.

Chaz didn't answer.

"Your reputation as a loving husband got shot when she said you'd called her 'fat and disgusting,' didn't it?"

"She put on almost twenty pounds," Chaz said.

Barb turned to the night before Kathy had collapsed. Chaz had gone home to tell Kathy he was going to file for a divorce, wasn't that right?

"She didn't want to talk that night," Chaz said. "She went to bed about eight forty-five."

Barb asked Chaz if Kathy had talked to anyone else that night. Chaz said she hadn't.

"Do you remember telling someone from the television show about this case [the *48 Hours* program] that you got up about four thirty that morning? That you drove around?"

"I got up at six thirty," Chaz said.

"If you got up at six thirty, that didn't leave you much time to fix your car, did it?"

Chaz again had no answer.

Barb asked if he had made coffee when he got up—at one point Chaz had said he was bringing coffee to Kathy in bed when he discovered that she wasn't breathing.

Chaz said that was wrong, he wasn't bringing coffee to Kathy, only attempting to wake her up, because she'd told him she wanted to get up early.

"You told Mr. Houston that while you might have seemed detached when the paramedics were working on your wife, you had 'turmoil' inside?"

Chaz agreed—he'd felt 'turmoil' watching the resuscitation efforts.

"Did you ever tell anyone other than this jury that you had turmoil inside?"

"Probably family," Chaz said.

"Her family or yours?"

"Mine."

Barb turned to Chaz's claim that Kathy had been receiving "threats" before her death from people who were unhappy about her candidacy for state treasurer. He wanted to match Chaz's claim against his actions. After all, running out on a woman who'd supposedly been receiving mysterious threats wasn't very heroic.

"What did you do to protect her?" Barb demanded. "Besides advise her to quit politics? Did you chain the windows and doors?"

No, Chaz said.

Well, Barb went on, wasn't it true that some months earlier Kathy had taken Chaz's gun from the house and given it to a neighbor—to keep it away from Chaz? If Kathy was really afraid that someone might come after her, why would she have gotten rid of Chaz's gun? In that situation, didn't you want a gun inside the house, not out of it?

"She was nervous," Chaz insisted.

"Did she display any fear?"

Chaz recognized this as a trick question. If he said yes, Barb would ask him why he'd decided to leave Kathy unprotected. If he said no, he would contradict his own testimony about the threats. Chaz realized that Barb probably had talked to others who knew Kathy, and that they might testify that Kathy hadn't told them of any threats. He decided to answer the question carefully.

"Not that I could see," he said.

Barb took up the subject of Chaz's suicide attempts again.

"Why do you do it where you can be found?" he asked.

Chaz didn't answer this.

"If you really wanted to do it, why not go out into the desert and just do it?"

Because he didn't have access to a car, Chaz said.

What about the Las Vegas attempt? "Why do you want to put your family and friends through this?"

"Because it didn't matter anymore," Chaz said.

Was he upset at the Augustine and Alfano families for thinking he was a killer?

"Yes," Chaz said.

Barb suddenly veered back to supposed threats against Kathy.

Did Chaz think that the supposed threats against Kathy had anything to do with her death?

"I don't know," Chaz said.

"Well, how would they know what you said to Kim Ramey about 'succs'?" Barb asked. "How else would they have known to use 'succs' to kill her the next day, unless Ms. Ramey had told them? Are you saying Kim Ramey worked for the people who threatened Kathy Augustine?"

"I don't know," Chaz said.

"If she didn't, they had to be real lucky to set you up with succinylcholine, didn't they?"

Chaz made no response to this either.

Barb ended his cross-examination without ever asking Chaz why he'd told Linda Ramirez he was afraid of what Kathy might do to him.

When it was his turn again, Houston decided to get Chaz off the stand. He had no more questions for his own witness. With this, the defense rested.

Chapter 32

The prosecution now called two rebuttal witnesses. One was Kathy's former executive assistant, Michelle Ene. Michelle said Kathy often discussed the state of her marriage while at the controller's office. Kathy's complaints about Chaz began within two months of the marriage, she said.

Why didn't Kathy leave the marriage? Michelle was asked.

"She loved him," Michelle said. "She told me she loved him."

Did she ever say she wanted a divorce?

Never, Michelle said. "She really loved him. If he wanted something, she'd go buy it for him."

The day came in 2006 when Kathy filed her candidacy for the state treasurer's job. Some people in the office had gone out for a celebratory lunch. Chaz went with them.

"I got the impression he was supportive and happy she was running for treasurer," Michelle said.

Had Kathy ever complained about her health?

Never, Michelle said.

Did she ever say anyone had threatened her?

Never.

On Friday, July 7, Michelle had gotten to her own home about 10 minutes after 10. Her husband told her that Kathy had called her "three or four times."

At 10:12 she called Kathy back, and talked to her for ten

to fifteen minutes. Kathy was upset, Michelle said. She told her that Chaz had opened his own bank account, and that he was going to leave her.

Chaz was with her when she called, Michelle said. At the end of the conversation, Kathy had turned to Chaz.

"Chaz, do you want to speak to Jim?" she asked, referring to Michelle's husband.

"No," Chaz said. Michelle could hear his voice on the other end of the telephone.

So much for Chaz's story that Kathy had gone to bed, feeling sick, around 9 P.M., without talking to anyone.

That was the last time Michelle talked to Kathy.

On the following Sunday, she received a telephone call from Chaz, telling her that Kathy was in the hospital.

"He was really calm," Michelle said.

Chaz met her in the ICU. He told her he'd been working on his VW in the garage about 6:30 on Saturday morning. He'd gotten back into bed with Kathy, then realized she wasn't breathing.

"How long?" Michelle meant, how long had Kathy not been breathing?

"About an hour," Chaz told her. Of course, that was impossible. Chaz meant he'd been working on his car for about an hour before finding Kathy without a pulse.

Chaz told her that he and Kathy had "worked it all out, they'd made an agreement." Chaz told her that it was too bad that Kathy had collapsed, after they had worked everything out. Michelle was non-plused at this observation, which seemed so far off the point.

Michelle also thought Chaz was lying about an agreement. "She never would have let it go," Michelle said.

Baum tried to water down Michelle's testimony by suggesting that Kathy was under stress from politics, and from the fact that people in the Republican Party were "ostracizing" her.

"Kathy was a very strong woman," Michelle said. "She

said [the impeachment] was behind her, and that she would overcome it. She was optimistic."

Hicks now called Nancy Vinnick, Kathy's long-time neighbor and friend from Las Vegas. She told the story of the Battle of Las Vegas, after which the Alfanos had left, and Chaz tried to kill himself the first time.

She recalled Chaz's words to Kay Alfano after the brouhaha.

"Your daughter is nothing but a fucking whore and a cunt," she said she'd heard Chaz say in the phone call to Kay.

"I couldn't believe he would call her mother and say something so despicable," Nancy said. Nancy admitted that she thought Chaz had been drunk.

While she didn't know Chaz very well, Nancy said, she'd had "misgivings" about the marriage from the start. "I was totally aghast that she married so soon after Chuck died."

But, she said, Kathy was "a very strong person." Even when Kathy was being shunned at political events during 2005, she'd kept up an optimistic front. Far from stressing out over the campaign, Nancy said, "She wanted to clear her name by running for treasurer." In other words, Kathy was looking forward, not backward.

"You recommended that she not run for another political office?" Baum persisted.

"Yes, I did," she said.

"But she did not take that advice, did she?"

"No," Nancy said.

That was the last of the testimony. Now it would be up to the lawyers for each side to convince the jurors to convict— or not.

Did I do too much?" Barb asked, as he began his closing argument. "If I offended any of you by my cross-examination of Mr. Higgs, write to my boss. But please don't let it affect your judgment."

The case against Chaz cried out for conviction, he said. He defined first-degree murder—"willfully and unlawfully, with malice and premeditation," taking another person's life.

"How do you poison somebody without being willful, without malice, without premeditation and lawfully?" The testimony over the days of the trial had proven the elements of first-degree murder beyond a reasonable doubt, he said.

"How can you know she was murdered? There is no other reasonable explanation for her death. Nobody testified that wasn't succinylcholine in her urine. Nobody. The 'succs' was there. It was not administered therapeutically, not by the paramedics, not by the ER. And what does succinylcholine do? It shuts down every voluntary muscle in your body. She was never going to recover after that injection."

And the only person who could have given Kathy Augustine that injection was Chaz Higgs, Barb declared.

"How do we know this? First, there was a very good witness—Kim Ramey. She told you that Mr. Higgs spoke to her about using 'a little "succs"' to get rid of someone. He said Darren Mack was stupid. He 'should've used "succs."' Kim Ramey wasn't lying. What's her motive? Why would she do that? Even if she had a motive, why would she pick 'succs,' which turned out to be true?

"How did she know that? The state submits that it's obvious—Mr. Higgs told her that, just as she said."

Barb traced the evolution of the investigation of Chaz, through Detective Jenkins, then to Anderson and Montgomery. And, he said, Chaz's own expert "did not disagree with the FBI's findings."

"What happened between ten twelve P.M. on Friday night and six forty-five on Saturday morning? Someone injected her with succinylcholine. There's no evidence it can occur naturally."

When Kathy was not breathing, what had Chaz done?

He claimed he'd tried to revive her with CPR, but he didn't even put her on the floor to facilitate the resuscitation—the firemen did that. And why? Barb asked. Because he was "overcome by emotion." But the rest of the time, Chaz *had* no emotion—he was too professional, too well-trained to let his emotions get the better of him. Chaz couldn't have it both ways, Barb said.

There was no credible evidence that Kathy had had a heart attack. There was no blockage, no arrhythmia—otherwise, the paramedics would have had to use the defibrillator. But they'd gotten Kathy's heart started without it, which proved there was no fibrillation from an arrhythmia.

"Dr. Nielsen said Mr. Higgs is not a sociopath, but then he defined one. I leave it up to you to decide whether Dr. Nielsen is right."

All the way through Chaz's testimony, Barb said, "it was 'poor me, poor me.' The best he could do was say, 'I love her and I want to be with her.' It just makes no sense.

"You heard Kathy Augustine painted in very unhappy colors," he said. "But even if she was a bad sort, even if she was 'a bitch,' the penalty for being a bitch is not death. You don't get to kill her just because she's not nice to you."

Barb sat down to await Houston's attempt to convince the jury that Chaz hadn't done it.

The prosecution was wrong, way wrong about Chaz Higgs, Houston said, when it was his turn.

"What we told you was not only proved, but proved to a greater degree than I had anticipated at the outset."

The burden was on the prosecution to prove that a crime had occurred, he said. They had to prove it beyond a reasonable doubt, and there was reasonable doubt all over the state's case. There was evidence that Kathy had suffered a heart attack, just as first had been thought. There was evidence that Madeline Montgomery's testing procedure was of doubtful validity. There was doubt that the supposed needle mark was even a needle mark, and doubt that it had been made on July 8.

Houston now digressed into a lengthy recapitulation of the trials and tribulations of the Kathy–Chaz marriage. What had begun so happily soon degenerated when Kathy's political enemies had ganged up on her in early 2004.

"That year began the unraveling," Houston said, "of what some have described as a high-school romance."

The stress of being shunned and condemned by her former friends in the Republican Party had affected Kathy to the point where the love in the marriage was crushed.

"He believed, if only the politics was gone, the problems between them could be removed. If only Kathy would get out of politics, the relationship could go back to what it was."

And who was Chaz Higgs? Was he really someone capable of committing a cold-blooded murder? Not only was there no evidence of domestic violence between Chaz and Kathy, Chaz had lived more than forty years "without so much as once crossing the line—there were no violations, he has been a law-abiding person his entire life."

The prosecution wanted them to believe that Chaz was cold-blooded.

"A significant leap, to say the least—based on speculation, conjecture, inadequate testing ... When Mr. Higgs testified, was there anything he said that caused you to say, 'This is absolutely not true'?"

The prosecution had "cobbled together a distorted image" of Chaz, Houston said.

Yes, it was true that Chaz had sent emails to Linda Ramirez. But that was only because Kathy had become obsessed with what was being done to her by the other politicians.

"He was lonely. He missed the affection of another human being. He missed another person loving him, valuing him."

There was absolutely no evidence that Chaz had ever

been in possession of succinylcholine, Houston said. It was true that the police had found etomidate at the Otter Way house, but the vial was sealed. Chaz had accidentally put it in his pocket, and hadn't yet returned it to the hospital when the police found it.

And there was the evidence of the respected Dr. Sohn, the chairman of the Pathology Department of the Nevada School of Medicine. He'd said the supposed puncture wound could not have been made on July 8.

"If it wasn't there on July 8, how in the world could Chaz Higgs have been guilty of injecting Kathy Augustine with succinylcholine? That theory of the state would simply collapse . . . You cannot let one part of the theory fall away without the whole thing falling apart."

By the time Kathy arrived at South Meadows on July 8, he said, the ER staff was preparing to intubate her.

"Consider the panic in the ER," he said. "There were two doctors, three nurses, two paramedics, IV lines. I suggest to you that there was an inadvertent administration of succinylcholine."

Houston quoted the testimony of Marlene Swanbeck, the ER nurse that morning.

"She told you, 'I was really surprised when I saw she was intubated . . .' If succinylcholine is in her system, what's more likely—that the ER did it, or Chaz Higgs? Context is very important in reasonable doubt."

The fact was, the jurors could not even be sure there really was succinylcholine involved in the case at all, Houston told them. Instead, there was substantial evidence of the possibility of a heart attack—sudden cardiac death.

Dr. Clark's repudiation of Dr. Sohn's aging of the puncture wound only showed that she was an advocate for the prosecution. Just saying that she didn't try to determine the age of the wound wasn't good enough.

"When a person is on trial for murder, he deserves to have the state's expert perform all the relevant examinations. It's not fair of the prosecution to use Dr. Clark as an expert when she didn't do the requisite wound analysis."

As for Dr. Montgomery—"she made it up as she went along," Houston said, referring to Montgomery's admission that she adapted the usual test for "mono" to look for "succs."

It was possible that Montgomery had mistaken "mono" for "succs" all along, he said. The only tests that had been completed, he added, were those of Montgomery. The defense was unable to replicate the tests. Houston sketched in some of the facts of the Sybers case in Florida, and told the jury that that conviction had been tossed when the FBI later admitted that "mono" could be found naturally in decomposing cadavers.

"Don't make the mistake the Sybers jury made," he warned. How could anyone say for sure that Kathy's body hadn't started to manufacture "mono" before she was revived? For all practical purposes, until that happened, Kathy was dead, Houston pointed out.

Then there was the sheer implausibility of the situation, Houston said.

"Why on earth would he inject his wife, then call the paramedics? Why wouldn't he just walk away for three hours, then come back and find her dead? All you have to do is wait. Why not *wait*? Why wouldn't he inject her and then just melt away? Why not do it in such a way that the heart can't be restarted again?"

It didn't make any sense, he said.

The prosecution had pointed out that Chaz didn't show the proper emotion, he continued.

"Well, it's not yet time in our history of jurisprudence where we convict people based on their emotions. You are damned if you do, damned if you don't—with his training, he should have been composed. But not *too* composed." It was unfair, he said.

And as for Kim Ramey: "They hang their hat on Kim

Ramey. Is it more likely that Kim Ramey brought up Darren Mack, or Chaz Higgs? Who was going through a bitter divorce? She says he was so cold-blooded, she got goosebumps on her arm. But then she invited him out for a drink. Where's the consistency?"

It was doubtful—reasonably doubtful—that Chaz had ever said anything to Kim Ramey about succinylcholine.

"The logic of that would be that this man, who talked to this woman for maybe fifteen minutes—he'd never seen her before in his life—is going to reveal his diabolical, undetectable murder plan the very night he is supposed to go and put it into motion. Is that even reasonable? Or possible?"

The whole case was nothing but speculation based on fantasy, Houston said. The jury should acquit Chaz Higgs.

As always, the prosecution got the last word, since they had the burden of proof.

"Where is the evidence that succinylcholine was *not* in Kathy Augustine's body?" Barb asked. "There is none."

"Let's say that Dr. Sohn was right," Barb told the jury, referring to the "punctate" dispute.

"Okay. If so, how did the succinylcholine get there? Dr. Clark said it was hard to tell the age of a bruise. She said, 'Well, maybe I didn't find it.' But the fact is, the 'succs' was there."

It wasn't reasonable that Kathy had been given "succs" by mistake in the ER, Barb said. There was no evidence that the rapid sequence intubation kit on the crash cart had its red seal broken, or that any of its contents had been used. Why? Because Kathy had already been intubated by Pratt at the Otter Way house. There was no need to use any "succs."

All the talk about Kathy being stressed before her death was bunk, he said.

"Mr. Higgs' testimony was entirely incredible. He said he didn't care about the money. You tell *me* he didn't care about the money, if you believe that."

Barb took up Houston's argument.

"Why didn't he just let her die? Maybe he thought she *was* going to die before anyone got there. Maybe he didn't expect them to be able to resuscitate her."

Maybe, Barb continued, Chaz had called the paramedics to give himself an alibi.

The hard fact remained, Barb said, that succinylcholine had been found in Kathy's urine, taken only minutes after she arrived at the ER, less than an hour after Chaz had called 911. At the time of her collapse, he was the only other person around. It was as simple as A-B-C. The suggestion that someone had gotten into the house and poisoned Kathy while Chaz was in the garage fooling around with his car was laughable. Anyway, how would the mysterious succinylcholine-wielding hit men have known what Chaz had told Kim Ramey the day before?

The FBI had no reason to fabricate anything, Barb said.

"Why would the FBI want to frame Chaz Higgs? What's he to them?"

The evidence clearly pointed to Chaz, Barb concluded. He was the only one with the opportunity, the means, and the motive.

"He hated her, he said it. He wanted to 'make her crazy.' He didn't mind telling people at work he wanted their help in getting rid of her. He told you he loved her. It's up to you to decide what the evidence is."

And with that, the case went to the jury.

Chapter 33

Chaz's jury received the case from Judge Kosach just before 6 P.M. on Thursday, June 28. The following morning, they returned to begin their deliberations. Throughout the trial, members of the Higgs and Alfano families had kept their silence in the rear of the courtroom, watching anxiously. Chaz's father, Bill Higgs, and his wife sat on one side of the room, separated from Chaz's mother and her significant other by a considerable distance. If the two ex-spouses said anything to one another, it wasn't apparent.

On the other side of the courtroom, the Alfanos sat quietly—Phil Jr., Phil Sr. and Kay, often accompanied by other relatives of the extended Alfano family. Dallas sat behind them, never exchanging a single word with her uncle and her grandparents. Dallas and Phil had been feuding over the trust—Dallas had hired a lawyer, the same man who had represented Kathy and Chuck in the Lori Lipman Brown fiasco years earlier, who was pestering Phil Jr. for a complete accounting. Phil said he'd already given one to Dallas. That didn't stop the lawyer, and Phil was fed up. He and Dallas hadn't said a word to each other since the day Phil had called Dallas and left a message, telling her that Chaz had been arrested. That had been in September of the previous year.

Houston and Baum fidgeted. They had done the best they could with what they had. It was too bad Walls hadn't testified for their side, Baum thought. Once Walls had said he didn't have enough information to contradict Madeline Montgomery, the only thing they could do was ask Judge Kosach for more time. When Kosach had refused, they were stuck with Walls; when Walls said he'd have to testify that Montgomery *had* found "succs," that was the whole ball-game, at least as far as succinylcholine was concerned. Now, all they could do was hope that the jury believed Chaz when he'd said he loved Kathy, and that she'd actually had a heart attack.

Barb and Hicks felt confident that they had proven their case. Barb thought he'd never had a case that had gone as smoothly. No matter what the defense had brought up, he said later, he felt he had it covered. They had hadn't been able to score at all—it was like pitching a perfect game.

The news media had washed into town at the start of the trial—television stations from Las Vegas, even representatives from two network magazine shows. Their trucks took up the whole curb on Virginia Street in front of the courthouse, antennas streaming bits and bytes into the heavens. One network even arranged for cameras in the courtroom. They sat in each corner, concealed in varnished wooded boxes behind glass panes, merging with the 19th-century decor. Cables snaked out the window and ran down to the street below, where air conditioners hummed day and night inside the trucks.

The *New York Times* had someone drop in, and so did the *Los Angeles Times*. Ed Vogel watched everything unfold, remembering the Kathy he had known as the *Review-Journal*'s correspondent in Carson City. The *Reno Gazette-Journal* reporter, Martha Bellisle, covered the trial from beginning to end, although in some ways the case was overshadowed by the looming trial of Darren Mack, scheduled to take place in the fall. While Kathy had been a big wheel, Darren Mack was bigger—at least in Reno.

"I always liked Kathy," Ed Vogel said, as the trial was unfolding. She had always been great with the press—funny, quotable, spirited, smart. It was just too bad she had such lousy taste in men, he added.

Across town, Jeannine Coward kept track of the proceedings by reading Martha Bellisle's accounts in the local paper. She still had mixed feelings about Kathy—really, a love–hate relationship. Sometimes Jeannine could remember the good times with her former boss, and her strange dream of the night of July 8, when the dream-Kathy had put her arm around her and smiled. But then the memories would come back of the screaming, the emotional outbursts, the intensity, the insensitivity to her employees' feelings. Jeannine was convinced she had done the right thing in derailing Kathy's political career. "Love the sinner, hate the sin," she'd said, during the impeachment trial. Jeannine guessed there was some dark secret in Kathy's past that had helped make her so aggressive, and yet so fragile; and if Jeannine really thought about it, she was pretty sure it had something to do with some older man, back in Kathy's most impressionable years.

Jennifer Normington soon left government service entirely—politics wasn't what it was cracked up to be, she had decided. Jeannine helped her find a new job in the hospitality industry, whence Jennifer had come, B.K.—Before Kathy. Jennifer had her own pet name for her antagonist: "Big Hair," she called her.

One night, after she'd quit and before Kathy died, Jennifer and her father attended a function at the Desert Research Institute, a Reno social mainstay. There Jennifer encountered Kathy, escorted by Chaz. Jennifer didn't know what to make of him.

"He reminded me of a cross between Ted Bundy and Jeffrey Dahmer," she told Jeannine later. Jeannine swore Jennifer told her this before Kathy died. Maybe Jennifer knew something about karma, too.

Just after noon on Friday, June 29, the foreman let Judge Kosach know that the jury had reached a verdict. They had deliberated only a little more than three hours. Then, apparently, the jurors went to lunch.

An hour passed, and another. Finally, just before 2 P.M., the jury filed into their box.

"Ladies and gentlemen, have you reached a verdict?" Kosach asked them.

"We have, Your Honor," the foreman said. The verdict form was passed to the court clerk.

"'We the jury,'" the clerk read, "'find Chaz Higgs guilty of first-degree murder.'"

Chaz gave no discernible reaction. Behind in the spectators' seats, Shirley Higgs let out a low moan.

"Thank you, thank you," Phil Alfano, Jr., whispered.

But the jury's job wasn't done yet. Now it had to fix the punishment, and for that, more testimony would be taken.

The state of Nevada had three possible punishments for first-degree murder when the prosecution wasn't asking for the death penalty—a 50-year sentence, with the possibility of parole after 20 years; a life sentence, with parole after 20; and life without parole. That meant a minimum term of at least 20 years, no matter what. The penalty phase was like a mini-trial—each side would present its case.

Both the prosecution and defense waived opening statements.

Hicks called the first witness for the prosecution, Dr. Pamela Russell, an anesthesiologist.

Russell said that as an anesthesiologist, she was quite familiar with the properties of succinylcholine.

"It's unique," she said. "It's a depolarizing muscle relaxant." Anyone given the compound would immediately suffer a "massive, taut spasm" of muscles, she said, which would last for thirty to sixty seconds. After that, there would be total voluntary muscle paralysis. The paralysis would wear off within fifteen to seventeen minutes, she said.

"Is it painful?" Hicks asked.

"Yes," she said. "Usually we give it with another muscle relaxant," like etomidate. "Every single muscle and bone hurts," she said, "from massive muscle contractions."

Anyone given the drug could hear, smell, and see, she said. If they wanted to scream, they wouldn't be able to open their mouth.

"They can't breathe," she said.

A person dosed with succinylcholine would know they were going to die, she said. "You will continue to feel things for six to ten minutes. After that, your brain begins to die."

Anyone injected with the compound not given oxygen would feel "pure terror," she said. It would be like drowning, without a chance to come up for air.

The defense offered no cross-examination.

Hicks called Dallas to the stand.

Dallas had written a statement. She had every bit of her mother's intensity as she glared at Chaz across the room. Tears came to her eyes as she looked at the man her mother had so suddenly married, and whom she had defended, even allowed to live in her house for several weeks.

Russell's testimony about the effects of succinylcholine had unnerved Dallas. It *was* gruesome to think about.

"After hearing your indifference to my mother's suffering, I know you don't know what it is to be a human being," she told Chaz.

Her mother was more important to her than Chaz could ever understand, she added. "I miss her every day, and will miss her for the rest of my life. Nobody can ever take away the pain I feel."

The defense asked no questions of Dallas.

Hicks called Phil Jr.

"I don't know where to begin," he said. "I've known two emotions over the past year, anger and sorrow, because of that man over there, Chaz Higgs."

His sister had referred to Chaz as her "angel," he said.

"But the fact is, he's the angel of death. I can think of no other individual who deserves punishment as much as he does. He robbed my daughters of their aunt. I've seen this tear them apart for the past year." He urged the jury to give Chaz the maximum penalty under the law.

The defense asked no questions.

Hicks called Kay Alfano.

Kathy was her first-born child, Kay said.

"It has been devastating, Chaz," she told him. "You don't know how devastating. To take the life of another human being is just . . ." Kay couldn't think of the words she wanted to express her dismay.

Since Kathy's death, she said, the Alfano family had received hundreds of telephone calls, letters and cards saying how much Kathy had meant to people. Kathy had always done her best to help people, she said, raising money for charity, going out of her way to do the right thing.

"Yes," she said, "she was political, but she was a wonderful human being."

Then Kay looked out at the courtroom and focused on Bill Higgs, and Shirley Higgs.

"I just also want to say that I feel sorry for Chaz's mother and father," she added. "Because what he's done to them is just as devastating."

That was it for the prosecution. Baum now called three witnesses.

Tina Carbone from the South Meadows ER, Chaz's former supervisor, led off. Chaz had always been a competent, caring professional nurse, she said. He'd never been a problem, and patients liked him. He had saved lives there. The jury should take that into consideration when they considered the sentence.

Baum called Shirley Higgs.

Shirley was in tears almost as soon as she sat down in the witness box. She described the upbringing of the twins—Cub Scouts, Little League, high school sports like football, track, golf and swimming. Chaz and Mike were very close, she said.

"They were all-around kids, they never had any trouble."

After high school, Chaz had joined the Navy, where "he had a fine career," Shirley said. He had stayed with her while attending nursing school after leaving the Navy.

Then Shirley made a plea for her son's life.

"I would hope," she said, her voice trembling, and finally breaking, "the jury would consider life with parole. For hope. Every person is entitled to hope. I would like my son to have that—hope."

Baum called Bill Higgs, Chaz's father.

"I was very proud of my son," he said. "Proud he joined the service." Chaz had never been in trouble before. "I don't think he even had a speeding ticket." He, too, wanted the jury to give Chaz hope—if they gave him life with parole, "he'd have something to look forward to."

Bill looked at the jury.

"I'm very sorry for what happened. We will be saying a rosary for her."

Both sides gave closing arguments. Hicks asked the jury to sentence Chaz to life in prison without the possibility of parole.

"Is this a person who deserves to be in society again?" Hicks asked. That was the question the jury had to think about. Hicks thought not. Chaz had killed Kathy Augustine in a heartless fashion.

"He had the audacity to come here and swear under oath that he loved her. He doesn't deserve to be in society again." That meant Chaz should spend the rest of his life behind bars.

"He earned that. Give it to him."

Baum summed up for the defense.

"I will not plead for mercy for Chaz Higgs," he said. "I

don't think anyone in this courtroom believes that Chaz Higgs will live out his term." Baum implied that Chaz would finally succeed in killing himself one day.

"I'm asking," he said, "for compassion and leniency for his parents. For whatever time they have left. Let them have their remaining years with hope."

The jury retired to deliberate Chaz's fate at 3:50 in the afternoon. At 4:25, just thirty-five minutes later, they announced they had reached a penalty decision.

At 4:35 P.M. on Friday afternoon, June 29—a little less than a year after Kathy Augustine had been found dying in her marital bed—the jury imposed a sentence of life in prison with the possibility of parole in 20 years. It was the lightest of the three sentences. They had given hope to Shirley and Bill Higgs, if not Chaz.

As the bailiffs escorted Chaz out of the courtroom and back to jail, Bill Higgs called out after him.

"We love you, son," he said.

Afterword

So did Chaz Higgs really murder his wife with the life-saving drug, succinylcholine? Or was his fate at the hands of the jury an awful miscarriage of justice, as his lawyer David Houston insisted, even after the verdict?

Chaz's mother Shirley left no doubt about what she believed. In a letter to the editor of the *Reno Gazette-Journal* published the day after his conviction and sentencing.

"Our family believes Chaz did not get a fair trial," she wrote. "It is obvious the jury completely ignored most of the evidence presented." Once the jurors had heard from Kim Ramey, Shirley said, they'd made up their minds. Then, she said, they had been "intimidated" by one member of the jury to rush to a verdict.

"It was clear," she added, "to anyone sitting in the courtroom that there were several obvious doubts why Chaz should not have been convicted."

But the true worth of evidence presented in a trial can sometimes be hard to perceive for those who are emotionally involved through ties of love. In the end a juror can only assess the facts presented in court, and vote their own, private sense of what's right, or what's wrong. In the case involving Chaz Higgs, if the prosecution's facts were accepted as true, there was only one person who had the opportunity, the means and the motive to kill Kathy Augustine, and that was Chaz Higgs. The failure of the defense to dent any of these three pillars left the jury with no other choice.

And how strange was it? Either Chaz Higgs was the dumbest potential murderer ever to use a sophisticated means of killing his victim, or the unluckiest man alive: as it happened, less than twelve hours after he'd supposedly said that he knew of a foolproof way of getting rid of a spouse, in some weird twist of fate, his own spouse had succumbed to the very same unusual means of death.

The fact that Kathy had been impeached and then abandoned by the Nevada Republican Party between 2004 and 2006 later led some to wonder whether her death had somehow been engineered by hidden forces lurking behind the scenes of the state's political establishment: perhaps some people were worried that Kathy would rise again from the ashes of her embarrassment, and wanted to prevent this, even by resorting to murder. But not even Chaz had seriously suggested this as a cause of her demise—in his view, the worst that the politicians had done to Kathy was cause her stress, and possibly a heart attack.

As Chaz had come into focus in the summer of 2006 as the most likely candidate for Kathy's murderer, Phil Alfano had at first tried to connect Chaz to Kathy's political enemies. Maybe, Phil theorized, Chaz had been the tool of Kathy's opponents—maybe he had murdered her on the orders of someone else. But it simply wouldn't compute—if Chaz had killed Kathy at the behest of Kathy's political opponents, why would he have named those same opponents as those who were responsible for her death by heart attack? So Phil concluded that Kathy's death had nothing to do with her political activities. The real reason Chaz killed Kathy, Phil soon came to believe, was simply that he wanted to get Kathy's money.

This was not to say that Kathy's political opponents weren't still after her, Phil later discovered. In acting as executor of her estate in the summer of 2006, he found several unpaid bills from the Las Vegas lawyer Dominic

Gentile. When he asked Gentile what these charges were for, Phil said, he learned that someone had referred Kathy to the United States Department of Justice's Office of Special Counsel—in April of 2006, more than two years after the impeachment, and just before she declared her candidacy for state treasurer. A new federal investigation file of Kathy's actions regarding Jeannine and Jennifer was opened, and was still active when Kathy died. It was clear to Phil Alfano that *someone* in Nevada was intent on stopping Kathy's renewed political ambition even before she succumbed to succinylcholine on July 8, 2006.

The notion that some sort of hidden, sinister organized force was actually behind Kathy's death was later termed ludicrous by prosecutor Barb. For one thing, he pointed out, how would Kim Ramey have known to suggest succinylcholine as the murder weapon, even before it was found? She'd have to be in on the plot, Barb pointed out, and that was patently ridiculous.

Because Chaz at one point had told a television magazine program that he'd left the house for a short period of time during the early morning hours "to go for a drive," that left the possibility that some other person had gained access to the property, and had administered the drug in Chaz's brief absence. But when Chaz later repudiated this statement, denying that he'd ever left the house, the possibility that someone else was responsible was severely undercut, Detective Jenkins later observed. And even if Chaz *had* left the house, the putative hit man's timing would have had to be so impeccable as to be virtually impossible.

"You'd have to believe that someone was able to make undetected, forced entry into a locked home, have access to Kathy, have access to the drug, and to have done all that within that three-to-five-minute time frame before Chaz comes back into the home and finds her unconscious, but *not* necessarily to the degree where she's deceased. And in order for her to be resuscitated to the degree she was, she could only have been unconscious for a matter of a few moments," Jenkins pointed out.

"So you'd have to believe that this intruder was able to access the Otter [Way] home during an absence that Chaz says didn't occur, have access to the body, then get out of the home with just moments to spare before Chaz returns from the trip he says he didn't take." Not only that, the supposed hit man would have to have known that Chaz had spoken of succinylcholine the day before, or at the least have enlisted Ramey in the plot to propose succinylcholine three days later as the cause of Kathy's collapse. The scenario was absurd, Jenkins said.

But why *had* Chaz broached the possible use of succinylcholine to get rid of an unwanted spouse, and this to a woman he had only met moments before? A possible key lies in Kim Ramey's description of Chaz: "I could tell right away he was a player."

In this scenario, a boastful Chaz, a "player," seeking to impress Ramey, would have mentioned "succs" as the "smart" way of doing someone in. The assertion that the drug would be undetectable at autopsy would be a way of further impressing Nurse Ramey as to his cleverness.

In turn, this raises the question of why Chaz immediately put his diabolical plan into effect. Why not wait for a week, since he knew that Ramey and her boyfriend were preparing to leave town within a few days? Then he could have poisoned Kathy, and with Ramey on the other side of the country, the likelihood of her reporting the conversation would have been very small.

The chances are, Chaz gambled that his information was correct—that there was no way "succs" could be detected at autopsy. It was only Pratt's success in resuscitating Kathy that led to the recovery of succinylcholine. Had she not been brought back to life, even if temporarily, Chaz could have gotten away with it. Then Chaz could have had the best of both worlds: he could have bragged about what he was going to do, then do it, but still with no one able to prove it. Best of all, Ramey, not yet having left town, would always wonder . . .

There were others who thought that Chaz's lifetime of unswerving loyalty from his mother Shirley played a role in the events.

"I don't think Chaz ever, and I mean ever, in his lifetime, ever stood up and accepted responsibility for any mistake or anything bad that he ever did," Barb said later. "I don't mean in a criminal way, but I'm sure he screwed up somewhere in his life, but I don't believe he ever, ever, had to stand up and say, 'Yeah, I messed that up.' I think he talked his way out of everything. I think his mother enabled him . . . to be like that."

Shirley's letter to the editor, in which she'd blamed the jury for her son's plight, only reinforced that notion, Barb said. "Lady, where were you sitting when this [trial] was going on? I think that that is evidence of his entire life, where she protected him from anybody ever being critical of his activities, whatever they were."

Dr. Neilsen, the defense psychologist, had another view. While not necessarily subscribing to the notion of Chaz's guilt, Neilsen observed that for all his life, Chaz had been seen as a golden child—excellent in his studies, a good athlete, handsome and attractive to women, the sort of person no one expects to fail. But when failures did come, Chaz had a compulsion to erase them—to wipe everything clean, and to start over. The marriage with Kathy had been a mistake, and Chaz had become caught on the horns of a dilemma: stay in the marriage as his self-image demanded, or flee in ignominious failure once again. The love had become poisoned, and had to be excised.

But why didn't he just obtain a divorce? Why all the talk about getting rid of Kathy, dumping her down a mineshaft, or the nefariously useful properties of succinylcholine? To

Nielsen, this might have just been blowing off steam, but to others, it spoke of darker motivations. The prosecution's rather weak theory—that Chaz simply hated his wife—was all that could be supported by the facts at trial, given the trust agreement. But that did not stop Barb and Detective Jenkins from speculating later that the real reason Chaz killed his wife was that she planned to divorce *him*. That would leave Chaz out on the street, with a part-time job, looking at yet another possible bankruptcy, another failure.

"I think he was afraid that at his age, he didn't have the assets," Jenkins observed. "He was going to be kicked out with virtually nothing. He had a 1966 Volkswagen to his name, and nothing else."

He'd married Kathy for her money, but then found the cost was too high, Jenkins said.

"I think everybody tends to undercut the level of hatred that he had developed for her. She was standing in his way of developing these other romantic trysts that he was actively pursuing, and if you listen to the tenor of what all of his co-workers said about the months before her death, he had nothing less than a hatred for her."

The truth was, Kathy *was* the controller, and if there was one thing Chaz could not abide, it was being controlled by a woman. In Chaz's world, women were supposed to venerate him, not the other way around. So in the end, Chaz had resorted to his own means of control—his own area of expertise, power that came in a vial—medicine to ease the pain. The fact that it was his pain he was easing wasn't beside the point—it *was* the point.

"I think it's as simple as, he didn't like her, he didn't see an easy way out," Jenkins said later. "Like most murderers, he was more concerned with his own personal well-being than that of someone else. He places *his* life, *his* comfort, *his* security above everybody else's, even his wife's, and she had become an annoyance."

Acknowledgments

The author wishes to express his gratitude to the large number of people who assisted with research for this book. The staff of the Washoe District Court patiently copied hundreds of pages of documents from the case of *State of Nevada* vs. *Chaz Higgs*. The office of Nevada Attorney General Catherine Cortez Mastro was instrumental in permitting the review of hundreds of pages of documents related to its investigation of Kathy Augustine. Defense lawyers Alan Baum and David Houston freely gave of their time, and provided answers to many puzzling questions, as did prosecutor Tom Barb and Reno police Detective David Jenkins. Dr. John Anderson, Washoe County toxicologist, went above and beyond in explaining liquid chromatograph/tandem mass spectrometer technology. Pharmacist Nancy Tardy was particularly helpful in explicating the uses and effects of succinylcholine. Dr. Ellen Clark, Washoe County medical examiner, graciously agreed to an illuminating interview. Jeannine Coward was vital in explaining the events that led to Kathy Augustine's 2004 impeachment. Abbie Goldman of the *Las Vegas Sun*, Ed Vogel of the *Las Vegas Review-Journal*, Clark County Coroner P. Michael Murphy and John Tsitouras were particularly helpful. Most of all, the author wishes to thank Phil Alfano, Jr., and Greg and Larry Augustine, for their recollections, without which this book could not have been written. As always, I'd like to thank Jane Dystel of Dystel and Goderich Literary Management, and Yaniv Soha of St. Martin's Press for their unflagging support.

Carlton Smith
Reno, Nevada
December 2007

Raves for *The Four Forges*

"Sevryn Dardanon is not your typical elf. In fact, the world of Kerith is not your typical elf world. In this spectacular series debut, the pseudonymous Rhodes (a prolific YA author) plays fresh variations on the standard epic fantasy tropes. Her elves, the Vaelinars, are outsiders, propelled by a magical cataclysm into an unfamiliar and somewhat hostile new environment. For Sevryn, a half-breed Vaelinar, life is especially difficult as he's neither of one world or the other. Meanwhile, human Dwellers take in the orphaned Rivergrace, an escaped slave of Vaelinar heritage, and raise her as their adopted daughter. Both Rivergrace and Sevryn struggle to survive as quietly as possible, until, by chance, their paths cross and they must help each other battle an unknown evil that's infecting Kerith. Sevryn and Rivergrace possess not only undeveloped magical powers but mysteries in their respective pasts that promise to keep the excitement level high in the next installment."
—*Publishers Weekly* (starred review)

"The first book of the Elven Ways series introduces the very detailed and well-drawn world of Kerith, in which four different peoples coexisted since the end of a devastating war, until a magestorm from another world brought a fifth people, the Vaelinars. Rhodes' use of detail will please those who like richly drawn settings and intricate plots."
—*Booklist*

"Rhodes evokes an atmosphere of urgency in her series opener, set in a world of ever-shifting alliances and unforeseen dangers. Strong characters and a compelling story make this a good choice for most fantasy collections."
—*Library Journal*

". . . a fantastic epic fantasy in what looks like it will be a special series similar to the works of Tad Williams and other great epic fantasists. The key cast members are believable individuals with distinct personalities. Jenna Rhodes leaves enough threads for readers to look forward to the next tale, but in a paradox *The Four Forges* feels complete."
—*The Book Review Forum*

"Rhodes has built a fully realized world with engaging characters with a dangerous manifest destiny. The characters are complex and real in perilous times and leave you waiting anxiously to see what is resolved. A bright beginning for a new light on the fantasy horizon."
—*ConNotations*

THE
FOUR FORGES

The Elven Ways: Book One

Jenna Rhodes

DAW BOOKS, INC.
DONALD A. WOLLHEIM, FOUNDER
375 Hudson Street, New York, NY 10014

ELIZABETH R. WOLLHEIM
SHEILA E. GILBERT
PUBLISHERS
http://www.dawbooks.com

First Paperback Printing, July 2007
1 2 3 4 5 6 7 8 9

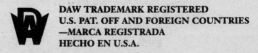

DAW TRADEMARK REGISTERED
U.S. PAT. OFF AND FOREIGN COUNTRIES
—MARCA REGISTRADA
HECHO EN U.S.A.

PRINTED IN THE U.S.A.